BEHIND THE LINES WITH THE SBS

MY LIFE IN **L SQUADRON** DURING WW2

Dedicated to all those who served in the
SBS, SAS, SOE, LRDG, LSF, GSS and
Cretan Resistance (The *Andartes*).

Des' handwritten memoirs on 200 foolscap pages and his SBS Commando knife. (Marshall Family Collection)

Often in Des' thoughts, he drew this sketch depicting the SBS and a Caique in 1986. (Marshall Family Collection)

BEHIND THE LINES WITH THE SBS

MY LIFE IN L SQUADRON DURING WW2

NICHOLAS JAMES MARSHALL AND
ROBERT DESMOND MARSHALL

Pen & Sword
MILITARY

AN IMPRINT OF PEN & SWORD BOOKS LTD.
YORKSHIRE – PHILADELPHIA

First published in Great Britain in 2025 by
Pen & Sword Military
An imprint of
Pen & Sword Books Ltd
Yorkshire - Philadelphia

Copyright © Nicholas James Marshall and Robert Desmond Marshall, 2025

ISBN 978 1 03613 481 5

The right of Nicholas James Marshall and Robert Desmond Marshall to be identified as the Authors of this work has been asserted by them in accordance with the Copyright, Designs and Patents Act 1988.

A CIP catalogue record for this book is available from the British Library.

All rights reserved. No part of this book may be reproduced, transmitted, downloaded, decompiled or reverse engineered in any form or by any means, electronic or mechanical including photocopying, recording or by any information storage and retrieval system, without permission from the Publisher in writing. NO AI TRAINING: Without in any way limiting the Author's and Publisher's exclusive rights under copyright, any use of this publication to "train" generative artificial intelligence (AI) technologies to generate text is expressly prohibited. The Author and Publisher reserve all rights to license uses of this work for generative AI training and development of machine learning language models.

Typeset by SJmagic DESIGN SERVICES, India.

Printed and bound in the UK by CPI Group (UK) Ltd.

The Publisher's authorised representative in the EU for product safety is Authorised Rep Compliance Ltd., Ground Floor, 71 Lower Baggot Street,
Dublin D02 P593, Ireland.
www.arccompliance.com

For a complete list of Pen & Sword titles please contact

PEN & SWORD BOOKS LIMITED
George House, Units 12 & 13, Beevor Street, Off Pontefract Road,
Barnsley, South Yorkshire, S71 1HN, England
E-mail: enquiries@pen-and-sword.co.uk
Website: www.pen-and-sword.co.uk

or

PEN AND SWORD BOOKS
1950 Lawrence Rd, Havertown, PA 19083, USA
E-mail: uspen-and-sword@casematepublishers.com
Website: www.penandswordbooks.com

CONTENTS

Acknowledgements vii
Foreword by Nick Marshall x

Chapter 1	War Breaks Out 1
Chapter 2	To the Middle East 9
Chapter 3	Time for a Beasting 14
Chapter 4	Off for a nice walk 19
Chapter 5	On to Cairo for Signals training 24
Chapter 6	Cairo Central to Palestine by train 28
Chapter 7	Arrival back at Azzib training camp 31
Chapter 8	Meeting Major Patterson and to the Sea of Galilee 35
Chapter 9	Return to base and preparation of kit for first operation .. 41
Chapter 10	Into Beirut, loading the *Tewfik* 43
Chapter 11	Sailing out of Beirut on-board the *Tewfik* 46
Chapter 12	Stop at Famagusta 49
Chapter 13	Les Stephenson and Onwards to Vathi Bay 51
Chapter 14	Stampalia Operation 53
Chapter 15	Landing on the Island 56
Chapter 16	Cave Recce and making contact with Cairo 58
Chapter 17	Recce for targets and visit from Stampalian shepherd 61
Chapter 18	Lying Up Position (LUP) 64
Chapter 19	Goats mistaken for Germans 67
Chapter 20	Attack Details 70
Chapter 21	Captain Anderson and Nixon Return 74
Chapter 22	Signals for Extraction 77

Chapter 23	The Extraction	79
Chapter 24	Return to the *Tewfik* (Had a nice holiday?)	82
Chapter 25	On Turkish Soil	85
Chapter 26	Fishing with explosives	90
Chapter 27	Signals for Jellicoe	94
Chapter 28	Culinary life aboard the *Tewfik*	102
Chapter 29	Guarding a ship at Penzik Bay & Shipwreck at Kiervasilli Bay	105
Chapter 30	Cable Line laying between *LS9* & the *Tewfik*	109
Chapter 31	Transporting German prisoners to Syria	114
Chapter 32	Cyprus Interlude	121
Chapter 33	Haifa & farewell to the German prisoners	126
Chapter 34	Parachute Training at Ramat David RAF Airbase	130
Chapter 35	Back to Athlit for more training	139
Chapter 36	Mock Attack on Cyprus	148
Chapter 37	To Mersa Matruh	153
Chapter 38	To Crete via Tobruk	158
Chapter 39	First Hide out on Crete	167
Chapter 40	Second cave hideout & Recce of target	171
Chapter 41	The Russian cook and the potential poisoning operation	180
Chapter 42	The Ambush	185
Chapter 43	The Bugout	193
Chapter 44	Wireless Problems	200
Chapter 45	Exfiltration from Crete	205
Chapter 46	Athens December 1944	214
Chapter 47	Athens January 1945	217
Chapter 48	The Istrian Operation	219
Chapter 49	The Final Chapter	223

Glossary	233
Notes	238
Bibliography	245
Index	247

ACKNOWLEDGEMENTS

When I first set out to discover more about Grandpa's wartime story in the SBS I could never have imagined that I would have learned so much. I assumed, although he and Nick had a lot in common and obviously through their military careers they would have shared stories, that I would only learn titbits or vague recollections of stories shared over a pint like the conversations he and my Dad would have when I was a child. Although I knew Nick and Dad would always listen with a keen interest and loved to hear his stories, I felt I would be very lucky to get any sort of detailed retelling. I wanted to know the who, when and where about the places he had served. I wanted to know everything, the finer detail.

First of all, I want to thank Nick. He has devoted so much of his time sending me email after email from his home in Perth, WA.

Grandpa's wartime documents, photos, memorabilia, maps, medals and of course his handwritten manuscript itself, all of these things appear in the following pages.

Through reading his manuscript and learning 'the finer detail' it has only served to increase my desire to learn even more about the operations he was a part of. Some sections of the book have been included by Nick and Myself to try and fill in the gaps and missing parts of Des' SBS story. These have been added for the enjoyment of the reader and for continuity in the story.

My collection of wartime SAS/SBS books has gone from a single book to now around twenty and whenever I enter a book store I am looking to see what I can add to my collection and learn from. One of these books is Gavin Mortimer's brilliant 'SBS in WW2 an Illustrated History'. It has served as an excellent resource for me and after discovering that there was an Illustration in his book referencing Des and his Brother Bill, I made contact with Gavin to pass on my appreciation and also, as I was quickly realising what an important and interesting document Grandpa's manuscript was, to ask if he could recommend a publisher that might be interested in the story. Pen and Sword was recommended and commissioning editor Tara Moran, Harriet

Fielding, Alana Brothers and Margaret Moran have all been great help and very encouraging throughout the process of getting this book made.

Gavin has also been very helpful in sharing some documents with me. For instance, the SBS Operational Report on Stampalia (modern day Astypalaia) which Des was a part of. As the pages of the manuscript are around 70 years old, and some of the writing at times could be difficult to read, this document helped to clear up some of the detail on other people who were involved in that operation.

I also want to thank my Dad Jerry, Uncle Iain and Aunt Andrea for their help and huge encouragement in getting this book made. Their interest has helped me to keep searching for the facts related to this story.

Nick's wife Cynthia has also been a massive help 'Down-Under', supporting him with each step and proof reading the work we have undertaken. Indeed my wife Emma has been very encouraging and our sons Ethan and Dominic have helped a little too.

I would also like to thank Craig Robertson, who administers the running of the fantastic website Specialforcesroh.com. To be able to put a face to some of the characters in these pages has made it an even more enjoyable story and I highly recommend you take a look at the huge archive of photos and documents on the website created by his late father John. It is a wonderful tribute to all those who have served in the Special Forces. Phil and Tim Williams, who run an excellent Facebook group for those who are relatives of World War Two SAS/SBS, have been a great help also.

Likewise I would also like to thank The Revd. John Russell of Little Gaddesden Parish Church for allowing us to use a picture provided by David Heard that is hosted on the website littlegaddesdenchurch.org.uk. The website has a brilliant page on Major Patterson of L Squadron with some impressive research carried out by the Churchwarden, Jane Dickson.

Thanks to Chris White for sharing his own knowledge and research of the SOE and SBS on Crete and also to Ian Layzell for allowing us to use a photo of Des in Beirut from his father Albert Layzell's personal collection and sharing with us his own excellent research into the SBS. We are also grateful to the SAS Association for giving us permission to use a small collection from their archives which appear in the following pages, as well as responding to many of our enquiries over the last couple of years.

Finally, I wish to express my gratitude for the warm welcome that my family and I received in August 2024 when we visited the village of Koufi in Crete. It has been amazing while working on this book how things have come together, whether by fate or by chance. Meeting Spyros in the Village who knew Manoli Kanakakis and was able to point us in the right direction to his home, then getting to meet Manoli's niece Katarina who was so welcoming and accommodating. It seems a miracle that almost 80 years to the day Grandpa

Acknowledgements

was covertly operating on the island that his children, grandchildren and great grandchildren were meeting the niece of one of his SBS comrades.

It has been my sincerest pleasure to learn the stories within these pages and I hope that you will enjoy reading about them as much as I have in the last two years.

Robert Marshall

FOREWORD
by Nick Marshall

During the 1960s both Dad & I worked (for different companies) in Holborn, London and for about three of those years I would travel alongside him in his company car on the hour-long drive into town. It was during this time that Des would often recount to me many of the details of his exciting SBS operations in the Second World War. These stories were fascinating and inspired me to join the Army Reserve as a Paratrooper and then 21SAS.

It also inspired me to go back-packing around Europe and the Mediterranean and to see places like the Greek islands, Cyprus, the Greek mainland, Italy & Yugoslavia. I wanted to visit the places where SBS operations had taken place in the Second World War.

Like nearly all fathers to their sons growing up, he was my hero and also a great role model.

If ever I asked for advice, he would give it and it was always good.

After the Second World War had ended and having been discharged from the Army, Dad returned to civilian life and found work in Central London. In the following years, he would return home from work to his wife Joan (my mother) and two young children (my sister and I) at their rented flat in East London then after supper would begin to write down the memories he had of his exciting and daring adventures on SBS operations in Southern Europe. Mum had encouraged him to do this, as often during the middle of the night he would suddenly wake up and sit bolt upright in a cold sweat, having been woken by one of the many nightmares he suffered about the war.

One recurring nightmare was of being chased across land by the pursuing German Army.

Today we would call this 'Post Traumatic Stress Disorder'.

Mum suggested that if he tried to put all his memories down on paper, this might clear his mind and help him dispel these nightmares. This remedy eventually had the desired effect.

Foreword

After many hours and years of putting pen to paper, the 300 foolscap page manuscript Dad had produced was sealed up, placed in an old fashioned hardback folder then put away on the top shelf of an airing cupboard in one of the bedrooms of the family home. By now we were living in Newbury Park and eventually it was forgotten about.

Sadly in August 1999 Dad passed away. He was 77 years old.

In 2015, Mum who was by this time aged 94, felt it was necessary to move out of the family home to an Aged Care Home in rural Essex.

With the impending sale of the property in order to finance her board, lodging and care in her new home, all the contents of the house had to be removed and it was only when clearing the house that to all the family's surprise we found Dads handwritten manuscript. It was agreed by the family that I should keep the manuscript as I had had six years of military experience (1965 – 1971, in 10 Para & 21SAS).

At the time I was still working and unfortunately had little time to read through all of Dad's copperplate handwriting style, which was difficult to decipher. I returned home to my wife and family in Western Australia and once again the manuscript was stored safely away.

In October 2022 the TV Series 'SAS Rogue Heroes' was aired on British television and Des' grandson Robert, who had previously seen Ben Macintyre's documentary series, watched the TV drama enthusiastically. He realised that although he knew his grandpa had served in the SBS during the Second World War, in reality he knew very little about what Dad's role was and where exactly he had served. He was eager to learn more.

Having contacted me in Australia, asking for any wartime stories I could tell of Dad's, I informed him about the manuscript. With mutual agreement we decided to have a crack at transcribing the entire document. And so, for the next twelve months, I would scan four pages of Dad's hand written manuscript and email them to Robert. He would then decipher the handwriting, word process the result and email the copy back to me for proof reading and to explain much of the Army, Navy & Air Force terminology.

This went on for a year and, as the story unfolded, we began to realise what an interesting and important story this was and indeed that others would certainly be interested to learn about the real life experiences of one of the pioneers of the now worldwide famous and revered SBS.

Des Marshall's life was exciting and varied. Des was a modest and understated man for all his accomplishments. He worked for the same company after the war, Crittall Windows, for over thirty years and was promoted to Export Sales Administration Manager. He had travelled all over the world. After the war Des joined the Army Reserve and rose through the ranks from being a Sergeant to a Commissioned Officer (Captain) and in 1966 he retired from the Army Emergency Reserve and went into the Army List as a Major. He was married to Joan for over fifty years and had five children.

Des had a great sense of humour too and was a dedicated catholic his entire life. Altogether he had served in the following Regiments: Royal Artillery, Special Boat Service, Intelligence Corps, Royal Corps of Transport and Royal Engineers. His medals and military ribbons bear testament to his British military service.

One of the remarkable things about this story is the amazing and vivid recollection Des had of the events he'd been involved in years previously, told in such detail that the reader of this story can feel as if they were there with him on SBS operations of the Second World War.

In a way it's a minor miracle that you are reading this story right now but, both Robert & I agree, it has been an absolute pleasure to bring Des' story & this book to life. This is a true story originally written by Des Marshall, who served as a member of L Squadron Special Boat Service Regiment (SBS) during World War 2 1943–1945.

CHAPTER I

WAR BREAKS OUT

September 1938 Munich Crisis. Joined Territorials, then a Royal Field Artillery Regiment at Stratford London E15.

August 1939 Attended camp at Bustard's Plain, Salisbury, for a fortnight.

1 September, 1939 Mobilization, as Hitler walked into Poland. Dashed home from work, met Bill, Des and John Murphy and Jack Jarvis who drove us to the Drill Hall. Great activity on office wallahs part. Stayed 'til nearly midnight, when sent home- lack of accommodation!

2 September Whole day spent checking slit trenches in parade ground and finally clocked out of billets at 11.00pm with Mrs. Bradstock (just married)!

3 September Marched to mass and ran back with air raid siren going full blast. Tin hats on and gas masks at alert- saw an old woman crying in the kerb. Ordered lie flat in Drill Hall, when a fat transport officer stood at the door sweating and waving two large service revolvers, warning that he'll shoot the first man that panics. No-one did! After that we spent the next few days being vaccinated, inoculated, having our kit checked and were paid out 10/- for possessing full kit, 10/- for years bounty, 5/- for being mobilised and for expenses for the year's drills, making nearly 13/-. We said we wished a war would start every year, as we thought this one would be all over by Xmas.

Our meals at that time stand out in my memory as consisting of kippers and brown stew!

When we went on manoeuvres to wanstead flats, we used 'Improvised' vehicles to draw guns. Our gun was drawn by a coal lorry!

In the first few weeks we had become Signallers and were able to avoid many of the odious tasks of the gunners and could loaf in the signal's stores. Parades were rather unusual. Battery Sergeant Major Black would stand before

Behind The Lines with The SBS: My Life in L Squadron during WW2

the whole battery and snap out orders, thrusting his square head forwards on his shoulders. 'On the right-cookhouse fatigues then latrines orderlies on the left'. The latrines orderlies, three of them, would then be inspected by their number ones, an acting unpaid lance bombardier supervising and an NCO by virtue of his office, which was indicated by a narrow yellow brassard worn on his right arm and earned him the title of 'Unclean'. He was a short fat cockney, who was given the job when no-one else would accept it. He was something of a comedian (self-styled) and after inspecting his 'Engineers', he would order them to 'Shape brooms', or 'Port buckets' and march them off the parade ground saluting the orderly officer with his brassard decorated arm and ordering eyes left as they passed!

Early in November, the buzz went round that there was a big move in the offing, but before it transpired the under 19 year-olds were posted away as being too young (presumably for active service) to an Anti-Aircraft (Ack Ack) regiment stationed in Norfolk. I was among a group sent to a 3-inch battery stationed at Watton Aerodrome and we were billeted in the village school under the charge of a weedy territorial sergeant who was too useless for operational use on the guns. He was assisted in our 'training' for seven to eight weeks by a large Norfolk bombardier, who was literally strong in the arm and weak in the head. All I can recall learning from the 'training' was how to smoke and drink, far more than was good for an eighteen-year-old soldier, or civilian for that matter. One outstanding feature of that horrible winter was a week's excruciating pain from toothache. There was no dentist in the station, and I had to wait until a civilian dentist came for his weekly visit from Norwich. During that week, we were marching, marching and marching in Field Service Marching Order, with and without arms and I thoroughly enjoyed myself all day with my jaw, but at night could get some relief by swallowing sufficient quantity of cider to remove all feeling.

'The Immatures', as we were known in that AA battery, were granted leave for Christmas 1939 (the war, amazingly enough, not having been won meanwhile!), and I went home with the princely sum of £2.0.0 for a week's enjoyment. This of course was spent to good effect on Christmas Eve in the company of Irishmen in the local club. It was a mouldy week, as my sister was sick in hospital and the family was very miserable in her absence. On 30 December I returned to Watton and arrived in the middle of the first snowstorm of many to come in that winter. We walked to the Aerodrome and were directed to the furthest perimeter where the unit my party was joining (our training having finished) was living in antiquated Nissen huts alongside their two guns and where we were to spend the next thoroughly miserable months of snow, cold and boredom, we London bred immatures being constantly derided for our ignorance of matters pertaining to Norfolk and Norwich.

War Breaks Out

Our unit had been recruited from a brewery in the county town and the officers were all the directors' sons and managers, the NCOs were the foremen and charge hands while the other ranks were just the other narks of the brewery too. Their minds were full of little else but beer and its merits, and they nearly all knew of its merits from experience other than brewing. There were, however, several who were very decent and helpful, mainly the older men. They taught us practically all we ever learnt about AA work, as those who were supposed to do the training weren't sufficiently interested in the 'immatures' to bother about them except to find fatigues and guards for them to carry out.

One of the most miserable periods of that winter for me was a week spent at the Regimental HQ at Honington Aerodrome as a clerk as they had found out that my pre-war occupation came in that classification. At the end of a week nagging at the RSM, I managed to get posted back to the lesser of two evils at Watton, in time to click for another posting to Mildenhall Aerodrome GOR, which was quite pleasant and brought out a couple of weekend leaves.

In March, I was recalled again as the battery was going to Watchet in Somerset for a firing camp. That camp was a tented place where we fired for a couple of hours each day between the incessant rainstorms. The outstanding feature of our shooting was our success (or failure) in shooting down the Queen Bee wireless operated plane by mistake. On our return to Watton after a fortnight I contracted a chill which developed into Otitis media (inflammation of the eardrum) which landed me stranded in the RAF sick bay for twelve days, after which time I had a week's sick leave. It was on this leave in 1940 that I met the girl who six years later was to become my wife.

On my return to Watton we were moved to Marham Aerodrome near King's Lynn where we started our nightly 'stand to's. These duties meant the whole section stood to the guns from dusk til dawn. When we dispersed, we

Des looking very young in the
Royal Artillery Regiment 1939.
(Marshall Family Collection)

Behind The Lines with The SBS: My Life in L Squadron during WW2

Des with his friend Des Murphy who after the war was 'Best Man' when he married his 'Girl' Joan. (Marshall Family Collection)

left a skeleton crew on the guns to keep lookout for aircraft and to take initial action while the main crew were getting to the guns from the huts after alarm.

One morning, we had just stood down at about six-thirty and were back in bed when after a few minutes, without warning, a succession of explosions brought us running half-dressed back to the gun site on top of the hill above the camp. A German Messerschmitt Me 210 had slipped out of the clouds about 15,000ft and dropped a stack of ten bombs across our gun site, fortunately missing everything important and making a line of small holes across the fields nearby.

Later on in the summer, (described in a book as 'amazing') we were transported to Duxford Aerodrome about 40 miles from London. We started our standard training operations in April and received no leave until September, when we were granted twenty-four hours per fortnight. During those five months we never spent one night in bed.

One September morning after we had closed down and were busy shaving, washing and some even having breakfast, we heard the alarm bells pealing frantically in the huts. The men dashed immediately to their places on the gun and installed with little time to spare before the shout of 'plane!' announced the appearance of a Dornier Do 17 dropping out of the clouds immediately over the aerodrome and preparing to make a run-in among the line of hangars and buildings containing the aircrews. The section commander gave the order 'action' and in a matter of seconds the routines of balancing acts on the predictor, assessing the height from the height-finds and setting fuses on the gun pits was being automatically performed by men who had done this so often in tedious practice runs day and night that the effort was second nature to them. Even so, each man was quivering with excitement at the first real opportunity of going into action against enemy aircraft, and the fuses being called by No.4 of the predictor crew were given in a tight, too-loud, voice showing the tenseness of his feelings, as he kept his pointer steady on the curves marked upon the fuse drum rotating slowly through the little window in his point of the predictor. This was one of the most important parts of the complicated routine of engaging aircraft and any slight miscalculations on the No.4 part would mean the failure of the action.

Today, however, there seemed to be no error on his part or on the part of any of the men doing their various duties, as on the order 'fire' from the Section Commander, both the 3-inch guns soared into action and in less than a minute five shells were soaring unerringly towards the plane glistening silvery in the morning sunlight. The first burst below the target, the second and third, in front and above and the best two appeared to explode upon the wing and fuselage. The plane immediately fell into a slow spiral as if the pilot were looking for a landing. It was some miles away when it hit and we couldn't see any explosion or smoke, but as we had the order to stand down, we saw the crash tender and ambulances speeding across the drome towards the last resting plane of several thousand pounds' worth of German war material.

Later on that day, we learned that the pilot and one of the crew, though wounded, were still alive and detained on the aerodrome, but the third member of the crew, who had lost an arm in the shell that had burst alongside the fuselage, had died on the way back in the ambulance. Our section commander called a parade and informed us that the general commanding our AA command had sent a telegram congratulating us on our cheap success and then the second commander ordered a barrel of beer to be opened and distributed free to the crews.

As if that success wasn't sufficient to keep the section talking for months, each man giving his quite unwanted account of the affair to everyone who in turn wanted to give their own, the following Saturday morning, exactly a week later, we engaged a small flight of Dorniers escorted by a long-range Messerschmitt fighter.

There were twelve aircraft altogether flying at 15,000ft, which is very nearly the 'in maximum range' for this gun but we opened fire and succeeded in downing one of the bombers. Unfortunately, through some error in the local GOR we had not been warned of our own fighters chasing the Germans and as our shells were travelling towards the formation of planes a lone Spitfire appeared among them and attacked the nearest bomber. Almost immediately one of our own shells burst below and behind the Dorniers followed by a cluster bursting all around the same place. The German aircraft suddenly started smoking and commenced to spiral down; as we watched the spitfire followed in its trail. We thought the brave pilot was chasing it down, but as the Germans fell slowly the Spitfire fell past it in a straight dive and continued to the ground where it burst into flames. The pilot however had bailed out at a safe height and a parachute was carrying him slowly to the ground, when one of the ME's peeled off from the formation and attacked the slowly swinging pilot as he hung in his chute harness.

The German fired several bursts at the helpless Britisher and the crash crews who picked him up after his landing found his legs almost severed by bullets; he died as they reached him. The sequel to that incident was the action of two RAF WOs who entered the guardroom wherein the survivors of that morning's German bomber were detained and who having sent the sentry outside for a while, spent several minutes in the guardroom cells, with the unharmed Germans. When the WOs left they told the sentry the Germans were sleeping and not to disturb them. When the sentry came to take their meal to the prisoners, two in number, he found them quite unconscious and badly battered. The RAF do not take kindly to Germans who machine gun pilots after they bale out and although the actual Messerschmitt which did the attack had got away (we had stopped firing as soon as the Spitfire had appeared on the scene and by the time the sky was clear of the unfortunate British plane, the German was out of range) the two WOs felt that their spleen was justifiably spent on two Germans, who would themselves not have hesitated to do as the fighter pilot had done.

The following summer and winter passed most uneventfully, as we simply carried out our stand-to each night which had become second nature to us, followed by a morning's rest and any afternoon spent filling sandbags and repairing our gun position, improving our camouflage and odd occasional hunting rats and rabbits in the woods at the back of the gun site. In the middle of August, we were relieved at Duxford and packed off to another Jimmy camp at Ty Croes in Anglesey, where we didn't shoot down any target planes but did quite averagely well otherwise. We didn't return to Duxford but were posted to Great Yarmouth and then Gorleston where we had the most action but did not have any great success in destroying any further German aircraft.

After Christmas 1941 I had the best news I had since leaving my TA unit. My elder brother Bill, who had remained in the Regiment, had put through a claim for me and after months of waiting, the RA records in London had finally got round to confirming my posting back to the Field Artillery. My brother's unit was at Beccles only a few miles away from my station at Gorleston, but in usual Army fashion I had to go first to Bungay where the HQ of the Regiment were installed. After a galling day waiting for transport, I was sent in a truck across the snowy wastes of Suffolk to Beccles arriving at my billet too late for supper and after the pub had closed.

War Breaks Out

From then until August, I had a busy if not entertaining time, going on schemes, training as a signaller and surprise of all surprises – stand-tos! These last were carried out in the most miserable place I ever had the misfortune to visit in England. Its name was Holly Grove. It was only after three months of gruelling hard labour that we were able to leave this dreadful place and life.

Each man had to spend several days every week digging down through feet of mud in the midst of this copse until we reached more or less solid gravel. We eventually did reach ground which didn't rise more than three inches or so above our boots and from then on, we laid down heavy bags of wood along three tracks to where they joined a fourth track. Alongside this we built a dug out roofed with elephant iron to form our Command post. The guns (four of them) were laid along the sidetracks on the extreme edge of the wood, well covered by camouflage nets and one object was to repel any attack from the nearby coast.

The forty-eight periods we spent in this manner each week is best forgotten as nothing, but unpleasant memories arise from them. In the summer we went to Sennybridge in Brecon, Wales for a firing camp and looking back on that fortnight I have only memories of rain and misty mountain tops, dragging guns or lorries out of muddy places and laying out and reeling in miles of telephone cable from gun positions to operating positions etc. After our spell at Sennybridge we returned to Beccles, but only for a few days and moved from there to Oulton Broad where we had a very comfortable set of billets and a dry easily accessible gun position, and we all felt we had finally clicked and prepared to settle down to a comfortable summer of drinking

Brothers Bill (left) and Des (right) 1939 in their Royal Artillery uniforms. (Marshall Family Collection)

and stand-tos. This optimism however was ill-timed for after a week or two of fairly uneventful soldiering the buzz went around that the regiment was going abroad. This was confirmed by the beginning of August, when we were officially notified and the exciting and interesting business of documentation, re-equipping etc. kept us busy until our embarkation leave.

In November I arrived home on leave in London in time for one of the 'warmest' parts of the blitz. This didn't bother me a lot as I spent most of the time with my girl who was an operator at Trunks Telephone Exchange in London and who had conveniently contracted a 'severe chill' which prevented her going to work, but not from accompanying me each day and night to what little entertainment we could find in those days of perpetual sirens and gun barrages.[1]

'His Girl' Joan Tingay 11th November 1943. (Marshall Family Collection)

CHAPTER 2

TO THE MIDDLE EAST

The Mediterranean is not an area with which the tourist associates rain. Nevertheless, as anyone can testify, who has spent the early winter in the Eastern Mediterranean, it can and <u>does</u> rain in the Levant coast, cold incessant demoralising rain, which often continues for several days without interruption. It was during one of these periods of unwaning wet weather that I had the first stretch of good fortune in my (up to then) not very distinguished career as a soldier. It was at that point when I finished with regimental routine guards and fatigues and began learning to be a soldier of the sort that fights and very often helps to win wars. It will be seen from these remarks that I did not like being a regimental soldier. This is no less than the truth, for I could think of no occupation which would be more repellent to myself than that of a member of the Territorial Regiment which has not been into action, and which is commanded by men whose experience of war is received at second hand and limited by schemes and exercises in England, Egypt and Iraq. I do not blame the inactivity upon these men, but I do blame the system which lays down the manner in which inactive soldiers must pass the time. This is, as everyone knows, by bull shine of every possible kind (bull shine is not the word, but the more expressive, less printable word will be recognised by those interested).

What the great ORs who become our military leaders fail to remember, in successive wars, is that civilian soldiers already accustomed to disciplining themselves before war makes it exigent that they be disciplined by others. The types who, between the wars, filled the ranks of our regular Army were not considered capable of self-discipline and were therefore the target of every petty aggravating chore that could be devised to compel them, by constant 'hazing' to 'fear god, honour the queen, stand straight and help others'.

However, many more competent to judge have dealt and no doubt will in the future deal with the rights or wrongs of war-time so-called discipline.

This stroke of luck came at the hour of the midday meal, on a streaming wet day when the regiment lay under canvas on the slopes of an olive-tree covered hill near the village of Zaghoria in Lebanon.

Behind The Lines with The SBS: My Life in L Squadron during WW2

Above: Members of 85th Field Regiment Royal Artillery Persia 1942. (Marshall Family Collection)

Left: Des' friend Arthur Wakefield. 463 Battery, 85th Field Regiment, Royal Artillery. Paiforce. Persia 1943. (Marshall Family Collection)

We were a field regiment of the Royal Artillery, who up until this time had been equipped with 25-pounder guns and 'Quads' for towing these weapons. On our arrival in the Lebanon a few weeks earlier however, we were informed that we were to become a mountain regiment, re-equipped with 3.7-inch mountain howitzers which would be transported by mules.

This last insult was too much to bear, especially as I didn't like marching (and we were promised plenty of that), so that when, one day, the orderly sergeant came the rounds asking for names of signallers interested in being posted to Special Service, I put my name forward as a last desperate, but I felt, vain effort to extricate myself from the horrible prospect of being 'valet to nag'.

I was crouching in the centre of our '180 pounder' tent trying to keep my kit as far from the muddy water which was overflowing from our drainage trench into the flow of the tent, bemoaning our lot in sympathy with the other nine signallers of my troop, when the flap opened to let in a flurry of rain and a soaked orderly sergeant, 'You're 885975 Marshall aren't you?' he read from a bedraggled paper. 'Yes, sarge'.

To the Middle East

'Right. Get up to the battery office, you're being posted' he said and withdrew into the rain before I could argue.

'What's this in aid of?' I had forgotten my application, but my memory was refreshed by the battery clerk who gave me the order detailing my move, medical exam and so on.

I was being posted to the 'Special Boat Section' of the SAS in Palestine. No further details were available, but the battery clerk commiserated with me on my bad luck! The following morning found me in the regimental transport on my way together with two others, supposedly strayers from other battalions, to Tripoli station.

There followed a week of frustrated enquiries at Beirut Transport Camp where the staff seemed less interested in passing-in the troops than finding enough mugs to fill the duty roster. We eventually prevailed on the office clerk to act on our behalf and were passed on to the Haifa Transit Camp where the comment was 'Special Boat Section? Never heard of 'em, you'd better get over to the cookhouse, spuds want bashing!'.

After a few more days of looking after the permanent staff's comfort, I noticed one afternoon a sergeant in strange dress wandering across the square. He was dressed in a beige beret with a cloth badge, a blue shirt carrying on its breast a pair of what appeared to be wings above an African star. The remainder of his attire consisted of a very brief pair of khaki drill shorts, hose fobs and of

Above left: Des in Kermanshah, Persia. (Modern day Iran) 1943. With 85th Field Artillery Regiment. RA. (Marshall Family Collection)

Above right: Bill in Paiforce, Persia. August,1943. (Marshall Family Collection)

Behind The Lines with The SBS: My Life in L Squadron during WW2

Above left: Des in Beirut, 1943. (Marshall Family Collection)

Above right: Bill and Des. Beirut, 1943. (Marshall Family Collection)

all things- a pair of brown boots! I picked up my yard broom, strolled across and asked him, 'What mob is that sarge?'

'SBS.' he replied.

'What? Does that mean Special Boat Section?'

'That's right'.

'Good Lord, that's the crowd we've been looking for a fortnight, the barnacles in this place say they never heard of them'.

I told him of our troubles. The sergeant made disparaging remarks about the position of the base wallahs but agreed to visit the office with me and 'see about it'.

The RSM was at his desk when we arrived and I was surprised at the respect he showed a mere sergeant, for when the stranger asked him if he'd ever heard of 'SBS', the senior man said 'of course' and smiled deprecatingly at the sergeant when he told how we had been bitched about.

'If they'd said "SBS" in the first place I'd have known what they wanted' he said.

"Ok, Will you arrange for transport for them?" asked our saviour 'Or shall I get it from Azzib?'

'That's alright Sergeant, I'll lay it on, don't you worry!' said the great man.

He was as good as his word and the following day saw me and my two comrades in trouble rolling up the dusty coast road, going north out of Haifa.

To the Middle East

An hour later our lorry slowed down and turned right off the road and started climbing up a gradient. The whirring complaint of the gearbox climbed to a high-pitched scream, dropped to a gentle moaning as we topped the crest and finally died as the truck rolled to rest.

We dismounted and found ourselves alongside a group of half a dozen huts, situated on the ridge of a long low hill running parallel to the north-south road which runs up to and beyond the Syrian Border at Ras-en-Nakurah.

Behind the huts were three or four EPIP tents which had been sunken into pits of a depth equal to half the tent walls.

The hill fell away slightly to the North and then rising again half a mile away it continued its undulating progress to the greater hills which marked the border of Palestine. At the top of the rise which formed the opposite end of the 'saddle' which begun with our own hill, stood moon tents and a hut or two, and between them a heaped collection of odd-looking craft, which looked more than anything like the canoes used by Eskimos, and called, I believe, kayaks.

I was to know a great deal more of these boats in the future, but at that time could only speculate on their form or purpose.

While I was surveying what I guessed to be my new home with the morbid interest of a soldier newly transplanted (albeit at his own will) a burly form came from one of the tents. He was a sergeant and dressed in such the same manner as the man I had met in Haifa Transit Camp, but this time I took the opportunity of studying his cap badge.

It was of a strange design and its very nature suggested exciting possibilities to my mind, so weary of trying to find the war and so fed-up with exercise and schemes. (All that I had experienced since being mobilised as a Territorial four years earlier).

The design of the cap badge was that of a vertical dagger with the hilt upwards and from each side of the blade, immediately below the hilt sprung a wing like that of a conventional angel. Across the lower of the blade just above the point a scroll fluttered bearing the words 'Who Dares Wins'. The whole design was in silver thread woven onto a dark blue cloth shield.

The newcomer looked at us, grinned and said 'Hello, who're you? Oh, I know you're the new Sigs, but only three?'

'That's right Sarge, and what a hell of a time we've had trying to get here. No-one's ever heard of this mob!'

'Didn't want to more like' he said, 'Still now you're here, get your kit down in that tent and get some scoff at the cookhouse yonder'.

We followed him into a tent, dumped our bedding rolls down on the trestle beds inside, grabbed our pots and pans and went off to have our first Scoff in the 'SBS'.

CHAPTER 3

TIME FOR A BEASTING

During the day of our arrival, we discovered quite a lot about our surroundings from information supplied by our new war-hardened comrades. The camp we were in was known as Raiding Forces Headquarters and was the base of the remains of the Special Air Service (of which Special Boat Section was a component) and also a newly formed unit to be known as Raiding Support Regiment.

RFHQ was a few miles from the Arab town of Azzib, 12 miles or so from the Syrian border, at Ras en Nakurah, and the nearest habitation of any sort was the Jewish resort of Nahariya, on the coast, a matter of a mile away to the south.

The main body of the SAS had returned to England, leaving only a few key men, such as the sergeant who welcomed us, to tie up the threads. The SBS, now to receive the title of 'Special Boat Squadron', was being reformed after heavy casualties in the 1943 autumn campaign in the islands. This was the reason for our posting, as a large number of wireless operators had either been put in the 'bag', killed, or posted home to help form the nucleus of a greater SAS.

In addition to myself and my two companions, half a dozen other signallers had just joined from their respective regiments, two from RA, four from tanks and one from Infantry. Only two of the others from the tank regiment had previously 'been to war', so we of the 'muleteers', weren't to 'feel out of it!'

The whole atmosphere of our new camp was completely unlike that of any in which I had previously 'suffered'. Every one of the old hands was friendly, the food was good, the canteen full of beer and chocolates, the tents dry and the NCOs helpful if inclined to pout their chests on which most sported 'Operational Wings'. This, I found out later, was the greatest honour which could be bestowed on an SBS or SAS type and was given for outstanding daring and resourcefulness, more coveted than a decoration, save possibly the VC. It was asserted that the wings, normally worn on the right shoulder after passing a course of parachute training, could be put on the left breast over the medals (if any).

As may be imagined by any reader who had not had the experiences for himself, the realisation that we should be called upon to jump out of aeroplanes

Time for a Beasting

gave food for profound thought and caused prolonged discussion among we new boys on the reaction this having to parachute might have upon us, and each one of us wondered if he would stand up to the test without weakening. It seemed to me at that time that no greater call could be made on a man's courage than to ask him to fling himself into space from hundreds of feet in the air! I'll wager that few, if any, of us went to sleep that night without having qualms and spasms of panic at the idea.

The following morning, we were all out on the eastern slopes of the hill, after breakfast, under the loving care of a man we came to know as 'Muscles'[2]. He was the physical training instructor, and was a man who appeared to have found his vocation! 'Muscles', an essentially cheerful man, roared with delight at the sight of a dozen or so regimental soldiers to play with; men whose muscles had become flaccid from riding in tanks or lorries and who had obviously never marched further than the cookhouse, or canteen! His favourite sport, I was to learn, consisted of lining us up in pairs, face to face on either side of a monstrous log like a telegraph pole and having told us all to lift, then proceeded to put us through all the most complicated back breaking evolutions it is possible to contrive with twelve men and a hunk of wood.

After ten minutes or so of this he gave us a 'break' by way of 'press-ups' which will be recognised as an anal torture beloved of PTIs in all services. This is a performance whereby the victim lies flat on his face with his hands flat on the ground below his shoulders, and with his body rigid, must press upwards to the extent of his arms, <u>slowly</u> and then lower again, slowly. The first one or two are easy, but the last dozen are fiendish! After an hour of this type of exercise, and many others too horrible to mention, the Muscles flung away his dozen or so ruined victims and we tottered off to the canteen to have a tea break of ten minutes.

The canteen was a cheerful little place with posters depicting soldiers' graves with the usual admonitions about not speaking to strangers and revealing secrets, etc., but one poster gave me a great deal of disquiet every time I saw it, and that was one of a man dressed as a parachutist tumbling out of an aircraft in the correct position of 'attention', followed by another picture of the same man during his descent, with the words 'Head well forward, shoulders round, knees together, watch the ground!' That's parachute lingo!

After our break we formed a class under the tutorship of 'Bunny', our sergeant friend of the first day. He and a corporal named Bob then instructed us until lunch on the art of wireless operation over long distances. As I had been a wireless operator in the Artillery for two years, I felt I knew something about this subject, but after an hour of their lectures and questions and answers, I despaired of ever being good enough. This opinion I found shared by my fellow pupils, in respect of their own abilities.

Behind The Lines with The SBS: My Life in L Squadron during WW2

The hour after lunch was devoted to practical wireless, which was more in our line, but I was amazed at the compactness and efficiency of the powerful little 'B' set we were to handle. Nothing so effective had ever been dreamed of by my stodgy RA signals officer and NCOs. Later on, when I had mastered the intricacies of theory and practice on their great little instrument, I wondered how I could ever have considered myself a wireless operator when applying for the transfer to the new unit.

The afternoon was finished off by the whole group being 'doubled' down to the beach at Nahariya, dressed in boots, drill shorts and hose lengths. We splashed about in the surf for an hour cooling off after our labours and were finally recalled to the beach at 4.00 pm by the sergeant. The activity in the mellow blue water had removed most of the aches and pains brought about by our drilling (or grilling) under 'Muscles', and I dressed feeling reasonably fit and looking forward to tea.

My exhilaration was soon beaten to its knees, however, for as soon as we had formed up to return to camp 'Bunny' looked back and forth at his small command and remarked 'Feeling fit?'

'Yes, Sarge!'

'Good, 'cos you'll need to be fit this evening, we're going for a run-walk!' The very prospect brought back all my aches and I wondered if these people ever gave you time to yourself.

'You needn't worry about hurrying over your tea' added Bunny, morse training won't be 'til six, and we'll go out at seven! It won't be for long either, I've got a solo school at eight so we'll be back by then!'

It seemed to me that a man who could look forward to playing cards after a day's strenuous activity such as we had enjoyed, was deserving of respect, so I didn't pose the questions spinning in my mind and we were off immediately after, trotting back up the long hill to the camp.

The sergeant was as good as his word and commencing sharply at six we played busily with pencil and paper translating dots and dashes (delivered at higher speed than I had ever hitherto been expected to 'read') into blocks of five letters. As I was missing at least one letter in ten, I began to despair, but when I was considering retiring from the contest, Bunny said 'Ok, that's enough, buzz off and get your skates on and be outside in five minutes!'.

At the appointed time we were lined up in a dismal group outside the canteen (wishing we were inside) and along came this prodigious man Bunny.

'Right, off we go, and we'll start with a double!' and he loped off down the hill like a young chamois.

We followed at a steady trot trying to forget our aching limbs and minds, as he led us along the dark road towards Azzib. The route was not involved, as we remained on the main road, trotting and walking at intervals of

Time for a Beasting

about five minutes each until we came nearly to the town of Azzib, where Bunny permitted a ten minute 'drag' on our cigarettes before repeating the performance all the way back to the camp. The outstanding thing I noticed about that particular piece of exercise and on subsequent occasions, was the speed of marching in the SBS. It was at least half as fast again as the speed to which I had been accustomed on the occasions on which I had been called upon to march. I found later that this rate of progress was invariable even across country and I was surprised how quickly one became used to travelling at this rate. It is my opinion that such fast marching does not cause the fatigue associated with normal route marching.

In this respect I would mention that we did not 'march' in the SBS, at least, not in the accepted sense. We moved usually in single file, but spaced out at irregular intervals and did not keep step with each other.

Later, when we really went into training, and did most of our travelling across hilly country, we carried Bergen rucksacks loaded up to about 60lbs weight. We rarely used roads, and often ignored marked tracks, preferring (at least, those in charge preferring) to keep to rough ground. I think each individual evolved the most comfortable way of moving according to his own ideas and I myself developed the habit of walking with my head down, watching the feet of the man ahead, regulating my breathing according to the gradient- so many steps breathing in, so many steps breathing out- my mind focused in the immediate present, without futile conjecture on how far it may to the top of that crest, or how soon we may expect a respite from the steady strain put upon our calf and thigh muscles, but the regular uphill climbing, downhill walking was equally hard of course, and the strain may have been slightly greater as one tried to support one's body under the weight of the pack, without losing one's footing or falling.

I mention this in passing, as it will be found later how much walking was involved in our training and finally in our operations. And one of the principal reasons I had left the 'Muleteers', was owing to the prospect of doing 'big walks!'

As we rounded a bend of the road the dark bulk of our hill came into sight through the clear night air and we noticed the few lights of the camp glittering a faint welcome. That scene was fairly typical of our early training, the weary sweating recruits running ever slower up the gradual incline, their heavy boots beating an irregular tattoo on the metalled surface of the road, the only other sound being an occasional gasp as one or other of us a released a lungful of air, breathing through the nose while our bodies were being subjugated to exertion to which we were so unaccustomed.

Bunny permitted us to walk up the final steep slope to the huts and tents and dismissed us at the top saying, 'Well that's not bad for the first day, but we'll really have to get down to this business from now on if you're to get up to scratch- goodnight lads!'

'Goodnight Sarge!'.

My tent-mates and I walked slowly over to our billet ruefully discussing the days ahead. Although we moaned in the accepted manner of soldiers, I felt and I am sure the others felt too, that at least we were aching in a good cause and looked forward beyond the initial toughening up to the time when we would take our place alongside these hard-bitten men we saw wandering about looking, for all their toughness, as though they enjoyed every second of their life. Their appearance suggested that they were only wandering aimlessly around the camp until such a time as they could again get away and carry on from where they left off at the end of the desert and Dodecanese campaigns.

The other members of my tribe started the inevitable bridge school when we had settled down in the tent, but as I am hopeless at card games and also because my feet felt like sacks full of broken bottles, I climbed carefully into my bed (to save the blisters from the unwelcome attentions of the Army blankets!), turned over, and slept.

Newly recruited to the SBS, Des signed this To Joan, With all my love. They would go on to marry after the war. (Marshall Family Collection)

CHAPTER 4

OFF FOR A NICE WALK

At the foot of the eastern slopes of the hill on which stood RFHQ lay a deserted plain running north as far as the eye could see and bounded on the south by orange groves. The eastern edge of this plain, about 3 miles across, was marked by the beginnings of a range of hills running roughly parallel to the coast, the nearest point of which was about 2 miles away on the opposite side of our camp.

After a number of days roughly similar to that previously described, and notable only for the gradual disappearance of various old members, (I found later that most of them had gone home to England to rejoin SAS, while others had gone to Cairo to establish a training depot at Abbassia), we were grouped together at the end of our afternoon bathe and exercise when Bunny addressed us:

> 'We're doing a scheme tonight, so I want you all ready at six with your shirts, battle trousers and boots. Draw weapons from the armoury and I'll give you the griff when we start.'
> 'Shall we need tin hats?' queried one soul. 'Tin hats? What are they for? I haven't seen one since I landed in Egypt four years ago!' the sergeant replied scornfully. 'Get off now and don't flannel, the Armoury's in that hut yonder'.

The Armoury was a joy to perceive. Always interested in small arms, I prevailed upon the enthusiastic armourer, (who needed little persuading), to conduct me on a tour round his treasures. There were weapons of all types, shapes and sizes; Italian Breda heavy machine guns. Beretta pistols and Sub-machine guns, German MG 15s, those first-class machine-guns whose vicious brrp was to become unwelcomingly familiar, Schmeisser machine pistols and American carbines, not to mention British Tommy-guns, Sten guns (most unpopular among the SBS!) Colt.455 revolvers and sundry other familiars. The Short Lee Enfield, though the most efficient of all rifles, was not widely used in the SBS, as automatic weapons were the order of the day, the rifle being only used, one to each patrol, as a sniper's weapon fitted with telescopic sights, but even so was rarely taken on a 'job'.

I chose for its lightness and compact ease of carriage, an American carbine, although it became accepted among the signallers later not to carry any other weapon than a pistol which was quite enough when it is considered that we always carried our own wireless sets in addition to only as much personal kit as was only essential. This meant that the signallers generally carried heavier, more awkward packs than the ordinary patrol-men; although it often happened that generous comrades shared our personal kit among them, leaving us only our sets and batteries to carry.

That evening we were briefed on the exercise by the instructor. It was a simple enough scheme and called for little skill or field training (a fortunate event for those of us whose last officers had not apparently considered us brilliant enough to learn more than the elements of map reading and whose training in that direction had consequently suffered).

Bunny spread his map on the table and showed us a point on a hill about ten minutes inland from the camp. 'That's the objective' he informed us 'I want you to get there, under your own steam, take any route you care to choose. I'll set you off in pairs at short intervals, those with the longest legs going last. Team up if you happen to meet, but this is the snag. I'll be at the destination with a truck and have a brew-up ready for ten pm. Anyone not there by that time will be unlucky, so make sure you keep going'.

I and my partner were despatched about mid-way through the 'hardships' and set off, for want of a better direction, straight down the eastern side of our hill on to the plain. It was by this time quite dark, the month being October, and the hour six-thirty pm.

The plain had appeared quite smooth and flat from our vantage point, but we soon discovered that this was not the case. At some time, I imagine some enterprising farmer had ploughed the arid soil, only to give up in despair before reaping the benefits of his labours. The ruts were deep and unevenly spaced, so that we were unable to make a fair judgement of when a sudden jolt up the leg would indicate that we had either stepped down into a rut or out instead of onto a ridge, or vice versa.

However, we made progress, even if it were irregular and uncomfortable. After what seemed like an age, I looked at the watch with which we had been issued (not without dire threat of what would be the result of its loss under our care!) and found we had been going for an hour. I judged from this that we must be nearing the further edge of the plain, and was straining my eyes through the inky blackness when my companion muttered 'What the b---?'. Before I could ask the reason for this sudden outburst I found the answer. We had wandered in the darkness into the gravity water tank which obviously had a disastrous leak. Disastrous to us as we were bogged down in six inches of body clinging mud which was all that was left of the saturated soil encircling the tank. Before we finally pulled ourselves clear of the bog, we were plastered with Palestinian soil!

My partner and I sat wearily on the nearest dry land and proceeded to clean off as much mud as possible, A hopeless task but gave us an excuse for resting those feet of ours. How often in the future was I to give thought to the feet so long neglected in the past!

While we were sitting there, we noticed a light glimmering a few hundred yards away and we rightly guessed we were at the edge of the plain and near a small hamlet which could have been seen from the camp. This not only marked the end of the plain, but also indicated the start of the rising ground, and after we moved off, we found that we were climbing a long gradual incline past the few darkened houses and then found to our relief that we were on a road of sorts. From the map it appeared that this road would take us nearly to the point indicated by Bunny as our objective, so we decided to stay thereon as long as possible.

By now the mud remaining on our boots and slacks was drying and made a brittle cracking noise with each step we took, until eventually it fell away leaving us dirty but at least more comfortable.

Further up the slope we found the road wound through groves of fruit trees so we took the opportunity to trespass and relieved our parched throats with the juice of half-ripened oranges. This, by the way, was a form of robbery not particularly frowned upon by the owners of the orange groves, as they were hard put to dispose of all their crops, the export side of their business being practically at a standstill, and I have on occasion seen large mounds of rotting oranges which have been surplus to the requirement of the marmalade and soft drink factories. These unwanted oranges were often used for feeding cattle and I remembered on one occasion seeing an enormous water-buffalo munching an equally large size in grapefruits, with the luscious juice dripping down his mournful chops!

Shortly afterwards we found ourselves nearing the summit of the hill we were climbing. As we reached the crest, a light flared a few yards ahead of us and we found two of our party lighting cigarettes. They had reached the top in front of us by coming up the rough side, not being lucky enough to locate a road, as we had. We joined them and after a short break we checked our position and found we were about 2 miles across country from our objective which lay at the top of a hill two valleys further east.

The four of us turned off the road and down through bracken and bushes growing thickly on the side of the hill. The going was much rougher here, and we lost a lot of time in diversions to avoid large clumps of thick brushwood. However, we came successfully to the top of the first hill and, from the light of the newly risen moon, made short work of the second valley.

It was nearly 10.00 pm as we scrambled up the last few yards of the last hill and arrived sweating and very weary on the main road running across the top.

Bunny had been as good as his word, and in the light of the headlamps of a stationary truck we saw him and his driver busily occupied over a Benghazi (dirt and petrol) fire brewing up a dixie of tea. Several other signallers had arrived before us and were stretched out resting luxuriously on the rough grass by the roadside watching someone else work.

We compared notes while gratefully drinking huge mugs of scalding hot sweet tea and looking forward to climbing into the truck and going home to bed. It came as a sad shock as Bunny and his driver packed up their brewing kit and loaded it on the lorry, said 'Well, lads most of you made it, only two more to come, so I reckon you'll do ok. Don't forget no loafing in a skip, tomorrow morning I want you all out at 8.00 am ready to meet our new sigs officer who's coming to take you off my hands. I'm pushing off now, so you can make your way back by any route, use this road if you like, it'll take you back to the houses on this side of the plain, and you've only got to go that short distance across country, so you'll find it fairly easy!'.

We had to walk back! This was considered a little hard, but no cajoling on our part could move this flinty hearted ruffian. 'It's all part of your training' he maintained, and we wasted no more breath in arguing. Soon after the truck had gone the stragglers turned up so we waited while they had a blow and we moved off on our weary way homeward.

We were loud in our condemnation of such Nazi methods and several of the more outspoken ones voiced the thoughts of us all in saying that we were beginning to think that life in Special Service wasn't much fun after all, and wondered if we had made a mistake in leaving the cloistered life of regular units!

Silence descended after a while however, as I for one was too busily thinking of the irreparable damage this sort of activity must be doing to my feet, and so lost was I in the interesting prospect of being a permanent invalid I didn't notice the sound which made the others stop. 'What is it?' I asked. 'Sounds like a bloody lorry or something' was the reply 'Coming this way too, same direction as we're going'.

One of the Tankies, a tall Canadian who had 'been around some' took charge and deployed us across the road in the path of the approaching vehicle. The whirring of the engine grew louder and eventually round the bend came- a bus! At first it seemed the driver hadn't seen us as the bus came at an unremitting speed almost up to us before we heard the brakes squealing in protest as he tried to push the pedal through the floorboards, in his terrified efforts to pull up.

Off for a nice walk

The bus rolled to a stop and the driver, a Palestinian, leaned out of his cab, his eyes staring from his head and his voice rising to a tinny falsetto as he demanded the reason for this attack.

One can understand his mistaking us for bandits, when it is appreciated what sight suddenly met his eyes on a dark and lonely road in the hinterland of the country.

Most of us were hatless, in shirts of various types, the only semblance of uniform being our Battle trousers and boots. We were dirty (and in my case at least) mud bespattered. Add to this the fact that all of us were nonchalantly holding our weapons at the ready, and it will be seen that our bus driver was justified in his error.

It had been 'Lofty's' idea, of course, to engender the idea in the driver's head, and he remarked afterwards 'Yes and if the bastard hadn't stopped, I'd have given him a burst in the tyres!' I have no doubt that this would in fact have been the unfortunate drivers' fate had he attempted to break through our control!

Lofty, among his other accomplishments, had a reasonable command of Arabic and asked in the tones of the innocent and benighted traveller, if we could possibly prevail upon the undoubted and obvious kindness of the Palestinian to such an extent as to beg a lift as far as he was going in our direction! The fact that a German Schmeisser was accidentally pointing straight up at him may have been an added encouragement to the driver to exercise his kindness, but he immediately agreed to the proposal, and we piled into his once clean bus and settled back comfortably till we reached a point as near as possible to our camp.

This point turned out to be a stone's throw from my old friend the water tank, and after bidding a fond farewell to our benefactor in which pledges of eternal goodwill were exchanged, we set off on our last leg (this was almost literal in my case, as the rest in the bus had given my feet a chance to forget that they were undergoing a course of torture), and the call on them to do more work that night nearly persuaded me to retire from the unequal contest and spend the night in heather.

We reached camp shortly after midnight, climbed into our friendly blankets and slept once more. I spent something of at least three quarters of an hour attending to the wounds abounding on my ruined stumps before I considered them ready for the morrow's bludgeoning and then, and only then, did I collapse into my temporary paradise.

Chapter 5

ON TO CAIRO FOR SIGNALS TRAINING

The officer in whose charge we were placed the next day turned out to be newly joined from the Corps of Signals, and he informed us, during a short address, that we were to go to Cairo for further training.

A day or so later, in an open 3-ton lorry, we were on the long road that led down through Palestine to Egypt. This journey took us down the coast of Palestine past Haifa and Athlit where the ruins of a Crusader Castle stand gaunt and deserted like a forgotten sentinel at the end of a spit of land formerly the north arm of a small bay.

The course of the road lay between the mountain range and the sea for several miles beyond Athlit until the mountains became hills and finally sloped away into the coastal plain. Across the brown and green plain our lorry rolled to Lydda where we saw a number of transport planes parked on the tarmac of a peace-time aerodrome. The monotonous movement of the lorry, as always, drugged my senses, and I slept on top of a pile of kit until I awoke to find that we were running through more hills into Beersheba. This was very much an Arab town, and I would have liked to stop and explore, but our long journey did not permit many stops, and we travelled on into the barren country of Southern Palestine, into the desert until we stopped to refresh at As-Luj transit camp. This halt was very brief, and we moved on into the gathering dusk for a few miles and then ended our day's journey at a point by the roadside which could only be described as a map reference. We didn't have tents to pitch so we rigged our tarpaulins from the side of the truck to the ground, sufficient cover only to prevent us from being saturated by the heavy desert dew.

Most of the following day we were occupied in the long monotonous journey across the Sinai Desert where the newly constructed road frequently ran alongside and sometimes over that built by General Allenby's forces in the First World War. It is difficult to judge distances when the scenery is never changing sand dunes, and I was beginning to think we would never reach the

On to Cairo for Signals training

edge of this desolate wasteland, when we came quite suddenly up to El Qantara on the Eastern bank of the Suez Canal.

After a meal we were treated to a singsong accompanied by the captured Italian guitar of one of the SBS 'veterans' and incidentally some very tall (but I've no doubt true) stories of their past campaigns!

I crossed the Suez Canal for the second time (the first time being on my way to Iraq) but transported by the ferry instead of the pontoon bridge our regiment had used on its eastern journey. Once again, I saw Ismailia, a town where I had spent several enjoyable evenings when we were at El Tahag Camp in the Canal Zone, and then on we rolled down the road bordering the sweet water Canal (I often wondered who the wit was responsible for the title of this foul ditch!). I remember on one occasion seeing, at separation points along the length of this canal, a woman washing the legs of a cow standing up to the udders in the canal, further on a man drinking from the same water, and a few yards away a young girl dhobying her filthy clothes!

It was said, and I believe it, that if a soldier were to fall into this canal, he would be given sixteen injections to inoculate him against the various diseases to which he would be prone from contact with the corrupt water.

We reached Cairo, an unpleasant town in my view, as the afternoon was drawing to its close and, moving through its streets of frantic movement dodging the overcrowded trams hurtling madly along at breakneck speed, we arrived at the gates of Abbassia garrison, on the further outskirts of the town.

This garrison is typical of Army quarters at home and abroad, so it was with misgivings that I visualised our being in the gloomy barracks, but my pessimism was unfounded, for we drove to the furthest perimeter of the garrison to where the sand starts and arrived at our destination, a tented camp known as 'Warren B'.

We were greeted by an officer of the Long-Range Desert Group and I found that there were several merits of this famous unit living in the camp and that they were the nucleus of a new LRDG

Wireless kit similar to what Des would have used while on operations. This is a later version the MK123 Transceiver. (Marshall Family Collection)

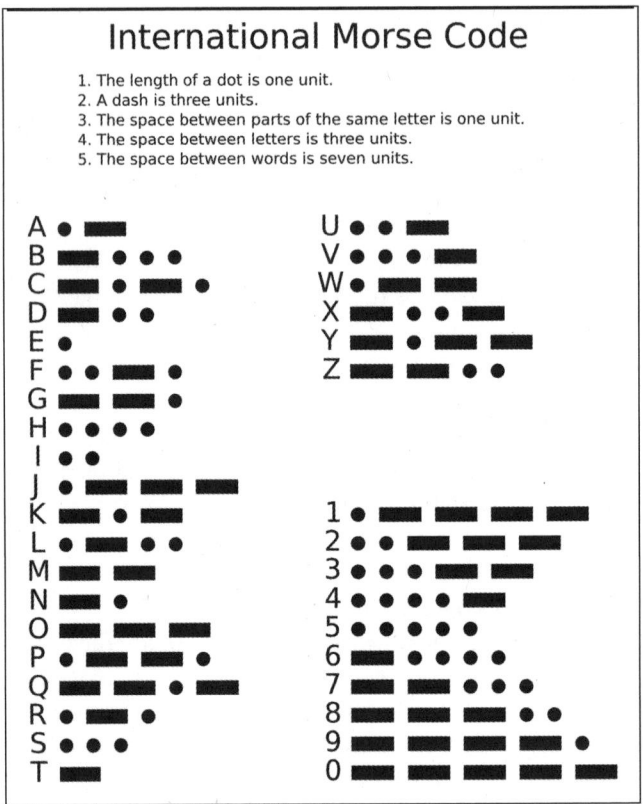

International Morse Code chart.

which was also being incorporated in R/Forces. This camp was to be the Signals Training Base for R/Forces and we were all under the instruction of a brilliant wireless man named Maric, a sergeant of the LRDG, who, before joining them in their daring desert raids had been a sergeant in the Palestinian Police and was full of yarns of both sections of his career.

    Our training started next day and was on similar lines to the routine we had followed at Azzib, with the exception that instead of a bathe in the sea with which to finish the afternoon, we were treated to a trot all-round the garrison for an hour! Another exception was that we had free evenings from 5.00 pm and could if we wished go into Cairo; I took advantage of this opportunity only on one or two occasions, because, as I said previously, I don't like Cairo and was never particularly happy sitting in its so-called cabarets or cafes drinking 'Stella' beer. Most of my friends from Azzib were card-happy anyway, so that I would have had to go alone, although the couple of times I did go down to the town it was at the request of one or other of these people who wanted an evening away from cards.

On to Cairo for Signals training

The period was not a particularly lucky one for me, as 2 weeks after our arrival, I was put in the garrison hospital with a poison which developed from an infected spot on my finger. This kept me out of circulation for a matter of days only, and I was back at the grind again.

Raiding Forces was at this time erecting a long-range wireless station out at Mena under the shadow of the pyramids and each day a small party of us were sent over to the new site, to give any labouring assistance which was required. My turn came after we had been at Abbassia about a month, and together with half a dozen others I was put on to the task of assembling a huge wireless mast built up of short thick sections.

We were given a stand easy during the course of the morning, and I was enjoying a cup of tea in the canteen, when a man came into the room whom I recognised as the driver who had brought us down to Cairo from Palestine. He looked around a while, saw me and came over.

'Blimey, I'm glad I've found you' he said. 'You're wanted back at Warren B, ak dum'.

'What for?' I asked.

'Search me, but I was told to find you, and no-one knew whether you were out training on the sets, down in the signal store or up here. I tried 'em all and this place was last. Anyway, come on. We'd better get cracking.'

We climbed into the seat of one of that type of signal wagon known to all as a 'Gin Palace' and we hared back to the camp. I felt sure that it was a matter of life and death, and from the reckless pace my driver kept up, it looked like being a matter of our death.

Our Gin Palace screeched to a stop outside the office of 'Warren B' camp, and the unit clerk was waiting outside to greet me with 'Get your kit packed right away and be back here in ten minutes- you're off!'

'Off where?' I was beginning to get annoyed at this tearing around without knowing the cause.

'Tell you when you come back- but hurry!' was all the satisfaction I obtained however, so I did as ordered, and by doing some remarkable packing, was back at the office within the time limit.

The major who was in charge of RF Signals met me in the office and told me I was to be taken to MEFHQ in Cairo where I would receive further instructions. 'Take this letter and give it to Major B in department Z' he handed me a folded envelope. 'You!, Oliver!!' he addressed my speed happy comrade, 'Take him to MEFHQ wait, and then take him where he tells you!'.

This secrecy seemed a little unnecessary for the movement of one humble signaller, but I must confess that I experienced a sense of excitement as we raced back into Cairo.

CHAPTER 6

CAIRO CENTRAL TO PALESTINE BY TRAIN

I was admitted to the HQ after being scrutinised by the MPs at the barbed wire roadblock in the road outside. Another Redcap led me upstairs to the second floor of the grand HQ building and up to a door marked 'RF Movements'.

The inmate of this office, a cheery young major accepted and read the contents of the envelope I carried. He looked at me for a moment and said 'I see, right! Hold on a second and I'll fix you up.' – More secrecy!

He appeared a sympathetic type, so I appealed to him to put me out of my misery and give me an indication of what was to be my fate. 'Eh? Don't you know?' he seemed surprised, 'Good lord, it's simple enough. One of your patrols is off on an urgent job, I know that much, and you are to join them in Palestine as wireless operator.'

'It wouldn't be Azzib would it?' I asked.

'You know it?'

'I do Sir, and I'll be glad to get back up there. I don't go much on this jewel of the East!'

He grinned 'Nor do I but I have to stay here and do a job any old dug out could manage. Still, we'll get you fixed up and at least you'll be off out of this unpopular town'.

The major disappeared into an inner office, and I heard the clatter of a typewriter for a few moments. He reappeared and handed me two slips of paper. 'This is your railway warrant and this your movement order. Show them both to the RTO at Cairo Central, and he'll see you're looked after'.

I thanked him and dashed off downstairs to the truck waiting outside. The driver looked at me for instructions and I told him to get over to Cairo Central to catch a train leaving in a matter of twenty minutes or so.

This was a bad mistake on my part, for the driver obviously thought his normal speed insufficient to meet the present emergency. I'm sure I had more narrow escapes in that short trip than ever was the case in action.

Cairo Central to Palestine by train

However, we arrived at Cairo Central in one piece and with time to spare. I thanked the driver, who took his leave and then I carried my kit over to the RTO office.

A sergeant took the slips of paper, read them and handed them back. He turned to a corporal wearing a white brassard on his arm and said, 'Take this cloak and dagger merchant on to the Palestine train and see him fixed up ok?'

We struggled through the usual maze of humanity wearing khaki and blue or filthy white robes and reached the train. My guide helped me aboard with my kit and then surveyed the scene in the crowded coach.

'Just a minute, I'll go get you a seat' he told me and moved off between the seats. About halfway down the coach he stopped by a Palestinian soldier sprawled out with his kit on a whole seat to himself.

'This your kit?' he asked. 'Yes? Well, move it, and make way for soldier.'

The Palestinian didn't appear to like his tone, and answered with a stream of his own language, but didn't make any move.

Apparently, the corporal understood his remarks, for he reached out a large paw, hauled the offender out of the seat and picking up the Palestinian's kit hurled it piecemeal out onto the platform. The other, screaming his protests, began trying to push my guide to one side, which action provoked his undoing, for the corporal leaned out of the window and called to someone outside.

A moment later two burly redcaps climbed aboard and, grasping the offender by each arm, marched him off the train. 'There you are mate, a nice seat for you.' grinned the victorious RTOs man. I thanked him and sat down a little shamefacedly into the vacant seat. Shortly afterwards the unfortunate Palestinian was flung back with his kit onto the next coach and that was the last I saw of him.

The infantryman sitting opposite me looked curiously at me and spoke. 'You must be somebody important chum, never seen those bastards so obliging before' he remarked.

'A bit hard on that poor bloody wog' I replied, 'I suppose these base barnacles must take it out of someone though'

'Don't worry yourself chum,' the other answered 'Those Palestinian wogs want kicking up the seat, the way they rob the squaddies in Haifa and Tel Aviv. Anyway, he should have done what he was told first time.'

The train started its crawling exit from the station, and I settled down to review the situation. Remembering the slips of paper, I brought them out and looked at the movement order. A most interesting document as it proved. At the head of the sheet was typed in red capitals the words 'MOST SECRET'. This was followed by my name and number but no unit. The text of the message was to the effect that 'to whom it may concern'. I was to be given every assistance to reach Azzib in the shortest possible time, and that all RTO staff were to ensure that I reached there in good working order. The last paragraph read 'This is an operational move and unnecessary delay will be treated with disciplinary action against the individuals concerned.'

I now saw the reason for the helpfulness of my RTO and Redcap friends, even they couldn't use their usual delay tactics in face of such an order!

The journey back to Palestine was tedious and I spent most of the time reading or sleeping, as the countryside through which the train ran was not such as to hold one's attention for any great length of time. We stopped on several occasions, including once during the night when we pulled up for half an hour to get a meal thoughtfully provided by the military authorities for the troops. At each stop the RTO train guard came along to see that I hadn't spirited away and felt content with everything. Such attention was embarrassing and had the result of evoking ribald comments from my fellow travellers until I began to wish that I wasn't quite such an important person after all!

CHAPTER 7

ARRIVAL BACK AT AZZIB TRAINING CAMP

Next morning at Haifa, which was as far as our train travelled, I was handed over to another member of the RTO staff and put on the Diesel Electric tram which runs up the coast to Beirut, in the Lebanon. These trams had little comfort and were obviously what they were designed for, that is, transporting troops. The 'coaches' were merely ex-cattle trucks with a wooden bench running round the inside of the four walls.

The last stage of our journey was a reasonably short one, and we very soon rolled to a stop alongside the Engine repair shops maintained by South African engineers at Azzib. I was the only passenger alighting at this point, and I stood alone by my kit beside the track as the train rumbled off on its journey north.

It was raining in an unpleasantly steady manner, and as I wandered over to the hut which served as a 'station' not a soul was to be seen. A couple of 'Springboks' were sitting inside the hut playing cards, so I asked them if any transport had arrived from the camp. When they told me that they had seen nothing, I asked if they would get RFHQ on the phone. They argued, and after much exasperated questioning and answering, eventually got through and having given my name to the people at the end of the line, told me that a truck would be sent 'immediately'.

Knowing the Army habit of exaggerating promises in this direction, I prepared for a prolonged wait on this rain soaked station but was pleasantly surprised when after only fifteen minutes a truck rolled up to my shelter, and the driver dismounted to help me up with my kit.

I was full of eager questions to the driver as we swished through the rain, but soon found that he neither knew nor cared what was to happen to me, so I relapsed into thoughtful silence until we pulled up outside the tents in the familiar camp on the hill.

I climbed down, and picking up the kit splashed through the mud to the section office.

Behind The Lines with The SBS: My Life in L Squadron during WW2

I was alongside the group of tents which I had previously seen from my original billet, those tents which had, stacked nearby, the odd looking craft I had noticed on my first day at RFHQ.

'This was at last the SBS proper,' I thought, and 'there'll be no more time wasted in training, the next move I make will be into action'. The thought revived the excitement and 'butterflies in the tummy' feeling which I had experienced in Cairo, but as I turned into the office hut, I had no suspicion of how wrong I was to be proved!

Disappointment tinged with relief (I must confess) were my feelings when I found out that my arrival was not the signal for frantic movement in the part of the office staff.

The clerk in the office, a lugubrious aristocrat known as the 'Duke', told me that they had no knowledge of my coming and that RFHQ had already sent two signallers to join the patrol which had been warned to depart to an unknown destination. He arranged however, for a message to be sent to Cairo immediately asking for instructions, and later on that day, splashed his way into the tent in which I had found the other pair of signallers to give us an answer.

It appeared that one of the others had been earmarked for the LRDG. and had been sent to Palestine by mistake, and that the 'Duke' was arranging for this unfortunate individual's return to Cairo the following day.

I had already asked my two comrades, one of whom had joined RFHQ on the same day as I originally came from the RA regiment, what was in the wind. They were no wiser than I was however, and said they too had been sent off to Palestine Post just a week before, only to find that no immediate move was anticipated.

After a few days of moving about the practically deserted camp we were told that an operation which was to have taken place had been postponed for a week or two and that we would, therefore, be taking part in further training with the patrol that we should have joined!

The training was not of the energetic kind to which we had become accustomed, at least not for some days, as all we did was draw operational kit and spend odd hours in small arms practice, mainly with pistols, these being the accepted weapon for wireless operators.

At the end of this period however, we were sent off with the patrol on an exercise under the command of a newly joined second lieutenant. We were taken by a lorry into Haifa to the top of Mount Carmel where we dismounted and started a march along the ridge of the mountain range. It was later in the afternoon when we started walking, and by nightfall we found ourselves on the eastern slopes of the mountain making our way down to the plain which lay behind Carmel. Our objective lay beyond the plain, but we never attained this owing to the fact that the by now familiar Palestine rain started and in a very short time was so heavy that we lost our way, and it was decided we would stay where we were until daylight, when we should be able to identify landmarks.

The place we stopped was under the lean of a sandy cliff, which afforded little to no cover, and we split up into small groups to try and find more comfortable quarters than this base, mountain side. One of my group said he had seen a light through the gorse when climbing down the mountainside, and thought it would not be far away, so we left the main party and made our way in the direction in which he thought lay this light.

My friends' surmise proved to be correct and about 200 yards along the hillside we came upon a Bedouin tent. This was one of those long low black hessian affairs which are seen dotted about the countryside in that part of the world, and we found on investigation that it was divided into two sections, one, the smaller half, being occupied by the head man, his brother, two sons and a nephew, the larger half containing the womenfolk of the household,

It was not necessary for us to ask for shelter, for the owner immediately invited us into his humble home and insisted that we should spend at least the night therein. Most of us had been in the Middle East for a year or more, and all had a smattering of Arabic, enough to make conversation with the various male members of the household.

We made ourselves comfortable sitting on the hard dry earth around the brushwood fire in the centre of the tent, and our host immediately started grinding coffee beans in a small but heavy wooden vessel, shaped like a cylinder with sides thicker than the centre opening. He used for the purpose a short thick piece of wood which almost exactly fitted the opening, pounding and grinding the coffee beans into a powder suitable enough for making the beverage.

While he was so occupied I looked around our temporary shelter and marvelled at two things. The first was that, although the roof and sides of the tent were made only of a rough, black dyed hessian, and apparently inadequate for the purpose of keeping out the rain, no sign was obvious inside of the torrent pouring down outside. The second point that struck me as strange was that although the fire had no chimney, nor was there any hole in the roof to allow the smoke to disperse, we experienced none of the discomfort usually associated with an open fire in an enclosed space. However, when I stood half upright to move my position, my eyes immediately started smarting from the smoke gathered near the roof but on sitting down again, this discomfort ended.

At one end of the 'men only' section of our Bedouin tent, were grouped a cow, two goats and a dog. At first, I found the odour given off by these animals fairly objectionable and wondered how our new friends could live in such an atmosphere, but as time passed, I ceased to notice the stink, for such it was, and realised that it is only in comparison with the fresh air that makes one object to smells, and that when one lives one's life in such surroundings, it is the fresh air which smells strange.

After we had drunk the strong unsweetened black coffee supplied by our hosts and eaten some of the tasteless bread and sour milk which accompanied the drink, one of the women came in bearing a large mattress and quilts. This bedding was spaced on the floor, and we were invited to make ourselves comfortable for the night. The idea of using such bedding in a tent occupied by goats etc. did not appeal to me, as I visualised waking next day with the addition to my person of more than that with which I arrived!

For reasons of politeness, and rather than give offence to our kind host, however, I crawled in between the quilts and mattress and within a few moments was in a deep comfortable sleep, remaining undisturbed until our friends woke us next day with more coffee. When on investigation I found that my fears had been ungrounded, and the bedding was as clean as anyone might wish to find.

The rain was still falling heavily, but we decided we must re-join our patrol, and taking a reluctant farewell of our Bedouins, we left to find the remainder of our party soaking wet, miserable and after hearing our story, indignant at our good fortune.

Our patrol commander decided it was useless to continue the exercise under present conditions, so we made our way back to Haifa, borrowed transport, and returned to our camp at Azzib.

The following couple of weeks were quiet and devoted to odd training of a desultory manner, the weather being such as to make it impossible to embark on anything ambitious. Just before Christmas however, a mixed patrol was sent up to Beirut to make the initial preparations for a new operation. We heard nothing from them until Boxing Day, when they returned to the camp to inform us that once again it was all off.

By this time the original flush of excitement of joining the SBS had worn rather thin, and the disappointment I felt was not relieved when we were told that, far from going on an operation, we were to be sent to Athlit on the other side of Haifa to join another patrol which was to set off what was to be our most rigorous test.

CHAPTER 8

MEETING MAJOR PATTERSON AND TO THE SEA OF GALILEE

The truck that brought us from Azzib deposited us outside a small group of tents just behind the desolate wind and rain swept shore beside the Crusaders Castle I had observed when on our way to Cairo a couple of months previously. This camp was about 12 miles south of Haifa and quite desolate, the nearest sign of civilisation being an enormous pyramid of salt about a mile behind us, then the small Jewish village of Athlit.

I was not at all pleased at the prospect of spending a winter in these uncomfortable quarters, but I need not have worried, for as we dismounted from the lorry, a tall fair haired giant wearing the crown of a major approached and addressed us in the patent accents of the Indian Army.

'Hullo, you the new signalmen from RFHQ? Yes? Well don't make yourselves too comfortable you know, we'll all be off on a walk tomorrow, and that will be the last you see of this camp for some while.'

He then proceeded to put us through a genial cross examination, asking our names, previous units, and what training we'd had, mountain orienteering training exercises with L Squadron undergone and so on.

This was my first interview with Major Ian Patterson, as such proved his name, who was the commander of the squadron to which I was posted, and in which I remained until the end of the war. He was not a lovable man but was as hard on himself as he was on everyone under his command and a man whose determination to have a "good" command resulted in drastic preening of those who joined the squadron, so that it became quite an honour to remain with him, as the single fact that he had not sent one back to one's unit meant that one must be of superlative worth!

After he had dismissed us by the customary vague wave of the hand, my comrade and I moved into one of the tents where we found ourselves in the company of L Squadron's marine patrol. I found that each of the three squadrons of SBS contained one patrol recruited solely from the Royal Marines and each

Above left: Major Ian Norman Patterson. OC of L Squadron from Nov 43 – Dec 44. Awarded the Military Cross in July 44 for his actions on the island of Nisero and "the personal inspiration he gave in leadership and in disregard to his own safety" also for other operations on Cos, Patmos and Pserimos. (Courtesy of David Heard and the Littlegaddesdenchurch.org.uk)

Above right: Capt. Morris Elliott Anderson. Commanding officer for the Operation on Stampalia (Astypalia). Awarded the Military Cross for showing "A high degree of leadership and courage, and has proved an inspiration to the men under his command." on operations on Stampalia and Piscopi.(Courtesy of the SAS Archives)

of these patrols was to attain a fame peculiar to themselves and shared by no other patrol. The members of our marine patrol were in the main HO 'Infants' straight from Chatham, but there was a Cadre of older 'Active service' ratings who served to keep the youngsters in order, and who helped to make from this raw material a very fine operational sub-unit.

The following day we were told what was to comprise the walk mentioned by the major.

Our informant was the captain, a South African, who was to lead our patrol on this particular exercise.

We were to walk from Athlit which, it will be remembered, was on the Palestinian coast to Samakh, on the southernmost point of Lake Tiberius, the Sea of Galilee of Biblical fame. The course of this walk, a distance of some

Meeting Major Patterson and to the Sea of Galilee

70 miles, was to lay directly across the ranges of Mount Carmel, the plain beyond, and then into the sprawling mountain ranges further inland bounded on the north by Mount Hermon. We were not to use any built up roads, and to make as little use as possible of any sort of tracks.

The time came to move off and we shouldered our packs, myself carrying a wireless set and sleeping bag, my co-signaller carrying the battery and his sleeping bag, and the remainder of the patrol carrying bergen rucksacks, personal kit, ammunition, bombs, and the residue of we signallers' essential kit spread among the various members of the patrol. Captain Anderson, our leader, strode across the fields and we strung out behind him on the first leg of our journey.

It was a distance of some 3 miles across flat country to the first hills of the Carmel range, and as a result of the rain, which had been falling for some days past, and which was still falling sporadically, the fields were inches deep in luscious mud. Our boots, heavy enough in all conscience without unwanted ballast, quickly become twice the size in a thick, tenacious oozing coat of this mud, so that it soon became a real effort to drag one foot after the other.

The three miles to the foothills would normally have taken less than an hour in dry weather, but in view of the foul conditions it was nearly dark before we came up to the road bounding the flat coast on the eastern side, the time we had taken covering the first leg being over two hours. After resting a few minutes and cleaning the heaviest mud from our boots, we moved across the road, and soon were climbing up a long wadi into the hills.

After about an hour's progress along the gradually steepening incline during which time I doubt whether we covered another mile, it became almost impossible to see the man next in line ahead. Our leader, who must have had an even more unpleasant time than we had as he was responsible for finding a way along which we might travel, called halt.

'I think we'd better stop for the night' he said. 'There's a small Wog village nearby, I think, and if we find it, we might be able to get shelter. One of you show a light, and I'll scout around to see if I can find it and use your light to find the way back.'

He clambered off into the murk and we took the opportunity to sit on our packs and light cigarettes. The captain returned in a quarter of an hour and led us along a narrow path up the side of the wadi.

The path gradually became less steep until eventually we found ourselves on a level piece of ground and moving forward gingerly through the murky darkness came upon a building.

A pale figure of a man in the dress of an Arab came forward and led our party further into the tiny village as such it proved to be, until we came to a rough gate. This gate enclosed a courtyard in front of a house larger than the rest and we were invited to mount stairs leading to the upper storey. I found later that this was the house of the Muleteer, or head man, and that the lower part of the house formed a byre and stable for the Muleteer's beasts.

At the head of the stairs, we found ourselves on a tiny landing with two doors leading from it. An elderly Arab came from one of these doors and smilingly invited us to enter the room he had just left. We moved into this room, which proved to be a clean, brightly lit chamber devoid of furniture, but with several heavy rugs piled up in groups around the walls. These walls also had rugs hanging thereon and as far as was apparent contained no windows. The light came from two modern pressure lamps suspended at each end of the room.

The man who welcomed us proved to be the owner of the house, the muleteer, and was accompanied by his small son who smiled shyly at us at first, but who soon became voluble and jabbered in the manner of small boys the world over. His father told us to make ourselves comfortable in this room and indicated that a meal was being prepared and would be ready in a short while.

I relaxed comfortably on one of the rug piles and placing my wireless pack behind me, leaned back and thought how wonderful it was to take the weight off my feet, which were beginning to suffer the effects of moving across the difficult countryside we had just traversed and had proved unequal to the task of supporting a soaking mud laden boot, and the chafing had caused blisters on each heel early on our march.

I painfully removed my boots and socks and found that on each heel I had developed a blister. These blisters must have been with me for some time, as they were no longer covered by skin and were quite raw and extremely painful, they were as large as pennies, had broken, and were now red raw wounds.

I had a small medical kit in my battle blouse, so I cleaned them up, removing the remains of the dead skin, spread ointment on the raw spots, covered this with thick lint and tied a long bandage tightly round each heel, taking the ends under my foot to give as much support as possible and at the same time prevent too much movement of the heel and ankle.

The night's rest in clean dry quarters served to dim the horrors of the previous days' march, and we set off again in brilliant sunshine and higher spirits. We marched for an hour and stopped to breakfast on the 'Arctic' rations with which we had been issued. At the end of the meal, if such it could be called, Captain Anderson told me to try and 'Get through' on the wireless to the base set at Azzib as this was all part of the exercise.

My co-signaller and I tried unsuccessfully for twenty minutes to establish contact but were forced eventually to admit defeat. This admission caused us to be the object of much derision from the rest of the patrol and annoyed criticism from the officer.

Meeting Major Patterson and to the Sea of Galilee

The cause of the lack of contact was never satisfactorily explained, as the sets were crystal controlled so that at least our signals should have been picked up even if we failed to hear the base set. We heard that neither we nor any other of the parties had established communications, and could only put it down to atmospheric conditions, or freaks in 'Screening' by the hills.

At the time however I was not aware of the general failure, and felt very disconsolate at our own break down, being so confident that we would immediately get in touch after our crammed training and hard work in mastering completely the operation of these sets.

When the expressions of disgust had died away, we parcelled up our belongings and continued the march over the top of the mountain, until finally just before noon we reached the foot of the eastern slope and stopped for the midday meal at the Palestine Police Post of Jenin.

Our wireless kit being now considered superfluous, we were instructed to dump it at the Police post in the care of the 'Garrison', and before moving on again we retrieved that portion of our personal kit which had been carried by the rest of the patrol, and in addition relieved them of some of their own gear, wrapping all this stuff in our sleeping bags and strapping the whole bundle onto the Everest carriers which had previously supported the wireless and battery.

Each man having a little lighter pack to carry, we continued across the plain at a greater speed than previously and by nightfall were well into the second range of mountains on the farther side.

It was nearly 11.00 pm when we stopped again for the night at a place called Tabor which was a camp for interning European refugees whilst they were being screened. Here again we were invited to be the guests of the police guards and spent the night sleeping on the floor of their canteen. It was New Year's Eve of 1943, but I couldn't have cared less and went straight to sleep in my sleeping bag, but one or two members of our patrol, Scotsmen of course, stayed up drinking what remained of a bottle of whiskey in celebration of Hogmanay!

My feet and those of several others were in a pitiful condition when we started again next morning, but after a short period of walking the pain became familiar and consequently less nagging, although after each stop the torture started again, magnified on each occasion.

This day was spent in crossing a wide plateau, and I visualised our journey practically ending by nightfall in a steady downward direction. My wishful thinking was dashed to the ground however, when as we neared the limits of the plateau the ground suddenly started rising again, and we were climbing into even higher and considerably more rugged mountains.

Darkness overtook us soon after we commenced climbing, but as the weather was fine and the moon had risen it was decided we should progress as far as possible that last night, in order to shorten the final stage of our walk on the following day.

This was extremely wild country, and no sign was obvious of any human habitation, nor even the usual goats, in the mountains. As we climbed, we still adhered to the policy of avoiding tracks, but it became necessary to drop this idea on some occasions when we were forced to follow narrow paths or a ledge round the shoulder of a peak or use the bed of a stream to find our way down into a gulley.

Our relentless leader finally agreed to halt for the night. This evening was spent in a saddle of the hills near the top of the mountains and the following morning we reached the peak soon after starting and commenced the long slow journey down the farther side. At midday we climbed once more to the crest of the last hill and looked down on Lake Tiberius and the town which gives this water its modern name.

We left the rough for good at this point and finished our march down the road leading through the town and alongside the lake to our objective – the Arab village of Samakh at the southernmost point of the lake. The people of this village and the village itself didn't appear to have undergone much change in the 2000 years since it first became news, and floating on the water of the lake were boats of the type which might easily have been manned by St Peter and his friends in the fishing expedition which resulted in his giving up his life and following his Lord.

Our camp, which in summer had been occupied by members of the Arab legion, those desert campaigners known as 'Glubb's girls',[3] was situated just beyond the village, and we climbed into the empty huts to find that we were the second patrol to reach there. The others came in during the rest of that day, the last stragglers arriving long after dark and all feeling completely worn out after this gruelling test.

CHAPTER 9

RETURN TO BASE AND PREPARATION OF KIT FOR FIRST OPERATION

The next day I visited the MO and as a result of his instructions did no more parades for ten days, walking gingerly round the camp in sandals enclosing huge bandages inside which were the raw pieces of meat I had once called feet!

It may appear that I have spent a lot of time discussing my under carriage, and if it has been thought that I have a one track mind, I can only admit to this being the case at that time, and apologise for the tedium which may have been the cause by my 'going on so'. The fact is, and I think all members of SBS will agree, that the greatest part of our training, and certainly the greater part of our operations were spent in marching, usually in rough mountainous country, and when one spends so much time on them, one becomes extremely attached to, and careful of, one's feet.

Almost as soon as my feet were healed and I was completely fit again we had the news that was to mark the end of the prolonged period of training that we had undergone, and which was to be the beginning of real living– SBS style.

My partner and I had been permanently attached to 'D' patrol, 'L' Squadron under the command of the South African officer who had brought us over the mountains, and one morning this officer came into our hut, sat on the bunk of the Scots corporal and called us all round to hear his news.

The news, so long awaited, was that we must draw operational kit, weapons, etc. from the store and armoury, and be ready to move the following day at first light. We were to travel by lorry to Beirut, and remain there, making final preparations for an operation, until the rest of the squadron joined us in a weeks' time.

As soon as he had dismissed us, we busied ourselves carrying out his orders. The first visit was to the QM store, where we drew that part of our equipment

Behind The Lines with The SBS: My Life in L Squadron during WW2

which was universally known as 'Operational kit' and comprised a string vest (for providing warmth at the same time as preventing lousiness), a heavy brown woollen jersey and white coarse woollen socks, which were heavily ribbed and felt uncomfortable until the foot became used to the roughness, and then, surprisingly, gave ease to the feet when marching.

Heavy treble soled brown boots with prominent studs, together with a pair of 'Desert boots', (soft suede boots) and a twill 'wind suit' completed the ensemble. This wind suit was like baggy pyjamas, the trousers being tied round the waist by a woven cord, and the jacket a loose hooded smock which also tied around and over the top of the trousers. They were to be worn outside the battle dress and were said to be both wind and rain proof. I doubted the truth of the latter claim and later we proved it to be quite wrong.

After completing my 'shopping' I called at the armoury and was issued with an enormous revolver described as a 'Colt.45' and looked like the sort of weapon one sees in films of the early conquest of the 'West'. I had previously been lucky enough (for exercise only) to have a Luger, but there was at the time a shortage of these fine German pistols, so I had to be content with my minor cannon.

In addition to this revolver, I was presented with a beautiful fighting knife, made like a stiletto of blue steel and manufactured by the famous Wilkinson Sword people[4]. This was in a metal tipped leather sheath, which was made to be sewn inside the leg of battle dress slacks, a slit being made in the material to allow the hilt of the knife to project outside within handy reach.

We packed up our heavy base kit and handed it into the store and the following morning, laden only with a bergen rucksack apiece full of 'ops kit', our patrol climbed into a 3 tonner and set off for Beirut. The lorry was like all SBS vehicles, uncovered, and the weather was as usual, wet, but we sat in the back of the truck perfectly content to know we were at last on our way on a real job.

CHAPTER 10

INTO BEIRUT, LOADING THE *TEWFIK*

Our lorry rolled into Beirut late the following night and drove straight into the dockyard, to spend the night in a naval store shed belonging to the Levant Schooner force, the members of which were to become as familiar to us as our own comrades. The next day we were installed in a large Barracks above the town, originally belonging to the French, but now occupied by a Veterinary Corps unit. That day was spent in settling in, drawing pay and looking round the town, while our Officer visited his naval counterparts to make arrangements for the work of preparation which we were to carry out.

We started work in earnest the next day loading stores of food, ammunition, medical gear, and explosives etc. onto the ship which was to be our forward base during the coming operations. This ship was a two masted schooner of some 180-tons and known as the '*Tewfik*'. Of its origin I knew nothing, but by the time it came into our hands it had undergone some drastic changes from its original appearance. The foc's'le was occupied by the crew of half a dozen Greeks, and was as evil smelling and murky as no doubt it always had been and always would be. The hold however, which took up the greater part of the interior, forward of the engine room, had been converted into a mess deck and running practically its entire length, bunks built into the ship's sides and on the fore and aft bulkheads, hooks for hammocks on each beam across the deck head, and of all things electric light! The power for this light came from a powerful generator mounted on the upper deck just oft the hatchway leading down to the mess and housed in a wooden hut built specially for the purpose.

Situated at the centre of the ship's length stood a tiny galley, just large enough for two men to feel uncomfortably crowded, which was to be the centre of all culinary activities on the voyage, and behind this the hatch leading to the engine room. About the engine room the less said the better, suffice it to add that without sails the movement of the ship under its engine power was hardly noticeable!

Behind The Lines with The SBS: My Life in L Squadron during WW2

Between the engine room and the wheel on the quarter deck was the hatch leading down to what had once been the captain's cabin, but which was now converted into a tiny wardroom for our officers. This later housed at least seven officers but how this was accomplished is a mystery, so cramped was the space therein.

Our little party worked solidly for a week loading and trimming the vessel, bringing truckloads of provisions from the naval stores, unloading at the wharf and carrying the goods across a narrow gang plank onto the ship where we then set about distributing them about the deck, until at the end of our week's labours only a very narrow passage was left all-round the rail of the vessel. The area bounded by this passage was piled with cases of food, ammunition, explosives and waterproof cases containing dismantled folboats and rubber dinghies (known to all as 'Jellicoe's Intruders').

Our daily tasks finished at teatime, after which we were free to enjoy ourselves in what I consider to be the best town in the Middle East for that purpose.

Each night I went down into Beirut in the company of one of the patrolmen who had become a firm friend, and he and I took advantage of every opportunity that presented itself for enjoyment, this usually taking the form of liquid nourishment in a dive bar on the front at the end of Avenue de Francais. The owner of this bar was somehow able to produce draught beer, no mean feat in the Middle East, and we soon became his best customers sitting in the bar till closing time (and after), then wandering into the café upstairs to our supper and to listen to a small salon orchestra doing its worst to *"Orpheus in the Underworld"*!

A few doors from this bar were a group of what the proprietors were pleased to call 'Pensions'. It was true that we could obtain a night's lodging and supper at these places, but there were always a sufficient number of young women on the premises to provide entertainment for the 'Lodger' should he be unable to sleep.

We occasionally wandered into these places for a while in the evenings and had a lot of fun watching the antics of nervous infantrymen trying to resist the blandishments of the entertainers. At that time they were used by British troops only, although later this rule seemed to be relaxed by tacit consent (probably because trade was not sufficiently flourishing), and one evening we were sitting drinking beer in one pension, the 'Sans Rival' and talking to the Madam when a burly gunner who had been glaring at us for some while came over to us and spoke. 'What the hell do you Polish bastards want, coming into this place?'. His accent told us he came not very far from the Gorbals. 'Get out of here or I'll break your bloody necks.'

'Just a minute Jock' I said, 'We're no more bloody Poles than you are.'

Into Beirut, loading the *Tewfik*

'You're wearing Polish kit' he answered unconvinced, 'Don't bloody well kid me, I expect you scrounged long enough in Blighty to pick up the lingo, but you're bloody Poles alright!' and he made motions indicative of going into the attack.

Before he could start his rough house however, the Madam raised a beer bottle by its neck and held it under his nose. 'You (F***) off, you Jock' she admonished him 'These two very good English friends of mine and drink beer and pay, not like you who just come and look at girls for nothing and then (F***) off without spending a livre!' She was a perfect lady during the whole performance, but I could see a free for all developing and always one for peace, I invited Jock to have a beer, and sit down with us. He grudgingly assented, and after talking a while was convinced and profuse in his apologies for 'Insulting us', and he in turn cleared up our puzzlement at the attack.

The explanation was a simple one. He had seen hundreds of Poles 'Crawling round Glasgow, hanging onto the arm of any bit of stuff, married or single,' and he had mistaken our winged badge for the similar badge worn by his by now already enemies.

I found later that his hatred of Poles was fairly well shared by most Scottish soldiers, and I often wonder now if they ever tried to carry out their promise to clear Scotland of the unfortunate Poles, or whether our far-seeing government took steps to remove the cause before the effect was felt.

CHAPTER II

SAILING OUT OF BEIRUT ON-BOARD THE *TEWFIK*

The end of this almost perfect week of hard work and hard relaxation came all too soon when the remainder of the squadron arrived in Beirut.

This marked the beginning of greater bustle and activity for a short while with individuals running here and there, conference at all levels between our officers and naval commanders, even to conferences between we humble soldiers and even humbler matelots!

Eventually however, the time came to embark, and we sailed out of Beirut harbour on a grey windy morning into a choppy sea, accompanied by three Harbour Defence Motor launches (HDMLs) and a couple of small Levant Schooners (LS).[5]

I remember that the scene reminded me of the preparation of the good ship *Hispaniola* for its trip to '*Treasure Island*' in Robert Louis Stephenson's famous book. This analogy was emphasised by the appearance of our people and the members of Levant Schooner Force. Most of us packed our Berets away during the subsequent voyage, and wore all manner of most unregimental clothing, including a gamely piece of material wrapped around the neck and a woollen scarf stuck on the back of the head in the best piratical fashion.

The weather worsened as we left the confines of Beirut harbour, and after several hours sailing the wind developed into a 'Force Eighter'. This was a naval term soon to become adopted by we lubbers, signifying a gale of a force marked on the Beaufort scale at figure eight.

I was allocated the second signals watch on the *Tewfik*, and two hours after sailing I climbed down from my hammock to find the deck heaving in an alarming manner under my feet. I didn't relish the idea of standing on the upper deck for two hours, even though the atmosphere would be an improvement on the stench in the mess deck. This smell was due to the fact that the movement of the ship had disturbed the bilge water and the disturbance had released the stink of the decaying matter floating therein.

Sailing out of Beirut on-board the *Tewfik*

Des' Silk map of Greece and the Eastern Mediterranean. Issued to him while in the SBS. (Marshall Family Collection)

As signaller on watch I had the task of scanning the accompanying vessels for signs of lamp signals, a job none too easy in a heaving sea when the low hulks of the other ships were often obscured by the waves which appeared to rise as high as the mast head of the smaller schooners of LSF.

My watch was not improved by the fact that, this being my first sea trip since landing in Egypt two years before, my stomach began to object to the unaccustomed gymnastics it was called upon to perform, and I hung on to the taffrail at the stern trying not to think of the hearty meals and beer I had consumed in the past week.

I soon decided that the upper deck of an overloaded schooner under sail is not the best place from which to watch the Mediterranean and was wishing I could retreat to the reasonable serenity of my hammock, away from this creaking, heaving, spray-drenched quarter deck. The Lebanon coast had long since faded into the murk and we were struggling through cold grey deserted seas, catching only occasional glimpses of our escorting motor launches.

Behind The Lines with The SBS: My Life in L Squadron during WW2

During one of the glimpses, I observed a signal lamp flashing and tried to reply with my own Aldis lamp. In order to hold the lamp with one hand while sighting it on the distant vessel and operating the trigger with the hand I had to release my hold on the taffrail. This proved a fatal move, as I pitched headlong to the deck with a sudden lurch of the *Tewfik*. I regained my feet however, and the signals officer stood close behind me, with an arm round each side of me, holding the rail, and I managed to read and acknowledge the HDML's message.

The message was an enquiry from the ML's skipper asking if we were alright and informing us that one of the small schooners had capsized in the heavy seas. Its crew had been picked up immediately however and were none the worse. No stores or equipment were aboard the schooner, *LS5*, so the loss by no means negligible was not as great a tragedy as it might have been.

We replied to the message in the phrase given to me by Major Patterson that we were alright, but that he had grave doubts about our engine which was doing 'Two knots and an Orion' (Two forward and one back).

The *Tewfik* and other vessels anchored of the coast of Turkey. (Marshall Family Collection)

CHAPTER 12

STOP AT FAMAGUSTA

Our little convoy battled its way into Famagusta harbour in Cyprus at dawn the following morning. This was not a scheduled stop, but it was decided that we should ride out the storm before continuing on our outward journey.

This was my first visit to Cyprus and in my opinion was not a success. After checking that we were still in a seaworthy condition and re-lashing some of the stores which showed signs of coming adrift, we were given permission to go ashore for the evening.

Famagusta is quite a fair sized port with modern shops and houses forming the greater part of the town, the remainder being known as the old city, and comprising headquarters of all the vice of the port of which there was an abundance.

Most of our people went into a large café bar known as 'The Argentina' and spent the evening drinking the various vinous products of Cyprus, Cognac, Muscata and an evil tasting local brew known as 'Commandaria'. Among this party was a Cairo Greek who had been attached to us as guide and interpreter for the forthcoming operations, and like most Greeks had no time for Cypriots.

Towards the end of the evening's pleasures, he made this fact clearly known to the native customers of the Argentina with the result that he became unpopular to such a degree that one of them made a knife attack on his person.

The attack was foiled by the intervention of one of our own men, a Birmingham corporal who was a giant of a man. His action prevented the sudden demise of the interpreter, but in the ensuing blood bath he was rewarded by a bottle being broken on his head causing a two inch long slash in the skin of his scalp. This became the signal for a general melee and in short order the Argentina presented the scene of a battleground, with damaged bodies lying on and around the wrecked bar and tables.

The Cypriots soon withdrew to the street outside the bar and, when our party made to follow, it was found that the 'enemy' had been reinforced by hundreds of other inhabitants of the port, who had completely blocked the exit and street outside. A council of war was quickly held, and the SBS sallied forth in a fighting wedge armed with chairs and bottles and were soon in the thick of it again.

I doubt whether we could have been successful in getting through the crowd unscathed, had it not been for the fact that someone 'borrowed' a revolver from a redcap who appeared on the scene, and started firing this into the air (or so he afterward maintained!)

At the same time a group of sailors from the ML's who had heard of the fracas arrived on the other side of the crowd, armed with Lanchester Tommy guns with bayonets fixed, and made a charge on the enemy's rear.

Anyway, we soon had a path cleared through to the road leading to the harbour and made our way down back to the ships.

As soon as we returned, all further leave onshore was cancelled, and the storm having abated, we left harbour at first light next day to continue our journey north.

CHAPTER 13

LES STEPHENSON AND ONWARDS TO VATHI BAY

We had not yet been briefed regarding our destination, but the signs on board gave us a pretty good idea that it was an attack on the Greek mainland, an idea which was supported by the presence of three Greek interpreters. One of these interpreters was not a Greek, but an Englishman named Stephenson from Liverpool, who had been captured on Crete during the German invasion in 1941.

He had escaped shortly afterwards by asking for permission to relieve himself while out on a working party, and simply walking into the hills. This handy individual had then supported himself for two years on the Cretan mountains, eating what he could, when he could, sometimes being helped surreptitiously by the natives at great risk to themselves, until finally he was put in touch with a British officer living with the *andartes* (partisans) and assisted to escape to Cairo in company with a young Cretan and several others who had become undesirables to the Germans and had been forced to hurriedly depart.

Stephenson had acquired such a perfect Cretan dialect in his Greek that Greeks we later met insisted that his speech was more Cretan than that of his little friend Manoli, who escaped with him and had also joined our squadron as an interpreter, (although in those early days his English was limited to "tourist dictionary" phrases plus a few Americanism's acquired from his father who had presumably visited the States). It is an extraordinary fact that whenever one meets a group of Greeks, there will always be one

Leslie Norman Stephenson. Awarded the Distinguished Conduct Medal in July 44 for actions on Stampalia and Nisero. Major Patterson cited "He has shown great resourcefulness and devotion to duty." (Marshall Family Collection)

who comes forward and says in an atrocious accent "Hiya fellas! Me – I speak English swell, yeah, swell – been to the States y'know" and so on!

As I mentioned above the presence of Stephenson, his friend and the Cairo Greek who caused the trouble in Famagusta, led us to believe we were bound for Greece proper, and many were the awful prophecies of what would be our final fate when meeting the Germans on their home ground.

These prophecies were quite wrong, as it later proved, for our belief itself was erroneous and instead of approaching Greece we turned Northeast and after another day's sail came under the shadow of the Turkish cliffs near the island of Castelorizzo.

The *Tewfik* and its escort sailed into a lovely cove called Vathi Bay on the coast of Turkey, where thickly wooded green hills sloped straight down into beautiful, still blue waters, and at the far end of the bay a small strip of silver sand glittered in the sunlight reflected off the sea. A tiny figure in what looked like rags was moving on this beach, apparently cooking by a fire, the smoke of which spiralled lazily upward in the clear still air.

We anchored in this delightful haven, and I hoped we might stay here for long enough to paddle a boat ashore and explore its confines. This was not to be, however, for after one night our patrol was told off to prepare for operations. This took the form of loading a folboat and rubber dinghy, into a Motor Dory along with the now familiar boxes of explosives and ammunition, and then with our bergen rucksacks, wireless set and batteries ferried to Castelorizzo, now clear of the enemy and occupied by the Navy, where we re-embarked an HDML 1283, which immediately cast off to take us on my first operation.

The *Tewfik* and Caiques used by the SBS. (Marshall Family Collection)

CHAPTER 14

STAMPALIA OPERATION

Twilight was falling as our ML moved its way in between the first of the enchanted islands of the Dodecanese, and we very soon saw a searchlight on the island of Rhodes probing its long finger into the darkness of the narrow seas. We steered a course very wide of its beam, and kept as close as possible to the Turkish coast, which we followed for the remainder of that night, until we reached a tiny bay at the end of a long promontory forming one horn of the Gulf of Cos.

This bay was chosen as the most westerly and therefore nearest point from which we could make a night approach to our objective, and we busied ourselves on arrival in rigging up the camouflage nets over the ML in order that our contours might blend with those of the rocky shore to which we had made past.

The operation of 'up camouflage' took a considerable time, and the sky over the cliffs to the east was lightening from pitch black to grey and finally light blue, before the skipper grudgingly admitted his satisfaction at the result of our exertions.

We spent the day in that cove, and after breakfast in the tiny and overcrowded mess deck of the ML most of us went over the side into the cool blue depths of the sea. The month was still January, but the water was not so cold as to be unpleasant, and when the first shock of immersion had passed, after diving from the ship's deck, I splashed about enjoyably for some while glorying in the freedom of swimming naked hundreds of miles away from the war!

As I thought this however, I suddenly remembered that only a few miles across the placid sea on the island of Cos, which loomed so near on the seascape and also on the other more distant islands, were thousands of Germans to whom we were to carry the war, and who might be the cause of our losing any further interest in its progress. This idea spoilt my enjoyment of the swim, and I clambered back onto the ML to re-join the others.

Captain Anderson came forward and called us up onto the fo'c'sle to tell us what was to be our objective. He spread an ordnance map on the deck and showed us our position.

'We are at the moment in this small bay just here' he pointed to a tiny indentation on the coast. 'Our objective is the island of Stampalia about 80 miles due west – here. We shall start at dark tonight, go straight to the south-west end of the island, and hope to arrive at about midnight. That will give us time to find our "hide" before first light tomorrow, and once there, we shall lie up for a day or so while I and the sergeant here make a recce and see what can be done to shake Jerry.'

'I can't tell you much of what is to be the main objective, but there is a certain amount of shipping, a wireless station and bridges which might be of interest in the big barges line. Anyway, we'll do as much as we can to make ourselves unpopular!'

I had not up to this point really formulated much idea of the type of work we were to do, and as most of the patrolmen were new anyway, had no one from whom to find out how the raids were to be carried out. There had been, however, at the back of my mind, the gem of an idea that we would do raids similar to those of Lofoten and Narvik in Norway.[6]

This business of lying up for a couple of days on an enemy occupied island only a few miles long didn't appeal to me in the least, so I spoke to the captain when he asked if there were any questions.

'How long do you think we should stay there Skipper?'

'Oh, about a week I suspect' was the reply. 'A day to get our bearings, a couple of days looking round, a night to get to the objective and lie up till dark the next night, and then a day or so waiting for the ML to pick us up again. Yes, I imagine about a week should do the whole job.'

In my ignorance it seemed to me that to spend a week under the nose of a German garrison was just asking for trouble, and gloomy indeed were my thoughts as we once again checked our wireless set and batteries to ensure their proper functioning when the time came.

Looking back over the years to that first operation, overshadowed by others more ambitious, I realise that my pessimistic gloom was more groundless then than on any subsequent occasion, but I can't remember a longer or more depressing day than the one we spent in that little bay.

As bad luck would have it (or perhaps it was good luck as it served to take our minds off more unpleasant things) a high wind sprang up at midday, and after being bumped against the rocks for a while, the skipper of the ML gave the order to cast off. Feverish activity was the order of the day, as we dismantled and stowed the camouflage nets, the sea becoming more vicious with each successive slap of the freshening wind, and the ship's side being subjected to more alarming bumps as we worked.

In record time however we were cast off and spent the remainder of the daylight hours cruising round the bay, during which time we nearly lost the ship's dinghy as it had been lowered to enable the crew to get at the camouflage spread on the shore and as time was so short, we had moved off with the boat in tow, until a heavy sea had swamped and capsized it so that it became a sort of sea anchor, dragging at the stern of the ML. The dinghy was eventually rescued however, and we finally set sail for our island into the teeth of the wind and an ever rising sea.

CHAPTER 15

LANDING ON THE ISLAND

I had a very uncomfortable time for the next couple of hours, as in the grip of a frenzied sea the ML was simply flung about in all directions and I was hard put to it to prevent my being seasick once more. As we sailed further out to sea however, the weather improved and by the time we came within reach of Stampalia I had mastered the overwhelming desire to be ill and looked with interest and apprehension at the dark bulk of the island as it loomed ever longer in the faint light of the stars reflected in the sea. The HDML had been chosen for the job of landing our party as its power comes from diesel engines which are a good deal quieter than petrol engines, and on the present occasion the skipper and engineer continued to bring our ship almost within the shadow of the island's cliffs with barely a whisper from the exhausts. Our motion was so slow and gentle that it was impossible to see any gleam from the wake, which at normal speeds shows up a fan of glowing foam stretching for miles along the ship's course.

There was no moon to light our way and incidentally reveal our presence to any watchers who might be on the cliffs, and no sound came from our small craft, as all speech, of which there was a minimum, was held in whispers. Occasionally someone was unfortunate enough to stumble against a metal bulkhead or piece of equipment, and at each faint clatter a chorus of hushed warnings was directed at the "clumsy bastard!"

This was the worst part of the operation, we thought; this creeping gingerly up to the island, wondering when and if the fire from a concealed machine gun would tear across the oily swell and rake our deck, or a German patrol vessel might appear from the direction of the harbour to make enquiries about our identity. If this latter had happened, it would not have gone at all well for us, as our low speed would not have enabled us to effect an escape before the enemy reached us and the HDML was poorly equipped for action against E. Boats which were plentiful in those narrow seas at that time.

As we approached closer to the island's bulk, the point almost directly ahead appeared to open as if to receive us and we found ourselves passing a

Landing on the Island

headland enclosing a bay. The ML's bows turned into the mouth of the bay and once inside on the calm waters, the skipper reversed his engines to stop the ship's progress, and after congratulating him on his expert navigation in finding the right place in the darkness, our patrol commander ordered us to lower the first folboat away for a 'recce'.[7]

This was the signal for silent but swift movement, and in a matter of moments the folboat was gently bumping against the shipside and Captain Anderson and his bodyguard swarmed down into their seats, took up their paddles and with a few strokes were skipping swiftly towards the distant beach.

After what seemed an age, the folboat returned with the patrolman above, who told us that this was the right place, and we prepared to leave. The remainder of the patrol then paddled ashore, leaving a corporal, myself and the other signaller.

By this time the ML's skipper was becoming anxious to leave, believing that at any moment the ship might be observed lying close inshore as it was, and as the engines were still in reverse, we had drifted a considerable distance from our original place, towards the mouth of the bay. He then decided he couldn't wait for the return of the patrol's boat and ordered us to take a rubber dinghy which belonged to his vessel. The crew unstowed this dinghy and fitting air bottles to the nozzles, quickly inflated the beastly coracle, which was quite circular in shape, and as we found immediately after we had set out quite unmanageable!

The three of us loaded our kit and the wireless set into the rubber dinghy and proceeded to paddle shore-wards. We then discovered that the ML had taken us nearly to the mouth of the bay, and we had the unpleasant task of propelling three handed this horribly designed craft a matter of nearly a mile to the beach.

Before we reached our landing place the ML had disappeared around the headland, and I have no doubt that once clear of the island it made record speed from the vicinity.

After an arduous and blasphemous passage, we came level with the breakers where we had to leap over the side into the shoulder high water and pilot our clumsy craft on to the beach. We found a fuming patrol commander awaiting us, wanting to know what the hell we had been up to, wasting precious hours of darkness taking a pleasure cruise round the bay and so on and so on!

We explained briefly and proceeded to deflate and hide our dinghy in thick brushwood which partly covered the beach near to the water's edge, dragging it behind us up the sand in order to sweep away signs of our footprints, should any inquisitive islander chance to see them and reveal the fact of our landing to the Germans.

CHAPTER 16

CAVE RECCE AND MAKING CONTACT WITH CAIRO

The bay in which we had landed proved to be the end of a long, narrow wadi with steep sides running inland for about a mile, when they came together as part of a range of hills. The island was shaped roughly like an egg timer, with a narrow waist, and these hills formed the longer part of the south-westerly bulge below the waist.

We shouldered our kit and proceeded up the wadi looking for the hiding place we knew to exist on the cliffs on its western side, information regarding this hide being gleaned from British soldiers who had escaped from the Germans and hidden in the same place during the short bloody battle for the Dodecanese of the previous autumn.

As we moved slowly up the rising floor of the wadi, scanning the cliff side for signs of an opening, the sandy bottom gave way to tangled bracken, stunted bushes and coarse grass tussocks which dragged and ripped at our clothing, making the going extremely difficult.

I soon realised a fact which I had forgotten in the excitement of landing; that is, that I was extremely tired, and began to long for a chance to lie down and sleep, but some half an hour had elapsed in clambering about the side of the cliff before one of the patrolmen gave us the news that he had found the cave for which we were searching.

We scrambled up the thirty odd feet separating us from the man who made the discovery and found that there were in fact two 'caves', with a common entrance. This entrance was about 5ft high and the same wide and immediately inside the cave split into two 'chimneys' each about 4ft in diameter and running upwards at an acute angle into the body of the cliff for about 20ft.

Captain Anderson, the sergeant and bodyguard together with a couple of patrolmen made their billet in the left hand chimney, while the remainder of us crawled up the steeply sloping and malodorous floor of the other. Fortunately, these chimneys widened out as they penetrated into the hill and we were able

Cave Recce and making contact with Cairo

to spread our sleeping bags across the width so that we slept with neither head nor feet downwards, both of which are an equally uncomfortable position. The lateral position had its disadvantages however, as whenever one of us rolled over in his sleep it was always 'downwards' and on several occasions small landslides of bodies were started, the nethermost sleeper bearing the weight of the several bodies which had rolled down upon him as a result of the highest one doing a slow roll!

Sleep we did however, notwithstanding the thought that a German patrol might be ranging along the ridges above us or scouring the floor of the valley about our feet. This thought had occurred to me while we stumbled through the weed-tangled brush of the valley floor, and I peered fixedly at the front line of the cliff tops looming above each shoulder, but I felt reasonably secure in the certainty that we must be even less discernible to those who might be staring down into the valley than they themselves would be to us looking up at their eyrie silhouette against the faintest light of the star spattered sky.

Hardly, it seemed to me, had I snuggled down into the smooth embracing interior of my sleeping bag, when the Scots corporal had my shoulder rocking in his urgent hand and sitting up, startled, I was informed 'come away noo, we've tae move tae another billet. Wi' all oor kit. Jillow!'

I grabbed my gear into a bundle and rolled down the slope of our pen to the cave entrance to find that my impression of a short sleep had been no illusion for the sky was still darkened, although a suggestion of greyness over the shoulder of the opposite valley wall gave sufficient light to see more clearly the ground we had covered in the night.

The remainder of the patrol were also on the move, climbing along the path traversing this section of cliff. I followed with my partner and the wireless kit, and passing an outcrop of rock we came into the entrance of a larger and more inviting cave than our previous tomb!

This cave, to be our home for the next week, was high enough to permit an easy upright stance, and about 8ft deep by 15ft long. The head of the entrance was low and a ridge of rock extending across the threshold formed a natural parapet about 3ft high. When we were all inside it would have been impossible to detect our presence, as the entrance faced down the valley at an angle towards the sea, and natural outcrops of rock on either side defended us from casual observation from the flanks. Our officer who, like others of similar responsibilities, had not been satisfied that our first discovery was the correct one, had gone on a scouting expedition after we were ensconced and had found this latter cave, and decided to move us at once, rather than wait till daylight when our movement might have been detected. He was considerate enough however, to permit us to return to our sleeping bags after we had settled into our new position, and I slept in comfort until 8.00 am when we were scheduled to make our first wireless call back to Cairo.

I pitched the aerial along the cliff in as inconspicuous position as possible, connected up the set, switched on and after sending my call waited to hear the answering signal, conscious of the anxious stares of my comrades and the wrath to come should my first effort prove a failure. So, it was with joy and satisfaction that I was able to give thumbs up as I heard at the end of my transmission the answering 'Dot-dot-dot-dash-dot-dot-dot-dash' repeated, followed by the introductory signal and Cairo's call sign! I replied and sent the message we had already encoded to the effect that the landing had been successful, and we were preparing for operations.

One message only was passed to us, which when decoded gave us the weather forecast for the islands!

Still, our success at 'getting through' was a relief and was a source of confidence to all, knowing that we were at least in touch with the outside world and able to call for assistance should the need arise.

CHAPTER 17

RECCE FOR TARGETS AND VISIT FROM STAMPALIAN SHEPHERD

The next couple of days were spent bored, waiting in our cave while the officer, Stephenson, and Manoli, our interpreter, went off to reconnoitre the Germans' positions.[8] We became pretty well used to the idea of living under the enemy's nose, as it were, almost literally, for in the light of our first day we noticed a concrete pillbox on the end of the opposite cliff, where the land ran out to form the southern spur of the bay. To this day I have no idea whether this was manned, but we did one day observe figures moving in its vicinity, although these might have been shepherds going about their lawful business.

On the second day after our arrival, we saw a solitary figure moving down the valley in our direction, and we all returned to the inner side of the cave not moving or speaking, but after a while we heard the rattle of stones then footsteps near the cave entrance and in a few moments a bearded face peered round the buttress of rocks by our home followed by a figure dressed in dingy rags. The islander, as such it proved to be, expressed no surprise at seeing us there, but instead smiled and addressed us as though we were expected guests.[9]

"*Kalimeris*," he said "*ti kanis? Kala?*"

Our Greek, although only smatterings gleaned from the crews of small fishing caiques which had accompanied us to the Turkish coast, was enough for us to recognise the greeting and I replied, "*Kala, efharisto*" in the accepted manner.

The stranger came into our small home and partook of some of our tea and biscuits conversing the while with Greek, interlaced with badly pronounced German which he obviously thought, and wrongly, that these odd words would help to convey his meaning. We managed somehow to understand most of his remarks in that mysterious fashion which I cannot possibly explain but which soldiers the world over will recognise and remember.

It seemed that he had encountered the captain and Manoli on the mountainside further along the wadi and after exchanging greetings with Manoli, he realised that this was no Stampalian, but a stranger from another island. Manoli had explained that he and a few comrades had come on to the island for a reconnaissance making no mention of the projected operations against the Germans.

This satisfied the islander and he promised to keep silent on the subject of their meeting when he returned to his village, but he implored both Manoli and ourselves not to attack the Germans for fear of reprisals which the islanders had come to expect from their new masters should any little antagonism be shown against the regime.

We assured our friend that our mission was a peaceful one, and he left, to return later the same day with a freshly killed kid and some eggs as a token of his friendship. This was a very great sacrifice on the part of the islander and one which we accepted only after a violent protest and in order to avoid giving offence, so earnest was he in his desire that we should be the recipients of his gifts.

I felt very badly about this episode, the reason being that we had been warned that the inhabitants of these islands were extremely poor at the best of times, and that since the German occupation their lot had deteriorated to such an extremity that many unfortunate islanders had actually died from malnutrition and neglect. In addition to this, I was very conscious of our forthcoming operation, and was guilty over having deceived this kindly creature with the assurance of our peaceful aims.

However, we found some little consolation in pressing gifts upon the stranger in our turn, so that when he finally departed to tend to his sheep and goats, we had prevailed upon him to accept chocolates, cigarettes, biscuits and a pair of socks which I had bought with me in my pessimistic anticipation of repeated wettings.

Captain Anderson, Manoli and Stephenson returned during the evening of the third day, and we immediately set about preparing plans for our effort against the German garrison.

The targets chosen by our comrades for consideration were five large caiques moored in a bay near the waist of the island, a seaplane at the same point, a bridge nearby and shipping and fuel dumps in the island's main harbour.

As our little party comprised only ten men including two signallers,[10] the idea of attacking all these targets was obviously ambitious to say the least, but by reference to each man's suggestions and ideas the captain was able to make a decision on what would be the most suitable targets, bearing in mind the length of time needed to carry out the operation, and that required to travel the not inconsiderable distance over the hills back to our cave.

Recce for targets and visit from Stampalian shepherd

At last, he announced that the main target would be the five caiques, as their loss would indeed be a serious blow, so short were the Germans of any form of shipping in the Aegean area.[11] The next target, which he himself would tackle, would be any shipping or dumps and as much damage as possible would be done to the island's telegraphy and telephonic communications.[12]

The bridge was discarded as a suitable target, owing to the length of time needed to prepare for and lay charges, and the exposed position it held in the centre of the island's narrow waist.

A further objective had been spotted by our captain, which was the house used by the Germans in the island's one town, but, as this town was in the other half of the island, an attack on this house would mean a return through the island's waist, which incidentally was overlooked by and protected by a machine gun from the wireless station and which would also almost certainly be met with an ambush by the Germans manning a small hut on the far side. Their number was not known but several of the enemy had been observed going to and from the brick built hut and it was thought that they must keep a patrol on guard at this compound.

Manoli Kanakakis and Les Stephenson. Brought together by war, their's became a Lifelong friendship. (Photo Courtesy of Marina Kanakaki)

CHAPTER 18

LYING UP POSITION (LUP)

During that day we were visited by a priest and doctor who came to plead with us to leave well alone. We pacified these frightened men and they left, leaving us to ponder the value of the word of our original islander, who had pledged silence![13]

By the following night all the patrolmen were ready for the fray, time pencils were affixed to the little bags containing the plastic explosive, incendiary 'candles' were prepared, Tommy guns and pistols had been dismantled, cleaned, oiled and reassembled, ammunition checked and loaded into the weapons, and first aid kits stowed safely in battle blouses.

Before their departure, Captain Anderson distributed gold sovereigns to each section of the patrol, in addition to Italian Lira, Greek drachma and German marks. This was to be used as 'Escape' money should any member be cut off from the rest of his party and have to bribe and buy his way to safety. It had been discovered that even the German soldier was not above being bribed by gold so that each man had a reasonable opportunity to effect his escape should he have the misfortune to be lost.

The long day finally came to a close and after wishing them luck the patrolmen slipped quietly from the cave down the long slope into the wadi, now full of drifting shadows as the westering sun dropped quickly behind the high cliffs towering above our eyrie.

As the last of them left, my co-signaller and I moved back nervously into the cave, wondering if we would ever see our comrades again, or worse thought, should the next footfall be those of a German patrol looking for the remnants of our party.

One of the patrol, a hardy Scots corporal, Jock Corner, had been left in the cave with us, suffering from a severe attack of malaria, a relic of his sojourn in North Africa a year before. He now lay, smothered in sleeping bags and various spare articles of clothing left by the other men, shivering and muttering deliriously in the back of the cave.[14]

Lying Up Position (LUP)

After blacking out the entrance to the cave with gas capes and ground sheets we prepared to brew up some tea for our restless comrade. As a means of cooking, we had been supplied with Tommy cookers – A small three legged folding stand on which was placed a round methylated spirit impregnated slab. This we lighted and in short order the water was bubbling in the mess tin we placed on the cooker.

Our brewing material was a compounded mixture of tea, sugar and dried milk which when placed in the boiling water gave us at least what was a reasonable substitute for properly brewed tea.

We piled more clothes on the sick man's bed and held a mug of tea for him to drink, so that after a while his mutterings ceased, and he fell into a pitiful sleep disturbed only by occasional violent bouts of shivering.

When peace finally reigned in our hideout, we decided to split the night into four hourly watches and tossed a sovereign for duties. I drew the first watch and strapping my revolver belt around my waist I crawled through our improvised blackout and took up my position immediately in front of the cave, from where I could watch the valley in both directions, as well as the hillside opposite. I chose a position in the shelter of the outcropping rocks at one side of the cave entrance, where I felt reasonably safe from observation, and settled down on a boulder to watch.

My comrades in the cave were soon quiet and sleeping, and an immense silence settled down on that deserted canyon. I have often read of feeling a silence, and I imagined then that the eerie emptiness of the still air had a tangible quality so I strained my ears to catch the slightest sound that might be made by an unseen enemy.

After a while I realised that the silence which I had imagined so complete was far from being even quiet for as I sat on through my watch in that group of rocks bathed in moonlight, I heard the constant rumble and muttering of the distant surf, and an occasional rustling down on the valley floor as some nocturnal animal made its way through the undergrowth, on its way to water or food at the head of the valley.

At one point the peace was even shattered by the passing overhead of a low flying heavy aircraft, the thundering beat of whose engines I had not even heard until the monster leaped into view low over the opposite cliffs, for a moment filling each corner of the valley with quivering sound, which as suddenly ended as the plane passed beyond its confines, leaving only the reverberating echo of its roar leaping madly from cliff to cliff and gradually receding into nothingness, leaving the quiet valley to its surf beat and a frightened soldier.

I awoke my comrade in good time for his spell of duty and thankfully crawled into my sleeping bag, relieved in more sense than one! It seemed no time however before he shook me out of my deep sleep, to report no movement, and suggested another brew up, which partly restored our not too steady nerves.

I took up my position once more in the rocky shelter and this time I strained my ears to catch the sound of explosions, which I felt sure must be heard when our friends had completed their task of blowing up the targets.

Although I persuaded myself on several occasions that a distant thumping had reached my ears, I was never certain however, and eventually decided that the formation of the hills was such that any distant explosion would be blanketed and lost before reaching us.

CHAPTER 19

GOATS MISTAKEN FOR GERMANS

Towards the end of my second and last watch I was staring at the dark shadow of the opposite hillside without actually seeing it, my mind drugged by the boredom and strain when I noticed a movement above me. I jumped and gazed up the cliff top opposite and after a few moments could have sworn to seeing figures moving slowly against the relief of the star speckled sky.

Crawling cautiously to the edge of my shelter I stared intently in the direction of the movement and was satisfied that I had not made a mistake.

I thought for a moment of waking my partner but decided it would not yet be necessary. I moved quietly back into the cave and brought out the Bren gun which had been left in our charge as a means of fighting it out should this become necessary.

By this time the movement on the opposite cliff was certain, and I also heard the scrambling of feet as the figures moved down the cliff face. I cocked the Bren gun, aiming at the floor of the valley at a point where I guessed the enemy must cross and prepared to sell my life dearly. I still didn't wake my partner, as I guessed he would be out with me at the first sound of firing, and I in my mind graciously consented to his having what might be his last sleep.

The figures moved quietly down the opposite cliff and by now I thought I could count at least half a dozen, presumably fully armed Germans. As they neared the bottom, I tensed myself to fire, when from their leader came a plaintive bleating. They crossed the valley floor, and I realised that I had not been mistaken, in my counting, but instead of half a dozen Germans, these were merely half a dozen very in-offensive and unhappy goats if their bleating was any indication of their feelings.

That long tense night finally ended, and the eastern sky was lightening as I shook my partner after brewing up another can of tea. Our sick comrade had quietened considerably during the night, and he awoke to full consciousness now as we discussed the various happenings of the night.

'Eh – is tha' a cup of tea ye have there?' he asked in a weak voice from his pile of bedding within the dark recess of the cave.

'Yes, here you are Jock'

We handed him a steaming mess tin brimming over with the dark brown stew. 'If you can call that tea, you're welcome to it. How do you feel?' 'Well, the heats worn off a wee bit, but ock ahm awful tired and weekly yet Still, this is a grand brew you've made, and while there's tea there's hope you know!'

We made the corporal comfortable, cleared up the cave as well as possible, and removed any signs of our presence from the ledge in front of the entrance. After making our routine call to Cairo and passing the information that the patrol had set off on its attack, we settled down to await the night and the hoped return of our friends.

During the day we took it in turns to take the three water bottles up the valley to a swiftly tumbling brook which peeped out of its rocky lair, raced down the valley for a few yards and disappeared into a hole in the eastern cliffs as though frightened of showing itself for too long a period in the light of day. To reach this reserve of sweet cold water we had to journey a matter of 300 yards along the valley floor, and it was a journey which, although I made it many times during our eight days on Stampalia, never failed to awaken a lively quaking in my heart, for although most of the passage to the water could be made along the cliff face, where rocks and bracken provided ample cover, the last 50 yards or so took one across the flat earth devoid of all protection, in full view of the cliff tops and that hateful pillbox.

However, once arrived at the grotto which marked the exit of the brook from its rocky home, and in the shelter of overhanging rocks I considered that it was worth the exposure to risk. This little tumbling brook burbled its way over a bed of large multi-coloured pebbles, winding between banks of solid stone, worn smooth by the years of the water's caress, diving suddenly under the shelter of a rugged boulder, and emerging quietly on the further side to continue its way for a yard or two in more dignified fashion until taking fright it leapt to the left into its final hiding place in the cliff face.

Standing by the water's edge and looking past the sentinel rocks, I could see the valley dropping steeply away from me between its steep boundaries, wriggling its way tortuously through the various green shade of bush and bracken, down to the silver strip of sand marking the edge of the sea. A sea which this day appeared so placid and kind that it was difficult to believe that it would become such a terrifying fury under the sting of the wind lash. The waters of the bay were now polished like glass, reflecting the smoky blue hump of the headland in its surface, and beyond the bay I could see the blue of the Aegean reflecting the light of the sun, so that its surface sparkled and glittered like a precious stone as the tiny waves threw the golden rays up towards the land.

Goats mistaken for Germans

The cliffs rising on either side of the valley were steep, and on the western side, where lay our cave home, they were covered by bush only about halfway up their height, the remaining hundred feet being bare and forbidding and suddenly sloping away out of sight from the valley. The opposite cliff was more decently clothed with a few stunted trees and bushes hiding the nudity of the rocks and upon the surface of this cliff I could see some of my 'Germans' of the night watch, placidly grazing through what foliage they might find, and taking not the slightest interest in the fact that their home was the scene of nocturnal attacks.

I carried the water back to my comrades and we again discussed the night's happenings. Neither of the others had heard any explosions or other significant noise during their waking hours, and we wondered whether the attack had failed, and our patrol put in the bag or worse.

'What do we do?' asked the corporal 'Supposing they don't come back the night?'

'Wait till tomorrow night and then the next and then the next and next.' I replied. 'Then if they're not back by three days we'll bung a message through to Cairo and ask for instructions.'

'That's all very well,' was his answer 'but in three days Jerry might locate this dump, and that'd be our lot! I'll no be much use for a few days, so it'd be up to you two to see to it, and I canna see you holding off an attack!'

This brought a flood of retaliation on his head for we signallers were always suffering criticism from patrolmen as we didn't carry guns for offensive reasons and were considered by them as 'passengers' until they wanted outside help and then they were all over us to 'get it through'.

He was right nevertheless in as much as two men with one Bren gun and pistols would not prove a very effective opposition to an attack, and we set about discussing plans for disposing our little force. There was little we could do, however, so we just sat around awaiting the patrol's return and trying not to think of the alternative solution to our problem.

CHAPTER 20

ATTACK DETAILS

The day passed uneventfully and at last the lengthening shadows crept across the valley until the light died altogether and night was upon us once more.

We commenced our watches again and I looked forward gloomily to the time when it would be my turn to sit at the cave entrance straining my eyes and ears to catch the slightest sight or sound. The time came all too soon, and I found myself crouching miserably beside the boulder outside the cave and staring blankly at the opposite cliff.

It was nearly midnight when I heard a stealthy movement along the cliff to my left and I stood up, straining back into the shadows, my revolver cocked in my hand tensed to fire as soon as I identified an enemy. It was no enemy who crept round the rocky eminence, however, and I almost dropped with relief as I saw the cheerful countenance of Manoli grinning at me from out of the dusk.

A moment later and the rest of the patrol piled hurriedly into the cave and sat down on their kits, gasping with their exertions. We waited until they had all rested and lighted cigarettes and then heard their story. I would mention that Captain Anderson and his bodyguard were not among this party, as the officer had chosen to attack his harbour targets by boat and would not be expected back until the following night.

The main party's' story was told in a scattered sporadic manner by the various members, but by piecing together the individual episodes, I gathered that the general sequence of events was this:-

They had reached high ground overlooking their objective by the early morning following their departure from the cave, after a long and arduous climb over a succession of heights, and had lain up during the day to observe the targets. With day light they spotted the five caiques lying moored a short distance from the shore, in the bay opening below them, exactly where they were expected to be situated. The seaplane, which appeared to be undergoing repairs, was anchored near the beach a few hundred yards beyond the caiques and Germans were seen moving casually about their work in the area.[15]

Attack Details

At the waist of the island, no great distance from the watchers, could be seen a brick building which was known to house the headquarters of the German garrison. This was seen to be the centre of activities, and so much coming and going was taking place that our friends began to wonder if our islander had spoken so freely of our presence that it had come to the Germans' ears and preparations were going forward to combat any attack.

The long uncomfortable day ended however, and the patrol were gratified to see the Germans leave their work for the night and retire in the direction of the other end of the island.

Corporal Asbery waited until the last of the enemy had disappeared, and darkness completely blanketed the scene before ordering his men to move. They gathered their equipment, made last minute checks of the bombs and weapons and began to move silently down the rugged hillside in the direction of their target.

As they neared the foot of the slope the moon rose beyond the shoulder of the hill, and in its light they could discern the hulls of the caiques lying motionless in the gleaming water, but on nearing the beach they found a complicated system of barbed wire entanglements impeding their progress. This had not been apparent from their hillside eyrie, as the wire was laid in a confused manner between and through bushes at the beach's edge.

After a quick council of war, the party moved along the beach towards the seaplane, as this appeared the target most easily approached; also as it lay

Left to Right, Bill, L/Sgt William (Jock) Asbery, Des, Curly Luke and Micky Rutter at Athlit Camp, Palestine 1944. Asbery was awarded The Military Medal for operations on Stampalia and Piscopi where "he has shown a remarkable aptitude for leadership and has been an inspiration to the men under his command." (Marshall Family Collection)

71

nearest to the garrison, it was the best choice for their first attention, as any pre-detonation in the bombs would draw attention to the seaplane which would lay between the patrol and the Germans as our friends attacked the caiques.

The approach to the seaplane was no more difficult than they had supposed, and a short journey through the water after negotiating the barbed wire and a dainty stepping across the sand being wary of mines, brought them up to the seaplane's moorings.

The patrolmen climbed aboard the pontoon and into the seaplane's interior, placing bombs in the positions where most harm would be caused and after a quick look round for loot (always a primary consideration in the SBS!) they returned to the beach.[16]

An approach to the caiques now seemed easier, so they prepared to move on to the next targets. A German sentry who had not been seen, however, saw the figures moving stealthily across the moonlit beach, and gave the alarm.

The Germans occupying the Aegean islands were noted for being quick on the trigger, owing to nerves brought about by the vulnerable positions of their isolated garrisons, and the Stampalia garrison was no exception.

In a matter of minutes, a heavy barrage of small arms fire supported by automatic weapons from ships and shore was disturbing the peace of the scene but, as always, no one seemed quite sure where to fire, with the result that our friends moved unconcernedly along to the beach near to the caiques.

These vessels were moored some little distance from the shore, and the attack would mean an unpleasantly cold swim before reaching the target. After a heated discussion as to who should risk pneumonia, Jock Asbery led three other patrolmen into the water and commenced swimming towards the caiques.[17]

The Germans had by now achieved some semblance of organisation, and parties of them could be seen moving on the uneven ground some hundreds of yards from the beach. It did not appear to occur to the enemy that their seaplane could be attacked as no attempt was made to investigate its vicinity.

Asbery and his men crawled slowly through the icy water keeping their bombs above their head, to prevent their saturation. The patrolmen on the beach withdrew to the shelter of bushes and prepared to defend the position should the enemy show signs of interest in the area[18]. At last, the swimmers reached the vessels and went from one to the other, placing the bombs in the engine rooms, on the deck immediately over the keel. On the last one they laid dummy charges which would never explode, as this caique belonged to a friendly islander who was known to be preparing a getaway as soon as a favourable opportunity presented itself[19] – so that the Germans would in any case be deprived of this particular vessel.

Attack Details

Their task completed and their bodies numb from the cold, they returned to the beach, dressed again in their battle suits and prepared to withdraw with the rest of the party.

As they moved inconspicuously through the bushes skirting the beach, looking for a gap in the wire, the seaplane blew up followed almost immediately by two of the caiques. This exhibition of fireworks attracted the Germans who proceeded to smother both targets with a withering fire, which was quite gratifying to our friends who paused a moment to admire the beautiful, coloured parabolas created by the hail of tracer ammunition being wasted on the empty boats.

Leaving the beach by means of heaving bushes onto the coils of wire, and climbing over the now innocuous barrier, the patrol started climbing up the hillside at right angles from the beach, in a direction calculated to mislead the Germans, who might follow their trail hoping to locate our hide. They soon realised however that the enemy were loath to make sorties into the hills (they never were anxious to do this unless in great force, we later discovered) and after leaving the vicinity of the attack they proceeded to locate and destroy as many telephone lines and posts as possible before returning to our cave.

CHAPTER 21

CAPTAIN ANDERSON AND NIXON RETURN

The following day was spent by the whole patrol sticking closely in the cave and we observed a certain amount of activity on the top of the opposite cliffs, but the height and distance made it impossible to identify the moving figures. It was decided not to give any possible chance to the enemy of locating our hide, and we therefore cooked no food, eating only biscuits and chocolate and eking out what water we had until dark when it would be safer to emerge from our hole.

Captain Anderson and Nixon returned on time the following night and told us their story. They had been unable to enter the island's harbour owing to heavy seas which made their folboat journey extremely perilous, and to avoid the risk of swamping they had tied up in a cove along the island's coast where they could watch developments of the patrol's attack.[20]

The bombs on the caiques had exploded successfully on two out of the four that had been attacked, as also had those placed on the seaplane, but the remaining bombs had apparently been damaged in the water during the swim out to the vessels, with the result that two caiques that should have been sunk were still afloat.

Captain Anderson decided that he would make an attempt to finish the job. On the following night after the 'flap' had died down, and the Germans, who appeared to decide that lightening never strikes twice in the same place had left the area unguarded, he and Nixon steered their folboat into the bay wherein lay the caiques. Creeping silently under the hulls of the vessels, they climbed aboard. They located the damaged bombs and replaced them with effective ones, climbed down into their tiny craft, and left the scene. While they were making their way back to their shelter of their previous hideout, they heard explosions and looking back saw fires burning on each of the two vessels, and immediately afterwards the fireworks display of the previous night was repeated, with the Germans firing again at the two burning vessels, and in several directions for good measure.

Captain Anderson and Nixon Return

Lying up in their cove during that day, they saw several German patrols on shore, moving about apparently looking for clues to the identity of the marauders. A German patrol boat was also seen moving slowly along the coast of the island passing within a few hundred feet of the two men's rocky cove and they could see from their cover an officer standing on the ship staring through binoculars in their direction, presumably scanning the cliffs and shore for signs of possible landing places for the attackers. Our two men had an unpleasant few moments when this happened, but the German boat passed on, and was not seen again that day.

After nightfall Captain Anderson, anxious lest our cave should have been located, brought his folboat back to our original landing place with a1 speed, and after caching the dismantled boat, arrived back at our hide about one in the morning. There still being several hours of darkness, he decided that we should try and find a more secluded spot than our cave, as the Germans would almost certainly make an exhaustive search of the island eventually, and we could not expect our relieving ML for a day or two. It was known that another cave existed higher up the cliff not very far from our own hide, so Manoli and Corporal Asbery were sent out on a search.

They returned in half an hour to report that they had located the cave, but that it didn't appear very accessible or comfortable. 'Never mind it's accessibility' said our officer, 'If It's difficult to find and get to, so much the better for us.'

So, we collected all our kit together and started off for the higher cave. It was a very difficult operation scaling that cliff, and my partner and I, with a wireless set, batteries and kit were the last to reach the new hide. Sergeant Wilson had stayed behind at the first cave with the Scot corporal who was still weak from malaria, and when we had dumped our kit, a couple of men were sent down to help bring up the sick man.

The new cave lay about two hundred feet higher up the cliff and being situated in a fold in the cliff face concealed behind a large rocky eminence, would be far more difficult for the enemy to locate. It was lofty, wide and deep, but by the light of our torches, we found that it was extremely damp, with moisture running down the walls and dripping from the roof. This moisture had been the cause of a beautiful formation of stalagmites and stalactites, but as one of the men remarked, 'it's some consolation to think you acquired your rheumatism in beautiful surroundings.' And we all had misgivings about spending an unknown period in the cave's dank interior.

During an examination of the cave, we discovered that it already had one occupant. This was a dead sheep, which had somehow become wedged in a standing position between two stalagmites in a corner of the cave. There was no way of telling how long the animal been locked in its damp tomb, but it appeared to have been dead some while, as the flesh had withered, leaving only a skeleton of a sheep covered by a hard smooth skin, almost devoid of wool. The animal's eyes were still complete, and with its mouth open in a silent bleat, made a weird impression of petrified horror in the light of our torches.

The discovery of an unexpected companion did not decrease our anxiety to leave the cold, damp cave, and when Sergeant Wilson arrived saying that they had tried but failed to get the sick man up the cliff, Captain Anderson acceded to the general desire to return to our former cave, notwithstanding the possibility of detection and capture. After all, as we pointed out, there were enough weapons and ammunition among us to provide a reasonable defence against a patrol, and if we were attacked, we could no doubt drive them off, or kill them, and by the time that happened Jock Corner would probably be fit to move, so that we could escape to this new cave before reinforcements arrived.

CHAPTER 22

SIGNALS FOR EXTRACTION

Next morning I had the pleasant task of reporting the result of the patrol's activities to Cairo on the wireless and at the same time asked for the ML to call and pick us up. It would be impossible for an answer to be received until the next night when our next call was scheduled as the request would have to be transmitted to our base in Turkish waters, the reply received and encoded for retransmission to us.

We had now been on the island six days and had had enough. Everyone wanted a square meal, and a decent bed, so my partner and I came in for abuse as usual, about not getting the message through yet regarding the ML's return. It was in vain that we tried to explain the legitimate delays occasioned by the need to encode and transmit, and retransmit messages to and from Cairo, and from Cairo to Turkey and back. They always appeared to consider such delays were just signallers 'Perks' and not at all necessary!

At our evening call, we received a message that the vessel would arrive on the night of the following day, so our friends cheered up and we were 'Good lads' from then on!

Towards midnight of our day of release (always the scheduled pick up time) Captain Anderson went down to the beach, taking me with him to flash the identification signal to the ML when it arrived and we took up position among the bushes at the edge of the sand. We waited there until twelve-thirty when the officer said, 'I'm going back to the cave to make sure everyone is ready. You wait here, and as soon as it turns up, flash them to come in, then double back to us at once. If you don't see anything by one-thirty come back anyway. I don't suppose they'll be coming if they're not here by then.'

I was left crouching in the shelter of my bushes until the appointed hour, by which time I had seen hundreds of MLs swimming through the haze of the starry night but never once did one of the phantoms prove to be the real thing. Eventually I packed up and wandered disconsolately back to the hide.

My adverse report brought a storm of invective down on my head!

One factional swore that the ML had arrived but I had gone back to sleep and missed it so that the skipper had gone away again, for want of a signal.

The other party had it that we had misinterpreted the message from Cairo, and that the boat wouldn't come for a week!

As soon as the next schedule time came round, we had a clarifying but disappointing message from Cairo to the effect that the weather had been too severe and that the ML had been unable to approach the island for fear of foundering. They went on to say the boat would come for certain, not the next night, but that following. This meant another forty-eight hours on the island, a prospect received by now with grave misgiving by all.

We received reports from a couple of islanders who chanced to bump into Manoli that the Germans were indeed quartering the island looking for us as they had discovered that the attack was carried out from an island base. It was reported that they had taken hostages, as reprisals against the citizen population. This was quite unlawful, as far as the Germans were ever within the law, for our men had made certain of identifying themselves by leaving notices in the vicinity of the attack, the notices bearing the following printed message.

"This raid has been carried out by British Commandos and any reprisals against the civilian population will be illegal. Any German official or soldier identified as being responsible for reprisals will be treated as a War Criminal and executed."

We made a practise of always leaving these messages for the Germans to find, but unfortunately as far as we could ascertain, no notice was ever taken of the warning, and in the present case, we realised that the temptation of handing us over in exchange for the hostages might prove too great for the, up to now, friendly islanders, so that our position was fast becoming untenable.

The anxious day was followed by an even more anxious night, with most of the patrolmen sleeping only intermittently, and all waking up when the sentries were changed. No unwelcome visitors arrived however, and the morning call to Cairo brought further confirmation that the ML would be calling the following night.

During the day we searched the cave and its environs almost meticulously, destroying and burying any signs of our occupation in case the Germans should recognise it as being a base. This was done on the principle that we or some of the patrol might come back to the island at a later date should the enemy install anything which might be considered a suitable target, and we could use the same cave as a convenient hide-out.

As a matter of fact another patrol did arrive on the island a couple of months later, which had more spectacular success, in as much as their commander captured and held prisoner for days in the cave the German naval officer commanding the area, evacuating this august person when they left the island. The patrol commander and his men earned much merit from this exploit.

CHAPTER 23

THE EXTRACTION

By nightfall all our kit was made ready, and we all moved down the wadi towards the beach. Captain Anderson and I went down to the beach at eleven pm and took up our position in the bushes as we had done on the previous occasion. The remainder of the patrol waited, concealed in a fold of the cliff side.

The time crawled slowly by and at midnight we were discussing the possibility of any bad luck holding up the ML's arrival, when to my straining eyes, the darkness at the entrance to the bay had seemed to move. I said nothing as I had already seen a dozen phantom MLs coming shore wards only to disappear at a blink. This time however, blinking my eyes did not disperse the apparition, and I gripped the officer's arm.

'I think she's out there now.'

'Where – oh yes, I think you're right, wait till she's well in the bay and we'll flash her. Don't be too anxious though, it might be a hun snooping round still.'

The shadow in the bay persisted and became larger until I felt rather than heard the beat of the ship's propeller above the sough and surge of the surf on the beach. Then the noise ceased, paused, and we both heard the engines again on a different note.

'She's going into reverse' I voiced my thoughts.

'Yes, go on, you'd better flash her now before the skipper decides it's all off and goes home –that is of course if it is ours'. The officer sounded as anxious as I felt.

Obeying instructions, I lay flat on the sand by the bush, raised my lamp, and aiming it in the direction of the ship, flashed the three dashes already arranged as our shore to ship signal. There was a nasty pause at that point, and we both flattened ourselves into the sand, expecting a burst of machine gun fire by way of reply, or possibly worse. However, the hoped for answer came in a few moments, when we saw the dash dot dash flicker out of the blackness.

'Good enough,' said Anderson. 'Buzz off and get the others, while I get my folboat ready.'

Behind The Lines with The SBS: My Life in L Squadron during WW2

I stumbled and thudded my way through the bracken and bushes to the point where we had left our comrades. Corporal Asbery suddenly stood in my path. 'What is it?' he asked.

'Ok, she's here Jock.' I gasped. 'Anderson's getting the first boat ready and you've all to *imshi* down to the beach now.'

The patrolmen grabbed their kit and departed while my partner and I slung our rucksacks on our backs, picked up the wireless set and batteries between us and staggered slowly after them.

At the beach by now all was hustle with the folboats being assembled at record speed, and a high pitched scream suddenly rent the silence, followed by a quieter hissing as the air was released from a compressed air bottle into the rubber dinghy. The boats ready, we launched them through the surf, loaded with kit, and the first half dozen men shoved off to paddle to the ML, now looming large in the darkness only a few cables from the shore.

We were waiting on the shore for their return, when the splash of oars announced the arrival of a sailor rowing the ship's dinghy.

'Come on, you bloody heroes' he said as his tiny coracle bumped the sand. 'Let's get out of this dump.'

We needed no further urging, and within a matter of moments we loaded our kit, launched the boat, getting a thorough soaking, and climbed into the almost capsizing craft.

The stalwart matelot pulled us slowly towards the ship which was drifting seawards against the tug of the idling reversed engine, and we eventually bumped her side where many hands reached down to heave us aboard.

As soon as we and the kit were inboard the vessel the skipper gave his orders, and we steered slowly out of the bay into the narrow seas on our way back to Turkey.

I would like here to pay a sincere tribute to the members of those small Special Service ships without whose help not one raid would ever have been successful. They navigated their way into tiny inlets through badly charted and largely unknown waters and almost took their craft ashore in their efforts to see we were landed or picked up with the least possible delay. The men and officers were always kind and helpful, giving up their bunks and rations to see that we were well cared for while aboard their ships, and permitting us to stand our turn of watches only under protest.

The crew of ML 1283, which picked us up on this occasion, gave us a bowl of good hot broth, lent us kit to wear in place of our sodden clothes, and allowed us the use of their bunks for the whole of the trip back to safer waters, while they performed the dangerous task of sailing through E-boat infested seas where they were at any time liable to run into and be attacked by larger, better armed and faster enemy ships.

The Extraction

Yes, I think all the SBS would be glad to give their thanks to such men as Coulter the skipper, his 'Jimmy; the tall, bearded Yorkshire engineer; his 'Stokes'; the taciturn but always obliging 'Swain'; and the rest of the crew, 'Nobby', who always lost his rum tot at scribbage, 'Pings' who in default of any anti-submarine duties did the work of steward to the officers, 'Lofty', that tall apostle-like Welsh 'Chef' who always had a good meal ready in the worst seas, working under the most appalling conditions in a badly equipped and tiny galley and all the others, whose names have unfortunately been robbed from my memory by time.

The men of these Special Service boats were, in the main, recruited from the fishing fleets, men who were used to putting to sea in small ships, hardy and tough as leather whose only ambition (when not ashore!) was to seek out the enemy and damage him as much as possible with their inadequate armour. It is significant that the title of these ships 'HDML' means Harbour Defence Motor Launch when it is realised that defending harbours was the last thing any of these would have wished to do, rather should the name be, 'Advance Attack Motor Launch'. If a name is to mean anything.

They were not content to accept the maxim 'They also serve who only stand and wait'. Theirs was a faith which demanded action, and by doing the job allocated to them in the islands they had all that any of them might wish for, and in going about their lawful occasions, earned the gratitude and friendship of their SBS passengers.

A Caique. Used by the Levant Schooner Force/Flotilla to transport the SBS on many operations. Fitted with quieter, more powerful Matilda tank engines, they were able to land them more stealthily.

CHAPTER 24

RETURN TO THE *TEWFIK* (HAD A NICE HOLIDAY?)

I awoke the following morning to find that 'ML1283' was tied up alongside the '*Tewfik*' in unfamiliar surroundings. The base had been moved during our absence to Kiervasilli bay in the Gulf of Doris –a delightfully picturesque inlet with an entrance which was practically invisible from outside until one was almost upon the opening in the cliffs of the gulf.

This inlet was even more beautiful than the first one at which we had stopped on our arrival in Turkey. The thickly wooded green and brown slopes of the shores rose steeply, almost perpendicularly, from the placid blue water on three sides of the cove and on the fourth and furthest side from the concealed entrance ran a narrow strip of sand ending at the foot of a steep sandy cliff. From this cliff, near the end of the beach ran a slender fall of water, which followed a swift narrow course along the foot of the cliff to the middle of the beach and then swung abruptly into the sea in a tiny estuary.

At the time of my first view of the bay I saw a ragged Turk sitting on his haunches on the sand by the stream, coaxing a fire into flame, and the wispy wavering pillar of brown smoke rising past the amber coloured cliffs into the sky made a scene of infinite peace and beauty. The sky itself, although this was only the beginning of February, was of a blue deep enough almost to match the rich colour of the sea in that bay, and over all the sun shone with a warmth and brilliance equal to that of an English summer day.

In addition to the '*Tewfik*' there were several other craft at moorings in this haven, a 'Fairmile' ML, two Greek 'Caiques', and a captured German motorboat known as the '*Bandy*'. When we went aboard the *Tewfik*, we learned that in addition to ourselves, only one other complete patrol was aboard, the other three being out on jobs.

We settled down to enjoy a few days' comfort in the well-appointed, and for the moment roomy, mess deck of the schooner, and my first task was to shave off all the accumulated and unwanted hair on my face. This was a fairly painful

Return to the *Tewfik* (Had a nice holiday?)

SBS Moored off the coast of Turkey. (Courtesy of the SAS Archives)

process, as my moustache and beard were still young enough to be stiff and bristly, but by dint of constant bathing and scraping I managed to get my face into the condition I'd been hoping for during the last few days. A number of my friends, more hirsute than I, had acquired beards of tolerable thick growth and they decided to leave them 'Just to see if they could grow decent sets', and in a week or two the men moving around the *Tewfik* had an even more pirated appearance than originally, with half of them sporting villainous growths of beards and flowing moustaches.

The next immediate requirement was a bath. A hot bath was out of the question, but I remembered the stream ashore, so collecting some clean underwear from my base kit, soap and towel, I borrowed a folboat and in company with my co-wireless operator paddled to the beach. The shore was quite deserted, my friend the Turk having gone about his business, so we stripped off our unpleasant clothes and I stepped under the tiny waterfall, standing in the stream at the same time. While I was having my 'shower' Jim was sitting in the stream having a slipper bath, and a more pleasant feeling we both avowed we had not experienced. The water was abominably cold at first, but in a few moments the shock of immersion passed, and we soaked ourselves literally, singing lustily the while.

So wrapped was I in the task of removing the fortnight's grime (Of greater volume than usual as that cave of ours had been pretty dirty and was at times used as a shelter for animals, of which fact there was a surfeit of evidence!) I didn't at first hear Jim's exclamations, and suddenly I noticed he had left his bath, and was tugging a towel out of his kit preparing to use it as a sarong. He was staring along the beach behind, and I turned to see what the cause of his concern was. The sight that met my eyes was that of a small procession of Turks, a man, a boy and two women, unbelievably ragged and poor, but two definitely women!

The party was only a few yards away, and I had no time to adopt evasive action as had my partner. All four of the strangers were gazing at me interestedly so I did the only thing possible, I turned my back in a dignified manner until the retinue passed and kept turning to present my blushing rear view to their eyes until they turned a bend in the cliff out of sight! I felt pretty foolish about the whole affair and was convinced that a blush of shame was creeping over my body from the ankles up, but my partner, between screeches of unseemly laughter, said that the Turks hadn't turned a hair at the unusual sight of an Englishman bathing himself in public view.

Our few days in that idyllic Aegean haven passed very quickly until one morning Tug Wilson, our sergeant, came to us and said that we were to prepare for another job. This seemed a little soon, as the other patrols had not yet returned, and we all had a moan about the imposition. He soothed us however, and said 'It's alright, you're not all going, I only want the two signallers, and three other blokes, and anyway it's not a shooting job so don't panic.'

We packed up our kit, drew some new batteries, tested the wireless set, and set about collecting some rations. While we were doing this, one of the small caiques, the *Etna*, came alongside, and we learned this was to carry us on the job.

CHAPTER 25

ON TURKISH SOIL

The loading of our kit took little time, and we were soon all aboard and prepared to cast off. This caique was about 40ft from stern to stern and 10ft in the beam. The engineer, a suffering invalid, was housed right astern, with a tiny cockpit off the engine room hatch, wherein squatted the helmsman at his tiller.

Our quarters were in the hold immediately ahead of the engine room, and from the evidence scattered thickly about the deck of the hold, it was obvious that this little ship had been used for carrying grain on its last trip. This hold took up most of the remaining space forward of the engine room, but right in the peak was a minute fo'c'sle which housed the three members of the crew. The cooking was done on the fo'c'sle head, and the heat was provided by burning wood on an unprotected piece of sheet metal guard nailed to the deck, a metal frame being erected above the 'fireplace' on which to rest the pots.

The rigging of this small vessel was simple, a triangular mainsail with an enormous boom which was a menace in any sea, and a tiny jib which always proved inadequate when a fresh breeze attacked it, and it usually simply came adrift and flapped like a pennant while one of the frantically jabbering crew wrestled with its folds.

This, then, was our new assault craft, or so we thought, but soon after we cast off, the sergeant told us that we weren't landing anywhere for a fight, but merely going to pick up some captive ships out beyond the gulf.

The weather was still like summer when we passed out of the cove into the waters of the gulf, and the sea was reasonably calm, but on our tiny cockle of a boat even the ripples caused by the breeze made the hull rock and pitch as though half a gale were blowing!

We saw when we came out into the gulf that our little haven was near its landward end and that at the rate of knots our caique could produce, it would be a day or so before we reached the open sea.

As the objective of this small expedition lay off Cape Krio forming the limit of the northern spur of the Gulf of Doris and our base was situated on the southern eastern shores, we sailed straight across the gulf until we reached the northern side. This trip, though short was sufficiently rough, (as we were sailing across the tide) to upset my fellow operator, and he lay on his sleeping bag in an uneasy slumber for most of the crossing.

As a result, I was compelled to make the evening wireless call alone, and a merry time I had of it, trying to balance the set, operate the key and keep my own position in that bucketing little ship. However, I established contact with Cairo and received one message, which when decoded proved to be the inevitable weather report.

It is amusing to recall, though not so entertaining at the time, that whatever sticky situation a patrol may have been in, and whatever dire calls for relief we might be making, we could always be sure that Cairo would pass at least one message during a schedule call, and that one would always prove to be a weather report. Still, these were often useful, and on the occasion in question it gave us the warning, already prophesised by the Greek crew, that a high wind was expected which would make sailing in our caique difficult to say the least.

The skipper of the *Etna* told us, when we advised him of the gale warning, that he intended to put into a small bay a short distance along the coast, where we could spend the night and ride out the gale.

He was as good as his word, and shortly before darkness fell, we sailed round a headland and found ourselves in a wide but shallow bay. Our crew and patrol being small, and the anchorage being safe, no watches were called for the night and after ensuring that our anchors were well secured, we all turned in and slept.

The following morning was grey and cheerless, and the waters of the bay restless and choppy under the impact of the wind, which we could see was whipping the sea beyond the bay into angry white capped rollers. There being no duties to carry out after my morning call, we took the dinghy ashore to have a look at Turkey and having heaved the boat high onto the pebbled beach we set off to explore the countryside.

The beach was bonded by small groves of fruit trees, and when we came through these, we found that they formed parts of an estate of a farm. There lay before us a field of poorly cultivated root crops and beyond, a cluster of mean looking shabby buildings.

Working near the edge of the field was a woman, dressed in miserable clothes and bending from the waist as she toiled at the ground. At our approach she stood upright, and we saw an incredibly old, tired face with the toothless jaws clamped tight together so that the bony pointed chin almost met the tip of the long angular nose. She gazed at us for a moment from faded eyes, half obscured by the shiny wrinkled skin of her eyelids, picked up a bundle from the ground and shambled off through a hedge in the direction of the buildings.

On Turkish Soil

'Don't like strangers it seems' grunted the sergeant. 'Let's go see what they've got to flog.' And followed the old woman.

Coming through the hedge we found ourselves on a farmyard which was filthy to great degree with a stench which was overpowering. Tethered by the wall of the house was a dejected looking goat sharing the little coarse grass there was with an aged donkey. Running about unrestricted were dozens of tiny chickens, smaller than any I had seen before, their legs and feathers clotted with filth from the ground.

As we approached the building a middle aged man came forward to meet us, dressed in a strange mixture of eastern and western clothes. His hat was the remains of a battered trilby surmounting a shaggy bearded head which was also encased by a cloth in the fashion of a balaclava helmet. A coat cut on the lines of a shooting jacket hung loosely from his shoulders almost in rags, and falling open, disclosed a waist wrapped in a cummerbund which had seen better days. This cummerbund supported a pair of those extraordinary trousers beloved of Muslims, with a full seat hanging in slack folds down to the back of his knees, where the legs were tailored to sit tightly on his limbs in the manner of jodhpurs.

It was obvious from his footwear that he had met other soldiers somewhere, for his ankles were covered by a good though dirty pair of Army grey socks, but his feet were wrapped in boots which had obviously been made from goat skin roughly sewn to pieces of wood which formed the soles.

The language difficulty was again overcome by means of signs, and when he understood that we were here to trade our host made off into the house, returning in a few minutes with a box filled with eggs. The old woman followed him, though still cautiously regarding us, and she carried a tall round tin, which we found to be full of honey.

'These people can't be as poor as they look,' said Tug Wilson, 'what do you reckon we ought to give them?'

'What about some of those crummy Vs' was a suggestion, and we all turned out our pockets to show our 'salesman' those foul cigarettes issued by the Army, and which we only smoked in times of great shortage, used as exchange currency throughout the Middle East.

The *Tewfik* had an abundant supply of these gems and each patrol had access to the supply (albeit unknown to the QM!) so that in our small caique we had a considerable quantity which we had brought 'just in case'.

The Turk regarded the 'V' cigarettes for a moment, examined one packet and looking up indicated by signs that they were acceptable, and that he would require so many packets in exchange for his eggs and honey. The barter was made, and we prepared to move on, when the Turk stopped us with a movement of his hand and disappeared within the house again. Mystified, we waited, and after a short delay, out he came once more, laden this time with a tin box full of almonds. Again, he indicated that so many packets would be required, but our current stock was exhausted, so we said that we would return to the ship for more.

As we prepared to leave with our purchases, he did a strange thing. He held a hand above the ground and horizontal to it, moved the hand in a circle and then with a stick wrote in the mud of the farmyard the word 'OIL'.

'Oh, I get it' said Jim, my partner, 'He wants us to flog him some oil.'

'Well, he's had it' replied Wilson and shook his head at the Turk.

The man looked blank for a moment, then a thought appeared to strike him. His eyes lit up, he shook his head violently and looked anxiously around the farmyard to find means of illustrating his requirements. In the corner by a well stood a battered pail, which he picked up and dipping it into the water, brought it over to us, filled to the top.

'What's this in aid of?' wondered the sergeant and was further puzzled as the Turk tipped the water on to the ground, rubbed his foot obscuring the word 'Oil' and then holding the empty pail aloft, banged vigorously on its side. Light dawned on me, and I said, 'He doesn't want oil – he only wants the empty drum, don't you remember how bucked those wogs were in Kiervasilli Bay when the matelots gave them a couple of empty drums, I expect the metal is valuable or something to these characters.'

We made noises and signs to show we understood, and leaving the Turk exhausted but satisfied, we returned to the boat.

On board the *Etna* we rifled the store of 'Vs', leaving about half the cache for future use, and asked the skipper if he had any empty oil drums. As it happened, one of his drums for the diesel engine was nearly empty and despite his protests (for after all it was a British oil drum, supplied for his use by the Navy) we emptied the remains of the oil into the engines tank and hoisted the drum over the side into the dinghy.

When we returned to the farm, we found that our Turk had been joined by a few of his neighbours, all as ragged as he, but a couple baring their wares. One had a pair of chickens; another had some more eggs. After a certain amount of bickering and 'knocking down' we secured our own Turks almonds, and the chickens, but left the eggs, as we had sufficient for more than the call of luxury. The egg vendor looked so crestfallen that I handed him several packets of the foul 'Vs' by way of solace, and for a moment I was afraid the dirty creature was going to hug me in gratitude.

The sight of our oil drum had driven our Turk to a frenzy of avarice, and he cast around madly for the wherewithal to acquire this glittering prize. It was obviously too good to be bought by mere eggs, honey or almonds, and after a mental struggle he dashed off to his house once more. When he returned, he was carrying a goat kid, freshly killed and skinned, which he offered in exchange for the drum. This was luxury indeed, after a diet of tinned M&V and we snapped up the bargain before he changed his mind.

Bearing our latest purchase, we returned once more to our vessel which began to look like a ration ship. The kid we hung up feet first to the mast, where it stayed for a few days, in order that the meat might become less fresh and consequently more tender, the live chickens were tethered on a running line to the bulwarks, and the almonds, honey and eggs we stowed just above our hold, forrard of the engine room hatch.

I had some qualms (I always did!) about the honesty of our barter, but as one of the others pointed out, the wogs wouldn't have sold the food unless it was surplus to requirements, and anyway they could probably get more for the cigarettes and oil drum than they themselves had given. In all the exchanges which we had made that morning I don't remember seeing a smile on the face of any of the Turks, and this seemed to be the case in all our future dealings with them.

They appeared to be a morose race, generally apparently poor, and ill dressed, but hardy and self-sufficient. My contacts were, of course, confined to the Turks along the rugged coast (although on one occasion we put into the fairly flourishing part of Bodrum but we didn't go ashore, and only saw the inhabitants from a distance), so that my impressions may be quite wrong, but it was easy to believe how fiercely and implacably they fought our fathers in the First World War, for you can't easily overthrow an opponent who takes himself and you so seriously.

CHAPTER 26

FISHING WITH EXPLOSIVES

Our shopping had taken most of the morning, but the wind didn't seem to have abated to any extent, so after lunch we cast about for more mischief to pass the time.

We had often seen the Greeks fishing with home-made bombs, so someone suggested we might supplement our already bulging stash of food with a little fishing by this means. To put the scheme into good effect of course, we should have had plastic explosive from which to make bombs, but in the absence of this material we decided to make do with '36' grenades or Mills bombs. The use of these bombs for fishing was and is strictly forbidden of course, but no greater authority being present than our sergeant Tug Wilson (who incidentally was the prime mover) we overlooked the illegality and loaded half a dozen Mills into the dinghy and rowed off to a point furthest away from the *Etna* on the shore.

Having chosen a spot which looked a suitable fishing ground we shipped the oars and lay to for a while in order that the absence of movement might persuade the fish that the area was safe for habitation. After a suitable period, we primed the first bomb with a four second fuse and pitched well away from us into the water and waited for the bump, but none came, so after a short pause we unshipped the oars and sculled over to the spot where the bomb had fallen. No signs of any fish were to be seen nor any upheaval in the water and looking down through the depths we saw that we had chosen an ill place for the experiment, for at this point the water was only a few feet deep as the cliff which met the water some dozen feet away, sloped only gently down into the sea making a shelf on which our bomb must have been damaged before the fuse had time to ignite the explosive.

Disappointed at this failure but determined to succeed with our remaining bombs, we pulled further out into the bay and pitched our second Mills well away from the cliff. This time the splash was followed by a dull thud and a sudden slight upheaval of the water. When we reached the spot, the water was obscured by a dense cloud of mud and if there had been any fish to be caught, we could not have seen them.

Fishing with explosives

This second wasted bomb was too much, and before going on with the by now not so fascinating sport, a council of war was held with each individual giving his views on the reasons for failure.

At last, we arrived at what we thought must be the solution. Four second fuses were too long, as the time allowed permitted the bomb to penetrate to too great a depth and the water of the bay must be less deep than we imagined, with the result that the bomb exploded near the bottom and disturbed the mud which in turn obscured the water to such a degree as to make it impossible to see any catch.

The remedy was obvious, but not too popular. We couldn't cut the fuses but we could reduce the time the bomb spent in falling through the water by retaining the bomb after the pin was removed for a second or two before pitching it into the sea! We all agreed that this was the answer, but nobody seemed very anxious to prepare our next bomb, until a little patrolman from Birmingham said 'Well, here's risking my neck for a bloody fish' and picked up the bomb, inserted the fuse, and pulled out the pin.

I don't suppose he held the live bomb for more than a second and a half but to the rest of us watching with anxious eyes and bated breath it seemed that the four seconds must be almost gone before he flung the grenade away from him with a look of vast relief on his face. This third bomb hit the water and immediately there was a dull thud which reverberated under the hull of our dinghy, and a respectable little water sprout over the point which the bomb fell.

We pulled over to the spot once more, expecting to see the water choked with fish, but at first the water was quite clear, and then in a minute or so, bodies began floating to the surface. Ready hands were over the side at once grabbing at the inflated corpses as they drifted by, but when we inspected the catch, it was more than disappointing. The fish were small and not very plentiful in number, some larger fish had been obvious victims of the detonation, but their size must have proved their undoing, for although we collected several pieces of what must have been fish of reasonable size, not one complete prize larger than a pilchard was caught.

Tired by now of persistent failure and convinced that Mills bombs were not the ideal weapon for catching fish, we agreed to call it a day, and returned to the caique, when we presented a puny catch to the Greek crew.

It was late afternoon now and nearly time for our call to Cairo, so I prepared the set and, after the usual exchange of signals, took the expected and inevitable weather report. This when decoded was encouraging, and promising a diminution in the strength of the wind, so that we might continue our journey.

At daybreak next morning the weather prophets were proved right for the wind had abated and the weather promised fair, with light clouds scudding across the blue sky and the open sea, though still active, by no means a menace to the caique's progress.

We breakfasted in the bay and set sail as the already warm sun rose above the Turkish hills, changing the colour of the sea from green to a deep blue.

The skipper of the *Etna*, always a cautious man, hugged the coastline as we sailed down the gulf towards the sea, his reasons, he explained, being that if we were attacked by a German plane, we could use the cliffs as protection, and if we were sunk, would have only a short swim to the shore!

We scoffed at the idea of an air attack on so small a craft, and urged him out into the sea, for the water under the cliffs was rougher than further out, owing to the back surge of the breakers making a double current and heaving the caique about as though it were on a switchback.

As the morning progressed however, it looked as though the skipper might be right, for low over the open sea at the end of the gulf we saw a seaplane moving backwards and forwards in our direction.

The crew immediately jerked into action, performing a ballet of fear in their excitement. They besought us to go below out of sight, as the German pilot would be at once suspicious if he saw so many figures moving on the deck of an innocent caique. We complied and went down into our hold, and in a few minutes the roar of engines beat down on the small ship as the seaplane flew low overhead and turned back to enable the pilot to have a second look at the vessel.

The inspection appeared to satisfy the airman, or possibly he didn't consider the small ship worthy of a bomb or machine gun attack, for the beat of the engines soon died again and our crew gave us the all clear to come up on deck.

As the day wore on we came near to our destination, and soon we saw, beyond a low headland, the masts of several ships pointing nakedly into the darkening sky. When we had cleared this point, we turned into a small inlet on the end of the cape marking the limit of the gulf and saw three fairly large schooners moored together under the guardianship of a Fairmile Motor Launch.

These three schooners had been used by the Germans to carry a cargo of oranges and a few Greek civilians into the island Garrisons, but it appeared that the Greek crews had conspired together to overthrow the few German guards on each ship and were steering a course for Turkey when they came up on the ML.

The skipper of the Fairmile, where the Germans were now captive, handed over custody of the schooners to us, with instructions to protect them on their journey down the coast as far as our base, where another ML would escort them to Beirut. The Fairmile itself was leaving at once for Beirut on urgent business so could not spare the time to act as 'Mother' and had asked for troops to come and take over.

That we were the troops and our ship the escort appeared to have shaken him somewhat, for he was a stranger to the SBS, but nevertheless he handed over his charges and departed.

Fishing with explosives

We spent the night alongside the schooner, in an atmosphere heavy with the scent of oranges, and during our conversations with the civilians learnt that they were all delighted to have been delivered out of the hands of the Germans and looked forward to going to Egypt, where the men proposed to settle their women and then return to the islands where they could help our people in their work against the Germans.

As soon as possible the following day, our little convoy set out on the journey back to our base, and it soon became clear that any ideas we might have of 'escorting' these bigger ships were hopeless. After an hour's sailing they were a couple of miles ahead of us and had to heave to in order that we might come up with them and so it was throughout the day, the stately schooners sailing gracefully onward under full sail and the power of better engines than ours, and then a sudden heaving to while they waited for our little caique to come waddling slowly up, its hopelessly inadequate engine chugging away in a determined manner, refusing to admit to the superiority of its more powerful rivals.

We eventually handed over the care of the three schooners to an HDML sent out to meet us and then we headed into the bay to await the decisions of the 'great ones' on our future activities.

Members of SBS between operations in the Dodecanese. (Courtesy of the SAS Archives)

CHAPTER 27

SIGNALS FOR JELLICOE

During our absence there had been a certain amount of coming and going among the other patrols, and the mess deck of the *Tewfik* being now more crowded than when we left, our little party elected to stay aboard the *Etna* until further notice.

I thought that this decision might mean a fairly reasonable rest from operating my set, as of course, we kept no wireless contact with Cairo whilst in base, this function being carried out by Royal Corps Signals operators based on the *Tewfik*.

My idea proved quite wrong however, for the night following our arrival in the *Etna* a dinghy pulled alongside and Lord Jellicoe, the commanding officer, came aboard. 'Any signallers on here?' he asked, looking down into the hold. 'Yes Sir' I replied.

'Got your set aboard? Yes? Good, I've got some messages to send and the main station on the *Tewfik* is overloaded with work at the moment so you can keep yourselves occupied with some of my work.'

His Lordship then handed us a batch of signal forms like a small book.

'I want you to encode those and send them on your next call. When is it scheduled?' he said.

I told him we could make a call in about fifteen minutes at eight pm.

'Good, then I'll wait till they are all gone' replied 'George' and proceeded to make himself comfortable on my rolled up sleeping bag.

My partner and I looked through the messages and saw that apart from encoding, the actual sending of such a formidable bunch would call for a couple of hours' steady work in the best conditions on the air. Such conditions were too much to expect, so we sat down miserably and commenced to encode the first messages before the scheduled time.

'George' had brought a naval 'Pig' with him (I use the word 'pig' with no offensive intent – this was how we thought of naval officers after our association with matelots for they never referred to their officers by any other expression, and I am writing of places, events and people and they come to my mind now and did so at the time).

Signals for Jellicoe

His name was, I believe, Seligman, and a man of great unpopularity among the men of coastal forces and Levant Schooner Force.

He and the CO sat in our hold gossiping away while we prepared our messages, and after I commenced sending, making things even more difficult than they already were, with a 'Busy' air and a fading signal from Cairo.

Still, by dint of my steady transmitting of the messages which Jim was meanwhile encoding and then reversing the process to give each other a break, we managed to get rid of all Jellicoe's message by ten-thirty, and just as I hoped we could rest and close down the set, Cairo sent the call sign which meant they had messages for us.

I suppose they had already decoded some of the messages from Jellicoe and realising his Lordship was 'on a line' as it were, they decided to pass all outstanding calls through my set. Anyway, the number of messages was such that we were still going strong at twelve-thirty when Jellicoe left us for his bunk on board the naval schooner *LS9* which was moored across the bay.

The last message was finally received by 1.00 am and Jim and I were in a collapsing condition having worked under the worst atmospheric conditions on the set for five hours without the comfort of an office seat (as had the Cairo operators) and with the CO nagging the while to get the incoming messages back into English as they were received. After we had closed down, we looked at the pile of messages still waiting decoding and I said 'Let the sods wait till morning – I am turning in.' Jim said 'Me too, even if it means RTU. I can't bash any more up tonight' and turn in we did.

The interval of sleep seemed all too short, and I was awoken by a heavy crash on the deck above my head, and Jellicoe's voice shouting:

'You Signallers, wake up, where are my messages?'

I sat up only dimly comprehending the meaning of this unpleasant awakening, but looking up I saw the irate face of our CO glaring down through the hatch.

'I said, where the hell are my messages?' he repeated, and not waiting a reply bellowed 'Who's in charge of the radio set? Come on speak up men, who's the senior man?' I looked miserably down at Jim who feigned sleep and looking back at the CO I gulped and answered:

'Er – well, we're neither of us is in charge, but I suppose I am the senior man Sir.'

'Well, get up man, and give me my messages' he howled.

Again, I looked round for succour, and seeing none I again procrastinated:

> 'There are one or two still to be decoded Sir.'
> 'What? You'll be lucky if you don't get an RTU for this, my man. Look alive and get them decoded at once d'ya hear? Then bring over to the *Bandy* in...' he looked at his watch, 'Fifteen minutes from now, and then I'll think about what to do with you two slackers.'

He stamped off the deck and I heard the splash of oars as he rowed back to his comfortable breakfast.

'Come on Jim, we'd best get cracking' I said, and he sat up with a rueful grin. 'You're a nice bastard, letting me carry the can.'

'Well you <u>are</u> the senior man' he grinned again, but immediately he dug out the messages and a pencil and we got cracking on decoding the last few messages.

It was more than fifteen minutes before I climbed into the dinghy and rowed over to the *Bandy*, so that I looked out for more abuse from the CO, but at the same time I had clipped a message to the top of the pile, where he would see it first, which was a congratulating signal from MEFHQ addressed to Jellicoe.

I tied up my dinghy to the stern of the *Bandy*, climbed onto the deck and made my way down into the tiny cabin. George and Seligman had completed their meal and were sitting back talking when I entered. He looked up and saw me, the smile fading from his face.

'You're late again signaller' he said. 'What's the excuse this time?'

I felt a little peeved at the unprovoked attacks on us, so I said without fore amble. 'We were working till one o'clock this morning receiving messages, we had decoded all but six of them and I felt that if I'd gone on I would probably have made mistakes. You can't keep it up indefinitely Sir and after all we had been going five hours solidly.'

He looked at me coldly for a moment and I expected the sack straight away, but instead he reached out his hand and took the messages without further comment.

I stood back by the door and waited. Jellicoe looked at the first message, which was the one telling him how good his men were, and I could almost see when he got to the part which read something like this...

'And first class communications being maintained in what we know to be adverse conditions...'

His stern cold face suddenly relaxed in the ghost of a smile, and he came to the end of the message, looked up and passing it to Seligman said,

'Look at that Adrian, the gods are pleased with our little offering!'

Jellicoe finished reading the messages and looked at me as though wondering what the devil I was doing there. 'I wondered if you had any more messages to send Sir.' I said, 'We have a schedule at nine o'clock and we'll have to encode them pretty quickly.'

'Eh? Oh yes, there is one' he said and looking round asked 'Have you a pencil?'

He himself had several sticking out of his battle blouse pocket, but I was used to his foibles by now and had come armed with both spare pencil (which I knew he would not return) and signal pad. When he had composed a suitably modest reply to the congratulations, he handed it to me with a charming smile and said, 'Thank you signaller, you've done a fine job, carry on.' And I was dismissed.

He was a strange, hard man to work for, was Jellicoe, but, as I worked with him on later occasions, I found he was usually scrupulously just and if a man worked as hard as he might, and as well as he could, George was always ready with a word of encouragement. But woe betide any man whom his lordship might suspect of slacking! Better were it for that man never to have heard of the SBS than to receive the final dressing down by this little Napoleon before getting his marching orders!

This little episode marked the end of our time on the *Etna*, and with one or two exceptions, the end of any interesting event in the islands so far as I was concerned. We did one or two more sorties, but they were more by way of grocery trips, delivering food by night to those islands which were known to be desperately short of even the essentials. These trips were hazardous, only as far as the sea journey was concerned. The landing was easy, unmolested, and for the most part, greeted by dozens of islanders who had previously been warned where to meet our provision ships!

There were of course other operations going on in the various islands of the Aegean. In particular one shooting match on the island of Nisero, but these have been written about in detail in 'The Filibusters' by John Lodwick and I won't attempt to describe any event which I personally did not experience, as this journal is being written from memory, assisted only by a few souvenirs, which I collected to act as milestones, and which are performing that function as I write.

The Nisero Operation

Early in March 1944, Major Ian Norman Patterson, who by this time had been itching to get out to operations himself, received intelligence from an SBS reconnaissance patrol on the island of Piscopi.

Behind The Lines with The SBS: My Life in L Squadron during WW2

Two German Lighters, laden with food, supplies and reinforcements were believed to be en-route to Cos with a planned stop at the island of Nisero.

With George Jellicoe abroad in Syria preparing to marry his fiancée and unable to restrict Patterson to a Base planning role, he seized on the opportunity. A patrol was quickly assembled that included lieutenant, Dick Harden, Les Stephenson and also Lieutenant Commander Ramsaur of the U.S. Navy, who had joined the party in an observational role. Des Marshall was also amongst the numbers assembled.

Nisero, at this point, was an island unoccupied by German forces and the SBS billeted themselves at the harbour town of Mandrachio to await the arrival of the German boats.

Dick Harden, Stephenson and one other were then sent to the nearby port of Palo by Patterson to observe any movements and with instructions to send a runner should the lighters arrive there.

At 8.00 am the next morning, a runner returned with news that the Germans' boats had indeed arrived at the port and were in the middle of unloading some of their supplies.

From a good vantage point Patterson observed and estimated the German strength to be up to thirty in number. The Germans looked very relaxed as they unloaded their cargo and on occasions left the quayside to wander into town, apparently unaware of any lurking danger.

Being fluent in Greek, Les Stephenson, wearing civilian clothing, was sent into the port town to try and gather any intel on the Germans' intentions but soon after and to Patterson's horror, the two boats weighed anchor and appeared to be leaving the island. Patterson thought he had missed his opportunity but was at once relieved to see the lighters sail a short distance along the island coast and moor up on the east side of the jetty in Mandracchio.

Meanwhile, the Mother Superior from the island's orphanage met with Major Patterson. To her distress, she informed the major of the Germans' intentions to remove children from her care and transport them to the island of Rhodes, an order she was most unhappy with.

Patterson devised a plan. With the Mother Superior's blessing, he asked her to take the children as far up into the mountains as possible, with the intention of taking the Germans prisoner when they arrived at the orphanage to collect them.

Instructing his men to keep out of sight, and telling Dick Harden to block any attempted escape from the rear, the SBS lay in wait at the orphanage for the Germans' arrival. In order to deceive them into thinking all was well, Patterson even went as far as donning the robes of an Italian priest.

At mid-afternoon the Germans could be seen on the approaching road to the orphanage.

Patterson greeted them on their arrival and led the unsuspecting men towards the orphanage through a narrow passageway into the refectory.

In a few short moments shouts of 'Hände Hoch!' could be heard.

The Germans turned to find Patterson, now assisted by Dick Harden. Bravely or foolishly, but with no intention of surrendering they opened fire and a bloody gunfight ensued which soon saw Major Patterson's own gun misfiring.

With no working weapon and now under attack from one of the Jerries, Commander Ramsaur took aim with his pistol and a bullet was put through the head of the assailant. Outmanoeuvred and outgunned, the Germans attempted to escape by jumping through windows, but were quickly mopped up by the SBS stationed in the surrounding area.

As soon as the last shots had been fired and the smoke cleared, the bloody scene was evaluated. Two Germans had been killed, seven wounded, including an officer, and three more taken prisoner.

Immediately attention turned to the boats. If the Germans didn't return to them soon, suspicion would grow and others would be sent to investigate. Leaving the wounded in the care of their medical Sgt. Kingsbury, the SBS made their way to the harbour. Now armed with a Bren gun, Patterson placed himself in a good position overlooking the harbour about 300 yards from the Lighters and soon, two more crew members could be seen making their way up to the orphanage.

Having likely witnessed the bloody scene, one of the investigators came running back from the area to raise the alarm. Patterson opened fire, killing him, then turned his attention to the boats. Providing covering fire and neutralising a Schmeisser and machine gun that had got into action, Harden, Corporal Long and Lance Corporal Clark advanced on the boats armed with carbines, grenades and primed charges. The Germans put up a good fight but soon realised the battle was lost.

Moments later a white flag could be seen waving from the enemy craft. Two more killed, six wounded and two more prisoners, brought a total of five dead, seventeen prisoners, and 40-tons of food and supplies into SBS hands.

Leaving behind an ecstatic local population who themselves had witnessed the entire shoot up, Patterson and the rest of the SBS set sail for the Turkish coast on the captured vessels, leaving behind Les Stephenson with the wounded German prisoners until the evening when a motor launch would arrive to remove them from the island.

Les Stephenson's adventures were far from over. On the journey back onboard an ML to the *Tewfik* on the Turkish coast, the naval Commander Sub-Lt. Hickford spotted two Lighters ahead that appeared to be in trouble. Believing these to be the enemy craft captured earlier, he caught up with them

Behind The Lines with The SBS: My Life in L Squadron during WW2

Des looking proud in his SAS Beret. (Marshall Family Collection)

and pulled alongside. Immediately it became clear that these were not the captured vessels, but two entirely new craft full of German crew.

Without a moment's hesitation and armed with Tommy guns, Les Stephenson and two of the ML's crew leapt overboard onto the German craft. They opened fire on the surprised Huns, at one point managing to turn the craft's own twin Breda's onto them. Some of the crew in the confusion turned their guns on one another.

Soon a third Lighter and an armed Caique appeared and began firing on the ML, killing two of the naval crew who were manning the ship's Oerlikon guns. Another shell hit a store of flares on board the ML and with smoke billowing from it, there was a brief pause in the enemy attack. Lt. Hickford used this moment as an invitation to escape the barrage and it was only later he discovered that he had left with Stephenson and the two sailors still on board the enemy craft.

Having seen the ML disappear off into the distance towards the Turkish coast, Stephenson and the others leapt overboard and began to swim the one mile journey to the shoreline. From there, they managed in their wet clothes to return to the *Tewfik* base along the coast riding on a mule.

Later it was revealed by captured German prisoners that there were twenty-six German casualties from the incident.

Major Patterson and Les Stephenson later received the Military Cross and the Distinguished Conduct Medal respectively for their actions mentioned above.

CHAPTER 28

CULINARY LIFE ABOARD THE *TEWFIK*

The two exceptional events which I mentioned above, and which are worthy of recall, are brief and at the time caused amusement to at least some of the parties concerned.

The first was on our return to the *Tewfik*, when I found my brother Bill, who was an operator to another patrol, had returned from Cos. For want of a better occupation, we both offered our services temporarily as cooks to the patrols on board at the time. It was necessary for someone new to take over this essential job as the patrolman who had previously had the task had become tired of abuse and handed in his chef's cap and ladle so that 'No food' or 'Cook your own' was the order of the day.

Bill Just Joined SBS 1943. Beirut.
(Marshall Family Collection)

Neither of us had any experience of cooking, however by dint of expert work with the tin opener and a plentiful supply of fat we managed to feed the brutes for a day or two on meals of fried bacon, fried stew, fried deserts and tea. Then we ourselves became tired of the diet and decided to try our hands at 'Toad in the hole'.

As mentioned above we were quite inexperienced and had no one to tell us that batter was one of the essential constituents. Anyway, with forty mouths to feed we prepared a mixture of flour and water. When this monstrous heap of grey rubbery mixture had almost filled the entire space of the tiny galley, we tried to press tinned sausages into it. This was found to be impossible as each banger insisted on sliding quietly to the surface as we tried to push the next one in place.

When we realised our defeat, we stood back and looked at the creation. We wondered what we should do. Then some kind soul poked his head in the doorway and enquired if we were preparing a patch for the hole in the ship's side. We told him what we hoped to do and he then pointed out the error of our ways. He confirmed that the correct basis for 'Toad' is batter. What we had prepared was more of a solid dough in his opinion.

This floored us for a while but then my brother said, 'Never mind, we'll make it into a cake'. We set to with a fruitcake in mind. We tried the pressing system with currants and sultanas. This was as hopeless as our sausage effort as by now the surface of our dough was something that should be seen to be believed. Eventually we poured a heap of currants onto the surface and then rolled the dough into a ball, then flattened it out and poured more currants on. Then rolled and flattened again and so on until all our fruit supply was exhausted.... And so were we.

Laying the mixture into greased pans it occurred to me that somewhere I had heard that brushing a cake with milk improved the browning. So we spread the contents of a tin of condensed milk onto each cake and placed them in our wood fired oven.

By midday the cakes were still not ready, a fact that we had ascertained by means of frequent looks into the oven in order to examine our efforts. After a couple more hours however the tops of the cakes showed a glistening appetising brown colour. Digging knives into the surface we decided they must be ready. So pleased with our success we lifted the cakes from the oven, cut them into squares and carried them down into the mess deck. The patrols greeted us with cheers, but we didn't wait to be complimented. A voice had whispered in our ears that all might not be as well as it appeared. We clambered back on deck returning to our galley to await the verdict of our 'Magnum Opus'.

The verdict was not long delayed, for in a few moments a stream of indignant and disgusted SBS men filed up to the galley door bearing their portions of cake and swearing that we had tried to poison them.

We disclaimed all malicious intent and examined the samples that our comrades thrust beneath our noses. They had every reason for being indignant. Although the top of the cake was a delicious crisp brown and the first half an inch well-cooked to the texture of a biscuit, the remaining depth of the cake became increasingly horrible varying through a consistency of a sticky yellow to a frankly foul, gluey grey mess of dough.

The remainder of the portions met their inevitable fate being tipped over the side of the ship into the Aegean. The men swore that a list had been steadily growing worse on the galley side of the vessel but was instantly corrected when the ballast of dough was jettisoned.

That effort marked the end of our cooking interlude. Other cooking volunteers came forward thereafter declaring that it was better to be poisoned by oneself than to leave it to a pair of ignorant blunderers......Or worse.

CHAPTER 29

GUARDING A SHIP AT PENZIK BAY & SHIPWRECK AT KIERVASILLI BAY

The other incident worthy of mention was our shipwreck, and this actually occurred before our period of cooking.

When we came back from 'escorting' the captured German ships, we did not stay in the bay for long, but were detailed off to sail to another harbour, known as Penzik Bay. In this bay lay the schooner which our caique and MLs were using as a fuel ship, and our duty was to guard this solitary vessel from any marauding German ships which were known to be looking for our supply base.

Very little occurred in the week or so our patrol spent on board the fuel ship, except that one of our men who located the rum store tried to annihilate one of the others under the mistaken impression that he had offered a grave insult. The combatants were separated and the offensive one placated by an officer who temporarily in command was known as 'Shorty' Wilsher.[21]

This officer, a grand individual, who was not one of the SBS, nor Navy, was a bit of a mystery, and we never did find out what he was doing in the islands, but after we left, we heard he had been killed in a way more mysterious and unpublished as his own presence. I suppose he was just another of the queer individuals who turned up occasionally on strange errands, who spoke little about themselves, and as quietly vanished again, who were unknown to regular troops and encountered by us when we ourselves were doing unusual jobs in out of the way places.

At all events, after a tedious wait in lonely Penzik Bay we were picked up one day by an ML bearing instructions for us to proceed to Kiervasilli Bay where we had found the *Tewfik* had gone and had been replaced by a rather dilapidated vessel which had escaped from the islands with a cargo of refugees and one German prisoner, who disgraced himself in an unmentionable manner when confronted with authority in the shape of one of our tougher officers.

Behind The Lines with The SBS: My Life in L Squadron during WW2

For some unexplained reason, we were to spend a day or so on this Greek schooner (now clear of Greeks) along with two other patrols, before proceeding back to the *Tewfik*, and we accordingly cleared the ship up a little, and made ourselves comfortable as possible. My co-signaller and I berthed in the tiny foc's'le where we had to take it turns to sit on the one seat, the quarters being so cramped that the other man must huddle in his bunk the while.

We managed to be fairly comfortable on the ship however, as it had been decided to use the bulk as a store for the food which was being distributed throughout the islands, and there being plenty of most kinds of food we did rather well in that respect at least.

The deck of the Greek boat was very badly caulked, and as a means of keeping the rain off the men who lived in the hold, a sail had been rigged across the width of the vessel, in the form of a canopy, and one day several of us were standing under this sheet frying pancakes on a made up fire, doing it as much as anything to pass the time away. There was a fairly heavy rainstorm going on at the time, and an ever freshening wind started up about noon. By mid-afternoon this breeze had become half a gale, and the waters of the bay were as choppy as many open stretches of water in a strong breeze.

The ship of course was not rigged at the time, but the canopy over the deck acted as a useful jib, catching the wind and causing the vessel to tug at the moorings. Nobody took a great deal of notice at first until it was observed that the shore seemed closer than it had been in the morning, and we realised the schooner was dragging its forrard anchor.

I would mention that there were no seamen aboard, nor any man who might claim a knowledge of sailing, so that we might be excused for what followed.

The first obvious thing was to unship the canopy, and this was done at cost of great effort, for by now the howling wind was first blowing the sail taught into a huge rigid belly of canvas, and just as we thought we might manage the monster, it would collapse on us and undo all the work which had gone into untying knots etc. However we did get the horrible thing down, and the tug on the line seemed to be eased a little. By way of further precaution however, one of our corporals showing, we thought, remarkable foresight, tied a heavy line onto a huge anchor which had been lying spare, and heaved it over the bows with the aid of three other men. This line being straight down over the ship-side they decided to heave it in and toss it once more, this time further outboard, in order that the anchor might be hauled back and catch in the seabed.

Their surprise was pathetic when they heaved the line back aboard, and found no anchor attached – apparently the corporals knot had been 'lubberly' and become untied in the handling!

We spent valuable time in trying to heave on the anchor chain out forrard, trying to pull the ship up to the hook and away from the shore. For a while it

Guarding a ship at Penzik Bay & Shipwreck at Kiervasilli Bay

seemed this might work for the slowly turning capstan was gradually pinching the anchor cable on to the drum, but we soon realised that something must be wrong, for the pull of the anchor seemed lighter and it became obvious we were only pulling in the anchor and not pulling our ship off the shore. The tug of the wind against the pull of the anchor was too great and the anchor gave up trying, leaving the great unwieldy bulk to look after itself.

By now the stern of the schooner was within a couple of dozen feet or so from the shore, and we were steadily moving to our doom. No one seemed to care much anymore, or to make any effort to stop the deadly progress of the ship, as most people were down below, bringing up as many weapons and ammunition as possible before the boat struck and sank.

Eventually there was a scraping noise, and a shuddering shock was transmitted down the length of the vessel. Immediately afterwards all was peaceful again and we were afloat but not for long. Another violent gust of the wind hurled us against the shore, and from below we could hear the shouts of our men as they warned us that the bottom was holed astern, and water pouring in through the breach.

This was the signal we had all been unconsciously awaiting, and we organised a landing party who went ashore over the stern and rigged up a line which we used to ferry our kit onto the rocky shore, rather on the lines of a 'breeches buoy'.

There were no women or children on board, so in order that the most ancient rule of shipwreck be observed, the officer in charge bawled out 'Signallers ashore with their wireless kit'. Possibly he thought we might be the means of obtaining help after we were all marooned! Anyway, my partner and I marshalled our kit and the wireless gear, marched down the now badly listing ruin of a ship and made a dignified landing over the stern.

Several bodies were now ashore, and chaos seemed to have been replaced by the stern British spirit of 'stiff upper lip' and 'save the kit', everyone moving purposefully back and forward on to the ship unloading the kit and dropping half of it in the sea in the process! After a while I became bored with nothing to do, and the excitement having worn off I was about to start an exploration when a sailor came over the headland to enquire if all was well. It appeared that the captured *Bandy* was moored in a small inlet round the point of the bay. Seligman had sent one of his men to see how we faired in the gale.

Our officer immediately saw this as a means of disposing of his precious wireless operators and sent us, with our gear, back over the headland to the *Bandy*, in company with the matelot, bearing instructions to go aboard and open up at our scheduled time with the glad news of the wreck.

We clambered over the hill and down among the rocks on the seaward side of the headland where we found the tiny *Bandy*. On board we found two naval officers, a German cook, two sailors and one of our own motor mechanics acting as engineer. When we had disposed our set and rucksacks in a corner and sent the required signal, we were told that as the best method of keeping out of the way we should get down in our sleeping bags in the bilge space on either side of the engine and stay there for the night, which we did, and spent a really unpleasant night sleeping and waking in the reeking area allotted to us. This was traditional naval courtesy – Seligman style!

Early in the following morning we decided enough was enough and told the Navy that we must return to the scene of the wreck, so, after using us as tow horses to pull the *Bandy* round the bay to a better position we were allowed to depart.

Over the headland all was peace and we found our comrades making breakfast on the shore under the guardianship of two Turkish coastguards who had arrived during the night, ostensibly to prevent any irregularities taking place on their sovereign soil, but really, I believe, in the hope of easy pickings. After we had eaten the group was split up into diving parties, taking it in turns to dive first into the sea alongside the ship and alternatively into the hold of the now fully submerged hull to retrieve what remained of the stores. In this way we reclaimed most of what valuable stores there were and spread the saturated articles along the shore to dry in the sun, until mid-afternoon the schooner *LS9* sailed into the bay as relief ship. We loaded her up with all the stores, piled aboard, and so the day drew to its close, we sailed out of the harbour past two desolate masts which stuck straight up from the water's edge as the last mark of a lost ship.

CHAPTER 30

CABLE LINE LAYING BETWEEN *LS9* & THE *TEWFIK*

By the middle of March the *Tewfik*'s final base had been set up at Port Deremen in the Gulf of Cos and a few men had been sent down to Castelorizzo to act as advance return party. A number of people had already returned to Beirut (among them an officer who had been sent down in charge of a captured German luxury ship full of champagne, cigarettes and wireless sets etc. originally intended for the island Germans). He disappeared for a while and when he turned up again, was richer by the value of the champagne, cigarettes and wireless sets – he didn't remain in SBS very long!)

Units of S Squadron had arrived in the islands to take our place and also a detachment of the Greek Sacred Squadron and some '*Kalpaks*'[22], so it was no surprise when one day Major Patterson came to me and said, 'Do you feel like going back to Beirut yet?'

'I don't mind Sir, why? Are we going?'

'I can't go yet myself, got to wait for the rest of S Squadron to come up, but I am sending the blokes back as and when I can now that our time is up. Anyway, I would like you and your brother to go with Sergeant Waterman and a few others to escort a captured German ship and some prisoners back to Syria, so get packed up and go aboard the *Etna* for a day or so until the rest are ready, will you?'[23]

We packed up again for the last time, and what a joy, we handed in our wireless sets to the newcomers, so we were now free agents, - or so we thought!!

The next day the major called us over to the *Tewfik* and asked, 'Have you ever done any line laying?' We informed him that we had cut our teeth on Dow 5 cable and laid enough line to reach from Turkey to England and back again.

'Good, I would like you to try and fix a permanent telephone cable from this ship to the *LS9*. These ships will now be static and as the *LS9* is about a mile away round in the next bay, we need constant communications without the need of taking a dinghy right round. Think you can do it?'

Behind The Lines with The SBS: My Life in L Squadron during WW2

We agreed to try and set about collecting the necessary gear. In addition to all the other vessels we had acquired was a tiny caique of about 5-tons with one engine which could throttle down to almost nothing, so we decided this must be our 'Monkey' truck (M being for maintenance) and we loaded half a dozen drums of cable wire aboard, together with a thing like a poker to act as a spindle and a spur to which we bent a wire hook which would do to feed the wire out from the ship's side.

Leaving about a hundred feet of cable on board the *Tewfik* we paddled across to the nearest point of land and tied back the cable to an overhanging rock. Then we started on our voyage, instructing the Greek skipper to sail as slowly as possible. I lay alongside the bulwarks near the stern holding a cable drum close in upon its spindle which we had lashed at right angles to the ship-side, and my brother with his pole crook guided the cable away from the wash of the propeller as it reeled off the drum, sometimes lethargically and at times when a wave lifted us forward the drum tended to spin madly at the tug of the cable, so that I had to use my hand as a brake to slow its progress when the boat dropped back to its normal speed.

The sea was fairly calm fortunately, but there was a slight irregular swell, which made our work all the more difficult as we were unable to regulate the speed of the drum's spin to the sudden thrusts made at the boat by these occasional waves. On two occasions the unexpected movement came as I was holding the drum, and before I released it, the cable parted with a jerk, and we had to turn the boat and travel backwards along the route until we came upon that part of the cable which hadn't quite disappeared. Then we toured slowly down its length again until we reached the broken end and wasted valuable time in making good the joint.

In order to facilitate the finding of the cable later, we had acquired a number of small squares of cork, stripped from a naval life jacket, and we fixed these to the cable at intervals along its length in the manner of buoys. This foresight was rewarded when we broke the cable a second time, for the line sunk immediately and we could never have regained it without returning to the starting point and working along its length, but as it was we had only to retrace our steps, as it were, for a matter of fifty feet to the last cork buoy, and pick up the loose end, make a joint and carry on.

The line laying took considerably longer, due partly to the necessarily slow speed of the boat and the setbacks we encountered and also due to the fact that to reach the *LS9* we had to round a small promontory, where it was necessary for us to land and make a series of tie backs to prevent the line being rubbed against the rocks. However, we reached the other schooner eventually at dusk, and proudly carried the last drum of cable aboard, fixed the end of the wire to the D5 telephone, buzzed the *Tewfik*- and found the line dead!

Cable Line laying between *LS9* & the *Tewfik*

This was a bitter blow, and was almost the last straw, for by now both of us were sick of cable laying, and ready for food, but we wearily climbed back on board our 'M' boat and started the long tiring business of checking for the fault. We found it eventually by tapping in at intervals and calling the *LS9* until we had no reply when we retraced our steps to the last tap in, pulled up the line and found it had been broken under the water by the weight of some drifting seaweed.

We attached a new piece to the severed end and chugged along to the next buoy, heaved up that end of the line, made a joint and received a reply to our call. The rest of the way back to the *Tewfik*, we received answers to all our tap-in calls, making the last one about 100 yards from the schooner, and then thankfully crawled back on-board the base vessel, sure this time that all was well. Our assumptions made the blow all the worse when we tried to ring *LS9* from the *Tewfik* phone and found the wretched line dead again, but we had had enough, and scrounging some food from our indignant chef, we went to bed.

We awoke next day expecting to begin the horrid business all over again, but before we could make a start Jack Waterman, the sergeant in whose charge we were to go back to Beirut, called us out and told us we were to set off at once to meet the German ship with the prisoners on board. I heard later that the telephone line did eventually work, so our labour was not in vain.

Having all climbed aboard the *Etna*, we sailed out of our bay for the last time and hove to once more in a small cove further down the gulf where later the same day a sleek attractive schooner arrived bearing the prisoners we were to take back to Syria.

The schooner was originally a Greek vessel known as the '*Arki Trieste*', and had been captured, along with its escort and German crews, by members of the Greek Sacred Squadron after a bloody battle of small arms. The Germans were really only guards, as the ships were manned by Greek sailors, out of Piraeus and one of these, an engineer on the smaller ship, had been wounded in the eye by a bullet which had ricocheted off the engine and taken half of his eye socket away but miraculously missing the eye itself which was still functioning properly. The only other casualty (apart from those killed) was one of the Germans who had a clean hole through his foot. We dressed the wounds of these two men as well as possible but sent the Greek back on the *Etna* to see the doctor on the *Tewfik*.

Our Sacred Squadron friends, an eager blood thirsty lot, were anxious to depart and get some more German scalps, so they handed over the ship and prisoners, clambered into a small caique which had come to collect them, and left us to it.

We commandeered the largest cabin in the stern just forward of the tiny wheelhouse, loaded our kit and bedding into the quarters we allotted ourselves and prepared to have a look at our new ship.

JULY 1943

Subject: Operational Wings.

To: Officer Commanding,
Special Boat Service.

"L" Squadron,
Special Boat Service.

NUMBER	RANK	NAME	WITH UNIT FROM / TO	OPERATIONS.	DATES.
14266591	Sgt.	WEBSTER J.	29.10.43 to Date	DODECANESE (Stampalia) CRETE. GREECE. ISTRIAN PENINSULA.	16.1.44=2.4.44. 4.7.44=25.7.44 23.9.44=19.1.45 13.4.45=25.4.45
3215566	L/Cpl.	AINSLEY K.	25.1.43 to 3.7.45	CRETE. 12.7.44 GREECE ISTRIA PENINSULA	=25.7.44 23.9.44 =19.1.45 13.4.45 =25.4.45
904073	L/Sgt.	GEAL R.	1.10.43 to 13.7.45	DODECANESE (Piscopi, twice, Fornoi). CRETE GREECE ISTRIAN PENINSULA	16.1.44.=29.3.44 12.7.44 =25.7.44 25.10.44=19.1.45 13.4.45 =25.4.45
	Rfm.	CLAYTON A.	30.9.43 to 29.12.44	DODECANESE (Cos, three times, Peserimo) CRETE GREECE	16.1.44 =2.4.44. 12.7.44 =25.7.44 23.9.45 =29.12.44
7900392	Cpl.	HILL R.	29.10.43 to Date	DODECANESE (Calimnos) CRETE GREECE ISTRIAN PENINSULA	16.1.44 =29.3.44 4.7.44 =25.7.44 23.9.44 =19.1.45 13.4.45 =25.4.45
6025782	L/Cpl.	DIGNUM W.	29.2.43 to Date	DODECANESE (Fornoi, Patmos, Kalimnos). GREECE. ISTRIAN PENINSULA.	16.1.44 =29.3.44. 23.9.44=19.1.45 13.4.45.=25.4.45
3909854	Pte.	NOURAHINE T.	23.12.42. to Date	DODECANESE (Cos, three times). NORTH AFRICA (In Hospital, no Op.) CRETE GREECE.	16.1.44=29.3.44 29.5.43.=28.8.43 12.7.44.=25.7.44 23.9.44.=19.1.45
887157	L/Cpl.	MARSHALL W.	11.10.43 to Date	DODECANESE (Peserimo, Patmos, Lipsos, Archi, Piscopi, Cos). GREECE. ISTRIAN PENINSULA	16.1.44=2.4.44 23.9.44.=19.1.45 13.4.45.=25.4.45
885975	Gnr.	MARSHALL D.	28.10.43 to Date.	DODECANESE (Stampalia, Misero). CRETE GREECE ISTRIAN PENINSULA	16.1.44.=2.4.44. 4.7.44.=2.8.44. 23.9.44.=19.1.45 13.4.45.=25.4.45
3530172	L/Cpl.	FOX. S.	28.10.43 to Date	DODECANESE (Amorgos) GREECE ISTRIAN PENINSULA	16.1.44.=29.8.44 23.9.44.=19.1.45 13.4.45.=25.4.45
14216715	Tpr.	HUMPHRIS T.	29.10.43 to Date	DODECANESE (Calimnos) YUGOSLAVIA (With "S") ISTRIAN PENINSULA	16.1.44.= 29.3.44 13.4.45.=25.4.45.

SBS wings document showing the places and dates of Des and Bill's operations. (Marshall Family Collection)

Cable Line laying between *LS9* & the *Tewfik*

It was one of the finest schooners I had yet been aboard, with a long hull, not too broad in the beam, a large hold amidships and plenty of deck space. The foc's'le was occupied by the prisoners and approached by a small hatch well up in the bows. On each side of this hatch and slightly aft of it were the galley on the starboard side and the 'leads' on the port. Both these houses were the same size, about as long as a wardrobe, and in the galley the space was almost entirely taken up by a wood burning stove.

Apart from the hold hatch the rest of the deck was clean, until about a quarter of the length from the stern where there were two small cabins, one on each side, one occupied by the skipper and bosun, the other by the engineer and his assistant. The only other deckhouses were our own cabin and wheelhouse right astern. The schooner had two masts and was well rigged with new sails, large enough to carry us at a good rate of knots even without the engine, which was the least attractive & efficient fitting on the whole vessel.

CHAPTER 31

TRANSPORTING GERMAN PRISONERS TO SYRIA

Our prisoners, with one exception, were pretty nervous and looked apprehensive as we studied them. Up to the present most of our captives had been German soldiers and it was a novelty to see real live enemy sailors for the first time. Most of us had a smattering of German and we spoke to the prisoners asking what made them look more than ordinarily upset – one expects prisoners of war to be unhappy, but these looked positively terrified. The one exception was the wounded hun, a tall powerful blonde Hitler youth who scowled perpetually and would have nothing to do with us. We found later that his comrades were all a little nervous of him and disliked his wholehearted Nazi outlook on life.

The leader, a Gefreiter, when we asked him the cause of their fear, hesitated, and being urged to answer, admitted that they were expecting to be executed on the spot! This was interesting and we asked him what form of execution they were looking forward to receiving. He looked even more miserable and replied that hanging was the death they had been threatened with by their Greek captors.

It appeared from what he told us, that reports of our activities in the Aegean had spread to the mainland, and the stories of the various exploits losing nothing in the telling, so that he and his comrades had a picture of us as somewhere between gangsters and pirates, with no thought of mercy and no time for prisoners, so that we usually executed our captives on the spot in the best tradition of buccaneers.

We assured the poor man that he had been misinformed.

'No.' I told him 'We have never hanged any German prisoners; we invariably make them walk the plank. So much neater really!'

Hans Haep looked hard at me when I told him (I would say not quite as fluently as that) and it was obvious a seed of doubt had sprung up in his mind. 'Is it that you don't mean to execute us?'

Transporting German prisoners to Syria

I set his mind at rest and told him we were peace loving citizens who did a job of work, and that was all, and who were to escort him and his friends back to a comfortable prison camp in the Middle East.

As he spread the glad tidings among his fellows, we saw their faces clear at once, and Jack Waterman having given the order to sail, they fell to, with a will, heaving and pulling at ropes and anchor chain, until we almost expected to hear them burst into song.

Eventually the sails were set and, the decrepit old engine coughing unhappily, we sailed east into the gulf on the first leg of our journey back to Syria. It was early afternoon, and the gulf was a picture of serene beauty, with the calm blue waters reflecting the warm spring sunshine, and the sky a brilliant blue flecked with wispy white clouds drifting gently inland over the heavily wooded green and brown shores of Doris. In the centre of this picture, or rather to one side, the southern side, of the gulf sailed our beautiful '*Trieste*', leaning gently away from the breeze under a full head of gleaming white canvas.

The breeze and the thrust of our struggling engine bore us down the Gulf towards the open sea at a fair rate of knots, so that by the time the westerly sun was going down behind the lowering hump of Cos and casting purple shadows among the scattered islands, and long slanting figures of golden light upwards into the sails and sky, we were nearly up to Iskandil Cape, which marked the point where we must turn south into the Aegean proper.

By the time we had cleared the point and were sailing towards Simi, the next milestone, the light had gone, but the indigo sky was cloudless and rich in stars, so that we had little difficulty in seeing the dark outlines of Turkey on the port side, and Simi dead ahead.

During the early stage of the trip we had taken a meal, settled our gear and rigged our hammocks in the small cabin, but now we sat around on the hatch covers over the hold and held converse with the Germans.

There were, as I remember, seven prisoners, (although anyone observing our conversation with these men would never have believed that they were prisoners and we their captors!) and in a very short while we came to know them by their given names.

The leader, a gefreiter, was Hans Haep, a mild enough man and as with all mild mannered men, was not much respected as a leader by his troops. Then there were Rudolf Schneider, a handsome youth from Sudetenland, Waldemar and Willi Kleine, a pair of 'cockneys' from Berlin, Walter, a better educated Berliner, who acted as their medical orderly, another Willi, from Luxemburg and lastly the tall blonde Nazi whose name I forget, but who never unbent to us in his bitter resentment at being captured.

The average age of the Germans was about twenty, the eldest being Hans Haep who was twenty three, the youngest Willi Kleine, who was just nineteen.

Behind The Lines with The SBS: My Life in L Squadron during WW2

Above left: Captured German PoW Rudolf Schneider from Niedereinsiedel, Sudetenland, now the Czech Republic. (Marshall Family Collection)

Above right: Captured German PoW Hans Haep from Holzheim, S/W of Dusseldorf. Germany (Marshall Family Collection)

Hans was the only one who had seen action before, the remainder being freshly called up and whose first sea going trip had ended in their capture.

During the many days we were with them, living and eating together, talking and working in their company, we came to like these enemy sailors who were, it appeared to us, not different from, in their outlook or ambitions, any British serviceman. They did not show any relish for the war, nor, with the single exception, any bitterness towards the allies. Hitler was regarded as a great man by all of them, but not infallible, nor semi-divine, and they each agreed it looked as though he would not be able to win the war, hoping, they said, to gain an armistice with less strings than had been the case in 1918.

We found that our low opinions of the Italians as soldiers were shared by the Germans, and they also had no very great respect for the American troops, saying that they were told (without any personal experience of course) that the Americans were pampered and decadent, were only useful in supplying the arms for others to go to war.

When the Germans expressed their dislike of war and lack of confidence in Hitler, we derided them, telling them that they were only saying these things because they thought it would please us and so help to ease their lot, but they were vehement in their protests that they spoke the truth, and asserted that they had expected death at our hands, and having been granted their lives, what more could they hope to gain from flattery.

I would say here, that although we came to like the Germans, and treated them in a possibly more lenient way than was proper, we never relaxed our vigilance and were prepared the whole time for treachery and attempts to escape. This may explain why we never experienced any trouble with our captives, but I, personally, prefer to believe that they were in the main honest civilians who were, like ourselves, forced to go into uniform under threat of punishment.

By 10.00 pm we had left Simi astern and picking our watches, the remainder of us turned in to our hammocks.

At 2.00 am it was my turn on watch.

That watch will be a permanently happy memory of mine, for it was two hours of perfect contentment. In the first place, although we were still in dangerous waters, where an encounter with a German boat would mean the finish of our war careers, we were heading for what was our spiritual home – Beirut.

Added to this was the fact that the weather was calm, and the night quiet, and I was on board a lovely ship. The scene is quite clear in my mind, the great purple vault of the sky glittering with millions of stars, the sea smooth, albeit with a gentle swell which acted as a sedative to the mind. I stood outside the wheelhouse in the poop of the ship, looking upwards past the spread of taut canvas shimmering palely in the light reflected on the sea, and watched the pendulum movement of the masts as they swung slowly back and forth across the heavens with the roll of the ship. I have read stories by sailors of such moments of serenity in the full rigged ships of a century ago when sailing through the tropics and I realised that night what a joy there was to be had from travel under sail, so that when my watch showed the time to be 4.00 am it was almost with regret that I called my relief.

The peaceful scene apparently was laid on for my benefit however, as when I was roused at dawn, I heard a familiarly unpleasant sound and came up on deck to find the sky grey and cheerless, the sea heaving in mighty rollers and our ship, with only a jib rigged in place of mainsails, rolling heavily in the grip of a force eight gale as it struggled to maintain headway against the pull of the sea and battering of the wind.

My brother, who had stood his watch late in the night told me that he had witnessed a strange scene during his 'trick'. It appeared that the gale had come up suddenly in the way familiar to mariners sailing the Mediterranean and the force of the wind had soon made itself felt, as it flung the ship over at a dangerous angle to the sea. The Greek on the wheel, being the only member of the crew on deck, had done his best in the situation, and to avoid disaster had swung the ship round from its course to force bows on to the westerly gale. This had the effect of righting the vessel, but the sails now being away from the pressure of the wind began to snap back and forth across the beam of the schooner, so that the constant swing and crash of its booms threatened to cause a disaster from another direction.

This crashing and rattling brought the captain on deck, who immediately saw another danger, not then apparent to my brother, who was anxiously watching the helmsman and preparing to rouse the crew. The fresh danger was that in bringing the vessel round into the wind, the Greek had automatically brought us on a course for Rhodes and even against the pressure of the sea and wind, the engine had been gradually drawing up nearer to the searchlight which was probing its long purge into the night from the eastern tip of the island.

The captain flew into a passion of curses and prayers, flung the helmsman from the wheel and grasping its spokes swung us away from the course to Rhodes, choosing the lesser of two evils, that of damaging his ship being preferable to capture. In any case he had the situation in hand at once, brought the crew on deck with his shouts, and gave the orders which resulted in the sails being reefed with the exception of the jib which would aid the steering without endangering the vessel. The motion of the ship quieted at once, and the rest of the night passed with no more disturbance than that caused by the heave of the sea and the lash of the wind as it cut its way into the rigging howling dismally at its failure to capsize our schooner!

Apparently another reason for the little Greek bringing us on a course for Rhodes was that like so many of his kind, he disdained the use of a compass and had been steering by the stars over the masthead until the clouds accompanying the gale covered the stars, so that he had lost his sense of direction completely, and being too short to see over the binnacle in front of him, had not realised that the bows were turned towards the enemy island.

Incidentally, during the gale the engine had retired from the unequal struggle and most of that day was spent by the engineer in trying to coax the ancient pistons back into motion. He succeeded after a fashion and the following day, which was spent in running down the coast to Castelorizzo, passed uneventfully, although we had two periods of mild excitement. The first was in the shape of a Junkers 88 which suddenly appeared in the Northwest and started towards us but turned off towards Rhodes, vanishing from our vision. The next surprise we had was when rounding a small cape, we came upon another schooner sailing towards us. We were carrying the Greek maritime flag, although we were in Turkish waters, but we saw the approaching vessel bore no ensign at all, which disturbed us, as it was not unlikely to be a German manned vessel. However,

Transporting German prisoners to Syria

we chivvied the Germans below decks, and the SBS men crouched down below the bulwarks, and as we passed within a few dozen feet of the other vessel we saw them run the Greek flag to the masthead, and we breathed again. It was by no means certain however, that she was not German, so we kept hidden until the ship had passed from view round the headland.

We reached Castelorizzo at daybreak next morning, sailed into the harbour thronged with British MLs and a few Levant Schooners. Our Greek crew was not very expert it seemed, for on approaching the berth selected by the captain, the *Trieste* sailed gracefully right up to the harbour wall – and poked the bow point through the wall of a derelict building!

The jar sent us all off our feet and was the cause of the usual feverish recriminations aimed at the crew by the long-suffering captain.

We reported to the senior officer ashore and asked if there were any instructions before moving on to Cyprus. It appeared that there was a job for us and we were told to bring the *Trieste* round to the south end of the island outside the harbour. This we did and found ourselves alongside a rough jetty loaded with high metal drums. The officer who escorted us to the berth then ordered the drums to be loaded onto the deck, as we were to carry them down to a harbour on the Turkish coast as fuel for the high speed MLs using that place as a base for operations.

The drums contained high octane fuel and were extremely heavy, but by dint of great exertion on the part of the Germans and Greek crew, (we looking on disdainfully!) fifty of them were eventually loaded on to the port side. We were then told we might depart, but when the mooring cables were unlashed and the engines started, the only result was a nasty grating and throttling – through the ship's length. The captain realised that the weight of the drums had so weighted the schooner that the keel was lying on the seabed, and this caused another outburst on his part, but by experimental moving and replacing the drums, we finally floated again and set off on our journey once more.

An hour later we realised that the air was foul with the fumes of the petrol, more than could be attributed to fact of sealed drums being on board, so suspecting a leak, we examined each drum, until we found our suspicions to be justified.

It was not possible to repair the damaged drum, as the welding at the base had cracked, so it was decided that the only measure would be to pitch the whole drum overboard and write it off; this we did, and then another thought struck us. A forty gallon drum of highly inflammable fuel floating free was a danger to shipping, so – always happy at the excuse of a little target practice we voted that we should sink it by rifle fire.

On board, apart from our own weapons, were a number of German rifles, and choosing them as a novelty, we waited till the drum had floated a safe distance and opened up on it with four rifles. We had expected the first few shots would ignite the fuel and burst the drum, but such was not the case, so that we exhausted practically the whole supply of German ammunition before we had made a sufficient number of punctures to ensure the sinking of the damaged drum. It may seem a little unorthodox and possibly dangerous, (although it was not really the latter) that we allowed one or two of the Germans to have pot shots at the drum, and very fair shots they proved to be!

The journey down to the Turkish harbour was made still in perfect weather, with the schooner heaving forward under full sail scudding, ostensibly aided by the engine, before a fresh breeze under a bright cloudless sky, while we lounged about on the warm deck basking in a sun which would not have disgraced an English midsummer's day. By now we were fairly clear of danger from enemy boats or aircraft, and all we saw that day were three British MTBs racing through the sea in line astern half obscured by the silver wings of spray flying up from their propellers. It was early afternoon when we came into the long narrow entrance of our destination, and by the time we had transferred our cargo of petrol to the fuel ship laying in the bay, it was reckoned too late to start off again that day, so we spent the remaining hour of daylight gossiping with the sailors in the MTBs and smoking. The MTBs moved off after tea, however, so for want of something better to do, we indulged in a little more target practice on empty tin cans pitched on-board. This was soon stopped however, for a Turkish naval cutter came racing out from the shore and an irate officer threatened to put us all under arrest for offensive action in neutral waters!

CHAPTER 32

CYPRUS INTERLUDE

We managed to edge our way down past the western point of Cyprus and with a steady westerly breeze filling the sails, we passed along the south coast of the island under a clear sunlit sky until we reached Famagusta.

On reaching the harbour entrance we managed to get clear into the crowded little harbour without fouling the mole, but once inside it was in a state of constant nervousness that we moved between the various types of ships, as they loomed suddenly ahead, almost upon us, then would swing away at the

Left to Right, Norman 'Barnie' Barnett, Des and Bill with two Greek boat crew in Famagusta, Cyprus. March 1944. (Marshall Family Collection)

last moment when it seemed certain a collision would take place. Our Greeks were not the best sailors in the Med! However, we did eventually bump quietly against a vacant wharf and were safely tied up in a short while without further mishap.

Once he had assured himself that we would not drift away again, Jack Waterman went ashore to report to the NOIC and we soon had a crowd of Cypriot stevedores and dock workers staring interestedly at our Germans, the first most of them had seen.

We did not take too well to the occupation of being stared at and shooed the nosy parkers away, and it was after a partial success that we were preparing to brew up when a young man with corporal's stripes on his battle blouse stalked up to the ship side.

He stared at us all for a moment, then spoke to the nearest man, who happened to be me. 'Er – are you English?' he asked smiling nervously.

'You're dead right Corp.' I answered 'Come aboard and see us. We're not dangerous!'

He clambered down onto the deck, looked round again and said 'I was rather looking for your CO, I'm from the FSP and I've been told to meet you lot. You are from the islands aren't you?'

I looked at the others and we all remained dumb.

'Oh, I really, um, you know, look here over my papers' and he handed over a bundle of papers with an AB64, FSP security card and a printed order. Dougie Croydon took them and glanced up 'Well Corp. The Skipper's ashore at the moment, but hang on a bit, he'll turn up in a moment.'

'Thanks very much' said the FS Policeman. 'I understand you've got some prisoners, but I'll wait to see him before anything else.'

'Ok. Have some char' said Dougie and he drank a mug of our own brew while we talked. The corporal was a little overpowering and inclined to be gushing in his awe at meeting 'Real Commandos' as he called us, but he was a friendly type and we treated him kindly.

After a while Jack Waterman was seen striding back to the '*Trieste*' and Dougie said, 'Here's the Skipper.' The young corporal leapt to his feet, jumped back to the quayside and as Jack came up the corporal brought his arm up in a beautiful salute and addressed Sergeant Jack as 'Sir'.

Jack returned the salute nonchalantly and asked the young man his business.

'Well Sir, I've been told to ask you if there is anything I can do to help you? Would you like us to take the prisoners away, do you need any food or clothing, how are you fixed for smokes?' and so on.

This was something we liked, and we all gave him our suggestions as to what we needed but were adamant in refusing to allow the Germans to be taken away as we wished to deliver them ourselves in Haifa.

Cyprus Interlude

The corporal left with our list of requirements and in short order we saw that he had been as good as his word to help us. A 15cwt truck arrived in about half an hour bearing a side of beef, a sheep's carcass, a load of vegetables and flour. The corporal came back while we were supervising the loading of this food and brought with him armfuls of cartons containing Navy issue cigarettes.

Having seen us well stocked he left again, to return in the afternoon with a mobile disinfecting unit, so that we stripped to the buff, wearing some spare clothes he brought while our own stained battle dress and underclothes were 'steamed' in the usual manner. When we had dressed once more in our own clothes, he told us he had organised a shower bath for us, and under his guidance we went in turns to our 'Army shower' hut on the other side of Famagusta. We wanted to take the Germans too, but orders were orders, and they were not permitted to leave the ship, at least not that day anyway.

By the morning, we all felt like new men. Clean, well fed and with plenty to smoke, so after scrounging some more money from the FSP 'Poor Soldiers Fund' half of us went ashore to have another look at the town.

I will not dwell on that evening which was spent in the 'Argentina' (the place which had been the scene of the battle on our previous visit) but suffice to say that the four of us who went ashore in a group came back separately. I don't remember the return myself, but the following morning I was told that I arrived in a state of drink taken, with one arm round the neck of the NOIC whom I spoke to as 'Jack' and my other arm around the neck of the NOIC assistant! Jack Waterman and Dougie Croydon managed after an appalling struggle to lift my lifeless form into a hammock and when they left to attend to the others I fell out, travelled five feet to the floor, and remained there sleeping peacefully in my birthday suit till someone mercifully covered me with a blanket. The others of my party were in no better state, but we all agreed next morning that it must have been an enjoyable evening!

The following day a ship from Haifa berthed on the next quay to us and we were treated to a staring visit by half a dozen very unsavoury looking Jewish seamen. They swaggered up to the quayside and stared insistently at us and the Germans.

The leader of the seamen spoke to his friends, and they laughed. I glanced at the Germans and saw that they all had worried expressions on their faces. The Jews went on talking and laughing, until I became fed up with the performance and stepped over to the quayside.

'What's the matter with you?' I asked the leading man. He stared me up and down, scowled and said, 'We are speaking of the Germans, What about it?'

I replied 'This about it. We don't like you or your nasty friends – *Imshi* and quick!'

Behind The Lines with The SBS: My Life in L Squadron during WW2

The Jew spoke again in his outlandish tongue to his comrades and turning to me sneered and said, 'Just like all the treacherous British, you prefer these swine to your own allies.'

'You're no Allies of ours, you're scum, now beat back to your ship and don't come back.' He looked very ugly for a moment, and I thought that we should have trouble, but just then my brother, always ready for such emergencies, leaned on the shipside, nonchalantly swinging his automatic by the trigger guard. 'You heard what he said, *Yalla!*' and he gripped his pistol in a business-like manner.

The seamen hesitated and then, seeing my other comrades unshipping their artillery, moved off, but before leaving the leader shouted words at the Germans.

'What was that, Hans?' I asked.

'They say they are coming aboard tonight when you are off guard – the English are never very thorough – and will attack us before you can defend us' he replied.

'Don't worry Hans. If they do come, they'll find a reception committee,' I replied. 'We'll carry a Schmeisser on guard, and a burst from that will quench their ardour.'

No amount of talk would ease their minds however, and that night we agreed to their request that one of them might stay on deck in turn with the British on watch and warn his friends if trouble threatened. As we expected of course, the Jews' talk had been all *braggadocio*, and nothing happened.

That evening we were treated to a visit by Doctor Campion, a resident practitioner in Famagusta who in peacetime looked after the ills of the English residents, but who now wore the uniform of a captain in the RAMC. We had expected him, for the FSP corporal told us that Dr Campion was behind all the kindness which had been effected by the corporal.

Dr Campion was a fine, god fearing, kindly man and we received much help and advice from him during our few days in the port, even to the extent of being invited to visit his home at any time! This several of us did and were treated most hospitably by the doctor's wife. She had a brother who was a professor or something or other who also visited us aboard the *Trieste* and interested us in the subject of his pet hobby. This was the scientific exploration of phenomenon as reported in the Bible. I remember one of his theories was that the flood, far from being the miracle expounded in the Old Testament, was due to quite natural (or un-natural) phenomena. He propounded that the moon had passed round the earth at least seven times in one day with the result that the sea following its practice and following the moon, raced to keep up with amazing speed of travel. This caused a huge tidal wave, many hundreds of feet high, to build up and sweep round the earth in the moon's path, inundating everything

Cyprus Interlude

in its passage, and so saturating the area that even after the moon regained its sanity the water took weeks to subside to its normal level.

The professor had many facts about him to use as evidence to support this theory. One was that in the Arctic regions, several prehistoric animals had been found frozen into the ice, perfectly preserved, but with their lungs full of water to indicate drowning as cause of death. This, he explained, suggested that the return of the water to the Poles after its subsidence, had carried the drowned mammals with it and they had been frozen into a state of perpetual preservation until the time they had been discovered.

After several days of quiet living on board the *Trieste* in Famagusta harbour, we were told that it could be a considerable time before her engine would be repaired and in a fit state to put to sea again, so we were advised by the NOIC to take the prisoners to Haifa on a captured Italian ferry boat which plied back and forth between Cyprus and the mainland, and would be sailing in a day or two.

Before we left however, we had another visitor. This time Lord Jellicoe, our CO, who had returned from the islands a few weeks previously and had in the interim been married to an English girl working in General Spears'[24] mission in Beirut. The duke came aboard one sunny afternoon with his bride – they were honeymooning in Cyprus - and was kind enough to introduce us to Lady Jellicoe using the English title of 'Mrs' when giving her our names. She was a very charming Lady and most gracious to us and even to the German prisoners who afterwards were struck with amazement at the democracy of so great an English Noble and his wife!

They both spoke to the Germans in the latter's own language, smiling and joking with the prisoners. This was a very different 'George' from the one who had shot me down in flames over the business of the decoding messages up in the islands!

At last, we were told to go aboard the Italian steamer the 'SS *Eola*' the afternoon before she sailed, and taking our prisoners on board, we were given a cleared space on the promenade deck, where we could guard our charges without being disturbed. The ship steamed out of Famagusta after darkness fell, and I thought that would be the last sight of the island – later events proved me to be wrong – as usual.

CHAPTER 33

HAIFA & FAREWELL TO THE GERMAN PRISONERS

It was an uneventful trip across to Haifa, and we berthed there in the fullness of time just before midday next day. Our little party stayed aboard until the ship had been cleared, and Jack Waterman went ashore early to make arrangements regarding the disposal of Hans Haep and his comrades. Before he returned, we had to go ashore onto the wharf as the crew were hosing down the decks and we waited there, an odd assortment of characters standing in a small circle round an even smaller heap of kit. After a while we noticed a group of labourers standing a little way off regarding us, and then a Jewish soldier who had been speaking to them and gesturing in a directive came towards our group. He stopped a few yards away and stared insolently at us and the prisoners.

He was a small undefined specimen of a youth. A member of the Pioneer Corps[25] or some such outfit and some of his compatriots were preparing to do fine work on the front line elsewhere, but his job seemed to be nothing better than to stand, hands in pockets, regarding the landscape. After a few moments he moved forward, right up to the nearest German, stopped, and turning round to see if his audience was attending, spat directly at the feet of the German. Having accomplished this daring feat he prepared to move off hurriedly, but not quite quickly enough for two of my comrades who grabbed him and hauled him over to the circle.

'Now then you....... Apologise or you'll go in the drink' growled Dougie.

'I don't apologise to German scum, nor to you English pigs', shouted the young man.

'Alright- in you go' said the big patrolman and made as though to heave him over the side!

'Don't!-Stop!' pleaded the Jew. 'I'm sorry, I didn't mean it for you, but these Germans, they have done many things to our people.'

'So what?' replied Dougie. 'You'd do the same to them in their shoes, and anyway, these are our prisoners, and we say how they'll be treated. Now *yalla* and don't come back.'

Haifa & farewell to the German prisoners

He gave the soldier a shove which sent him staggering for a dozen paces.

The young man turned round at a safe distance, scowled at us, and making a rude sign moved quickly to the protection of the mob of spectators which had by now grown to a considerable size. He stopped and spoke loudly to them waving his arms in the air in our direction.

'Wonder what he's up to?' I muttered.

'Don't know, but if he comes back, he will go in the mire' growled Dougie.

We soon saw what the Jew had been doing, for as Dougie spoke, the sullen crowd moved slowly across the quay towards us in a half circle whose ends reached the edge of the quayside. As they drew closer, we saw many of them had lumps of wood and pieces of iron in their hands, their purpose being only too clear.

With one accord, we unslung our Tommy guns and Schmeissers, and gripping them at waist level we aimed them at the crowd, as we ourselves formed a half circle opposite to their own. This made them hesitate, but I could hear a voice, presumably that of the soldier, (now safely out of sight behind the crowd) haranguing them and after a moment the solid body of men moved again closer to our tiny group.

Things looked a little grim, but at a word from Dougie, the corporal, we made a great show of cocking our weapons, rattling the bolts as we did so and gripping the butts even firmer raised the stubby black snouts in careful aim at the front line of the attackers. This apparently was enough, for the whole phalanx stopped and were silent for a space. Then when it seemed as though we should indeed be compelled to fire, they drifted slowly back again and waving their fists at us, and shouting threats, dispersed about their business.

It was clear as soon as they had broken up that our guns had not been entirely to blame for their dispersal, for we saw a Military Police lorry winding its way along the side of the rails towards us with Jack Waterman standing on the running board directing the driver.

The truck pulled up alongside our group and half a dozen MPs jumped down. The sergeant major in charge, a typically bull necked, red faced regular sergeant major came forward and stood, hands on hips, gazing at our prisoners.

'Aw right,' he said, using the only opening phrase known to his profession 'Now you lot, get on board the lorry' to the Germans who, not understanding his words but recognising the symptoms, promptly moved to obey.

Walter, the medical orderly, passed the SM carrying his small medical box.

'Ere you. What's that you've got?' asked this kind copper ''and it over, you can't take it with yer!' He reached out his hand to take the box, but Dougie Croydon moved forward and caught his arm.

'It's alright Sergeant Major, we've had these blokes for a fortnight, and you can take it that they've nothing more than they should have. That chap's only carrying his medical kit. He's their orderly.''

Behind The Lines with The SBS: My Life in L Squadron during WW2

The SM looked at Dougie, taking in his huge frame topped by a slick black head and beautiful beard. 'An' who might you be? One of the ruddy Apostles? Stand aside soldier, these are my prisoners now and I'll say what's what- aw right?' The SM pushed Dougie aside, grabbed the medical box and shoved Walter onto the truck.

Dougie looked as though he was about to make more of the incident, but a warning look from Jack Waterman stayed his hand and he fell back beside us as we watched the last of the Germans climb into the truck.

'Aw right that's the lot!' said the SM to Jack. 'You can take your men home now Sergeant' and he himself climbed aboard the truck preparing to move off, but before they could go, we all crowded round, shaking the hands of each prisoner and exchanging spiritual wishes of good luck.

The MPs' eyes popped out of their heads at the sight of our apparent fraternisation and the SM's red face became the colour of his cap until he burst out 'Now that's enough – drive on' and the truck moved away.

The last we saw of our captives was half a dozen hands waving unhappily from the back of the lorry, and so they moved out of sight round a nearby warehouse. We realised that this was really the end of our island adventures.

It was not quite the end of our chapter however, for one more character is deserving of mention. His name was 'Scruffy' Beaumont and was the embarkation staff officer at Haifa. It was he who went to endless pains to see us provided with a meal and arranged to have us driven back to our camp at Samakh in his VW lorry. With our naval friends disdaining all interest in half a dozen scruffy commando types, and no other transport of any kind being available, 'Scruffy' had sympathetic leanings towards us, as he had himself been a member of Parachute Brigade, and was so badly smashed up in Sardinia that he could no longer jump or take part in the sort of activities demanded of Special Service types.

The kindly MEFHQ had therefore deposited him in the comparatively safe backwater of Haifa docks to supervise the arrival and departure of sea going soldiers. Beaumont was indeed a character, for he insisted on retaining his Balmoral and below his battle blouse stretched a pair of tartan trousers (he had been in a Scottish regiment apparently!) and even went to the extent of declaring his individuality by sporting a ginger moustache which grew up his cheeks each side until the ends merged into his ginger sideburns coming down from under the jauntily worn Balmoral.

A more jovial, obliging and energetic man I have never met before or since.

We found on returning to Haifa after a week's leave in Beirut, that the unit's base had been moved for the summer from Samakh to Athlit, the place from which I started my cross country march of 70 odd miles at the end of December. On arriving at the camp, I renewed my acquaintance with the desolation

Haifa & farewell to the German prisoners

abounding therein. The only building was a small badly appointed tin hut being used as a cookhouse. There was no water laid in to the camp, the only supply coming from a daily-filled water truck, and the only accommodation were the EPIP tents which we ourselves erected. The floor of the tents, in common with the ground covered by the whole area of the camp, was silver sand, interspersed by patches of rough gorse. The western end of the camp rose slightly to a low crest, and beyond that a long even beach sloped down to the sea.

Our camp was situated on the southern point of a bay, the northern end of which boasted the ruins of a Crusaders castle, now occupied by a tribe of Arabs who lived in the remains of the dungeons beneath the ancient pile.

The month was then April, and the warm Mediterranean spring sun was beginning to make itself felt, so that after a week or two in the camp, during which time we became acclimatised to once again living under canvas, life began to take on a more rosy aspect.

Our days were spent in further training, folboating, small arms training, swimming with the Davis Escape Apparatus, physical training and so on.

Des getting some well-earned rest at SBS HQ Athlit camp, Palestine 1944 (Marshall Family Collection)

CHAPTER 34

PARACHUTE TRAINING AT RAMAT DAVID RAF AIRBASE

During those weeks, parties of more men were despatched to Ramat David aerodrome to undergo their parachute training, and in the fullness of time it became the turn of my brother, myself and half a dozen other people to depart for our jumping course.

There was little warning given, presumably to prevent undue brooding on the supposed dangers of parachuting, so that it came as a nasty shock one day when we were detailed to pack our kit, climb aboard a lorry and leave for the airfield.

The journey, which lay along the coast road to Haifa and then eastwards round the northern end of the Carmel Range, took about three hours, and we arrived outside our billet at Ramat David in time for tea, which few of us felt like sampling, preferring to nurse the greasy feelings which we all by now experienced in our middle regions. I imagined that we would be taken up in a plane, harnessed in a parachute and dropped out almost as soon as we arrived, so that I felt by no means hungry and only wished I'd stayed safe in the RA where at least one kept one's feet on solid ground!

Our gloomy surmises proved quite wrong however, for in the morning following our arrival in the RAF camp, we were loaded onto another lorry and transported down to the airfield, where instead of going into a plane, we were herded into line outside a huge blister hanger and presented to our instructors.

Into the hands of these men we were placed in batches of eight, and in their hands we remained for the best part of the succeeding fortnight. These instructors, all young RAF flight sergeants, were to my mind as good psychologists as any who earns his living by the practise of the subject.

They took we nervous ground worshippers and in the space of a few days had made men anxious to do their first jump, and this by no other means than that of continual talking, discussing every aspect of parachute jumping, and by constant reiteration instilling the idea in our minds that there was very little in the business after all.

Parachute Training at Ramat David RAF Airbase

There was of course an excessive amount of ground training, physical jerks and running to ensure our fitness, and hours on end of simply falling down and rolling on the ground. This last may sound easy, but it was not until I met my instructor that I ever realised that there is a very definite and not easily acquired art in falling. After a few days of falling and rolling, my neck and back gave me ample evidence of muscles of which I was not even aware, aching and swelling to abnormal size with the constant unconventional exercise to which they were being subjugated.

In addition to rolling, we also spent many hours jumping out of the door of a plane fuselage which formed part of the Para school's equipment. Also running along a raised platform and jumping out through a door frame on to the ground and of course, a great deal of time was spent in what looked like a fair ground! This was a huge hanger, fitted up with swings, ropes, a trolley on a rising and falling track, and square raised frames, which proved upon inspection to represent the aperture in certain types of planes used for Para training.

Behind the swings, at a distance of about 20ft, were raised platforms about 15ft high. The drill was to clamber up to the platform, adjust our parachute harness to one's body and step off into space. This was a fairly unpleasant business the first time I tried it, for one fell suddenly straight down towards the ground, with a nasty upward movement of the stomach and, just before hitting the ground, the ropes to which the harness was attached and which were suspended from the roof took the strain, and one found oneself swinging gently back and forth as on a swing. While swinging in this manner we were taught how to turn and check our motion in the air, that is, reaching up to the full length of the arms to the two straps which stretched forward at an angle, one from each shoulder and connected to the rigging line. By pulling these straps downwards, the front of the canopy would be flattened vertically slightly, spilling a little air, and acting as a stop or break against the air. This gradually reduced the swing until this effect was fully vertical. In the training of course, this effect was not obtained, as the shoulder straps merely connected straight to the roof and the only effect was to raise one by the length of one's arms. After the swing had been reduced to a small pendulum motion, we were taught to unharness ourselves while still holding the straps and, at the correct moment, to release these straps and fall to the ground on a forward movement, using the falling and rolling drill which formed a part of every aspect of the training.

Later we were put in groups in the trolleys at the higher end of the track, the trolley was released and ran down the gradient until it reached the lowest point before rising again; at the lowest point, when the trolley had reached a speed of about 10 miles per hour, we had to jump from the platform onto a flat square of sand alongside the track, using the old familiar rolling drill. This gave us the idea of what it was like landing by chute in a breeze, when one doesn't fall vertically, but is carried by the breeze in a forward dropping movement.

Behind The Lines with The SBS: My Life in L Squadron during WW2

All the drills were gone through time and again for about ten days, when by constant reiteration we had become familiar with the idea of jumping and landing and were considered ready for our first drop.

At one point during our training we were taken on a tour of the packing shed, where we saw what meticulous care was taken in the drying, folding, packing and testing of the chutes and I think it was there where I fully gained the confidence without which I think I could never have finished the course.

The chute packers treated the parachute as though it was a particularly weakly and beloved child of their own, handling it with wonderful care, and spending hours of resource, ensuring that the whole thing was packed correctly, patiently repeating the process several times until they were quite satisfied that nothing more could be done to decrease the very slight element of risk of a parachute failing to open.

We were also given an old parachute to train with, each man adjusting the harness on himself in turn, and his comrade holding the canopy until he was ready, when they released the chute, and it became filled with air.

The day was, I remember, fairly windy, and when it came to my turn, I stood ready harnessed, when the others released the canopy lying horizontally on the ground before me. At once, I felt the tug as the canopy filled with air, and in a moment, I was thrown to the ground on my face and began to be dragged along through the dusty grass of the aerodrome. We had been shown how to twist onto the back, and by twisting the cap of the harness close in the chest to release the straps and slip out of the harness, but so great was the pull of the wind, that before I finally turned over and released myself, I had lost the skin from the underside of both forearms.

At one point in our training, we were taken on a practice trip in a Lockheed Hudson and flown around the dropping ground to enable us to see just what it looked like from up there. I was not a bit impressed with this my first trip in a plane and took a poor view of the small dark brown field as a prospective place for alighting from the moving vehicle!

However, at the end of our training we were warned that we should be doing our first jump at 7.00 am on the morrow, and as concession to our peace of mind, we were given an evening off, and a truck was laid on to take us into Haifa. I went with the others, and we attempted to enjoy ourselves with the forlornness of outlook that the Christian martyrs must have regarded their last night in the cell, before going to their certain death on the morrow!

I remember that we went to a café in town and put in some pretty heavy drinking by way of celebration (or so we told ourselves), that the course was nearly ended, but for all our pretended high spirits and high speed drinking, we none of us enjoyed ourselves, especially when, as it is always the case at such times, one of our members kept harping on the possibly tragic ending to our first jumps in a humorous manner, believing I suppose that it was in the finest tradition of heroes to belittle and make fun of the dangers facing us!

Parachute Training at Ramat David RAF Airbase

Going back to camp that night a heavy silence fell on we very sober and sombre soldiers and our individual beds were entered without so much as a 'Goodnight' all round, nor even a merry quip on the next day's proceedings.

I slept well, much to my surprise, and was awoken at 6.30 next morning by a nasty, hearty instructor telling us that we were to climb on a truck waiting outside to take us to the airfield.

'What about breakfast and a wash and shave?'

'You'll feel more like them <u>after</u> the jumps lads.' was the cryptic reply, and so it was that scruffy, but not very hungry, we hurried 'like snails' on to the lorry and were whisked down to the aerodrome and deposited outside the packing shed.

Here we were each issued with two parachutes and told to adjust the harness of each in turn.

With fumbling, nervous fingers, I managed to carry out our instructions, and leaving one chute nestling against the wall of the sheds with my name chalked on the envelope, I found the 'stick' of eight men who were to accompany me on my first 'death defying leap into space'.

As we walked across the field towards the waiting Hudson, my chute felt big and clumsy on my back, and I was sure that the harness was incorrectly adjusted. I repeatedly looked down to see that the lid of the box retaining the straps on my chest had not been twisted round (in case it came undone in the descent) and the strap of my crash helmet seemed to be too tightly adjusted round my throat which felt larger this morning than it had before, and possessed a large lump which insisted on trying to climb into my mouth against the pressure of the huge gulps with which I was forcing it back into place!

All too soon, we came up into the slipstream of the waiting plane, and were hurried into the dark comfortless interior of the fuselage. Once inside, the instructor bundled us all up towards the nose of the plane for the take-off, and in a very short space of time, we were trundling down the runway, then racing down its length, with the roar of the engines and the rumble of the wheels mounting into a crescendo of noise, until one felt that we would never take off and then – we were airborne and climbing up to the required height of 800ft, with the engines singing a deeper, more even note, and the wheels still rumbling with the momentum of their spin as they were folded up into the body of the plane.

As soon as we had become airborne the 'stick" was distributed down the length of the plane with number one sitting on the 'Lavatory' seat abaft the open door, number two was facing him on the other side of the door, and the rest of us placed at odds and evens on each side of the fuselage.

The instructor, without parachute, as always, a blasé young man, strolled about among us with a morbid quip here or a word of encouragement there if one face looked greener than the next.

Then the awful moment of waiting commenced as we circled over the dropping ground at the required height – waiting for the precise moment when the pilot judged himself to be at the start of the run in for the numbers one and two.

This first jump was known as 'Slow Pairs' – that is when only two men jump out on the first run in, each of the pair waiting for the instructor's go ahead before leaving the plane.

I wonder now who had the worst of it, numbers one and two, who went first, or numbers seven and eight who had to circle the field three times watching their comrades exit before it became their turn! I was number five on that trip.

Suddenly the Instructor said 'Hook up one and two' and we knew that this was almost it! Then after ensuring that the straps of the first two chutes were securely clipped to the static line inside of the fuselage he ordered 'Action stations number one'.

The first unfortunate with a dreadful grin on his green face presented himself to the doorway in the prescribed fashion, standing crouched to ensure his chute did not foul the lintel and at once it seemed the Instructor yelled 'number one, Go!' With a parting farewell slap on the pack.

The man leapt forward and was gone with only a small bang against the fuselage to mark his going – I learned later that this was the empty envelope of the parachute which being attached to the strap connected to the static line, trailed behind the plane until all the stick had left, then the instructor had the unpleasant task of leaning out and heaving the empty envelopes back inside the plane before landing.

A few seconds after the first man had jumped, the procedure was repeated 'Action stations number two', then 'number two. Go'. After his exit the plane did a circle of the field and it became the turn of numbers three and four to return to earth.

After they had gone I moved up onto the 'Lavatory' seat by the door while we circled again and then as the light flashed in the bulkhead of the fuselage, the Instructor said 'Ok. Number five and six, hook up!' and I stood up from my seat, reached over and clipped the steel hook of my strap to the static line, making sure that after the hook was in place, the securing pin was firmly thrust through the hook to avoid the danger of the hook coming away from the line,

Then the awful words 'Action stations number one' (I had now become number one) and I realised that this was the culmination of my training – the moment when I must prove whether I was worthy of membership of SBS.

In the few seconds I had stood crouched in the doorway, I suppose I could have thought of jibbing but for some reason it was not until later that I recognised my last chance, and I felt profoundly relieved that I had not remembered to back out.

I think that so profound was the effect of the psychological training as well as the physical training we had received, that my mind was too busy remembering the correct exit drill to dwell too closely on my fears.

Parachute Training at Ramat David RAF Airbase

It must have been only two or three seconds between the orders, but as I crouched low in the doorway, with my feet close to the sill, and my hands gripping the jamb, I felt as though it had always been like that, and I would be stuck there quaking for all eternity.

However, at last it came, 'Number one. Go!' and I flung my body out and upwards in a desperate attempt to make a good exit and reach the 'position of attention' before the wind whipped me in accordance with the textbook.

As soon as I was clear of the doorway, matters were out of my hands, for the slipstream took hold of my body and flung me violently backwards towards the tail of the plane and for the following couple of seconds I had about as clear an impression of events as one retains when under gas in the dentist's chair.

It seemed that I was buffeted about in all directions with my arms and legs (so carefully trained to 'keep to attention') fluttering uncontrollably like broken wings, then without prelude, I was swinging swiftly on the downward stroke of a giant pendulum, and I saw above and in front of me, the white comforting expanse of my canopy.

As soon as I reached the radius of my swing, I recalled the drill for correcting the motion and reaching up I pulled down the webbed straps holding the rigging lines. This did not wholly stop the swing, but it decreased its intensity so that in quite a short time I found myself hanging vertically below my canopy and looking down I was surprised to find that ground was only about 100ft below and moving slowly away behind my feet.

By this time, I felt an elation such I had never before experienced and one which I am sure is shared only by those who have made successful parachute descents. However, there was not a great deal of time for reflection, as I had to compose myself for the difficult business of landing.

Holding firmly to the straps pulled down to the level of my shoulders, I remembered the drill 'Head well forward, shoulders round, knees together, watch the ground' and having attained the correct position, I twisted my body slightly so that I should land with my feet at right angles to it, forward position of the chute.

Hardly had all those actions been accomplished than the ground suddenly appeared to be rushing up to meet me, and then my feet were whipped away, and I found myself automatically going through my landing drill, first the legs, then the hips, then the shoulders and over- and I was lying on my back on the ground in the soft earth and my canopy fiercely fluttering a dozen or so yards away.

Still carrying out the drill, I clambered to my feet, pulling in the rigging lines hand over hand, until the chute lay folded neatly in layers in the bag which I had carried strapped to my chest behind the harness straps. Then only did I look up to find several others had already completed their drops and were in the process of collecting their parachutes ready for their return to the airfield.

I picked up the bag and joined my earlier comrades, who were waiting in a truck at the edge of the dropping zone (DZ).

As soon as our 'stick' had all arrived we drove down the road at breakneck speed to the aerodrome, stopping once more outside the chute store.

Here we retrieved the chutes we had earlier adjusted, and no sooner as these were fitted onto our shoulders we were marched off once again and inside another Hudson motoring down the airfield for another take off. This second jump performed almost before we had time to think about the first one was, by myself at any rate, made in a dazed state and it was not until I was floating down to the ground once more, until I realised fully, that this was at the end of my second descent!

The realisation filled me with an even greater feeling of joy than the emotion I had experienced thirty minutes earlier when dropping for the first time.

This second jump was a 'quick pair'. That is that when two men were ready at the exit door, one as close as possible to the other and holding on to his harness, the instructor would shout 'Action stations numbers one and two' a pause then 'number one go – two go!' and both men would be gone.

I expected to stick to the man in front of me that time, but as soon as we were through the door, the wind flung us apart and I didn't see my partner until my canopy was open and we were swinging quietly to the ground.

As soon as the eight men of my stick had all landed, we climbed once more into the truck, unloaded our used parachutes and returned to the camp where we did justice to the special breakfast prepared quivering with excitement and proud of our accomplishment.

We sat for the rest of the time discussing our courage and by evening I think each man had recounted each moment of both drops a dozen times to ears that weren't interested anyway, as the owners were only waiting a chance to air their impressions of the daring feat!! Most of the chatter had died down, as the shadow of the following day's jumping cast itself over us, and when someone suggested going by liberty truck to Haifa, he received no takers, we were all too busy worrying about the repeat performance.

The only thing I remember about the next day's jumping is that it became my turn to go as number one and sit on the lavatory seat by the exit door, and I never felt so sick and terrified in my life as when I sat staring along the fuselage at my unhappy comrades, I was determined not to look down at that vast green space below. If I had I doubt whether I could have done the jump.

However, I did and experienced the wonderful feeling of elation which seemed to repay the terror of waiting a thousand-fold. We only did one jump that morning as the second jump was saved until the evening for our 'night jump'. It was dusk as we marched down to the parachute store to prepare for the jump and we could see the hazy glow of the setting sun reflected on the tops of the Carmel Range to the west. Along the runway as we plodded, loaded with

Parachute Training at Ramat David RAF Airbase

our chutes, we could see the navigation lights of our aircraft and the flames spitting from the exhaust as the pilot warmed up his motors for the flight.

We clambered aboard our Hudson for the sixth time, and found ourselves in a fuselage dimly lit, sufficient light only to find one's place in the plane. In a few moments we were off trundling down the runway, bouncing as the engines took the load, and then we were airborne once more.

This moment always seemed honestly surreal to me, as though we had a taken a step which could not be redeemed – although, of course we could have 'jibbed', I don't think the idea ever entered our heads once we were on board the plane.

After what seemed an age, the fuselage was lit with an eerie glow as the pilot put on the small green lights which indicated we were 'running' them. As he eased back the note of the engines changed and the fuselage suddenly seemed to be full of flickering light.

I glared over to the window and saw to my horror that flames and sparks were shooting past in a positive shower, the instructor howled above the motors 'Don't worry lads, those gremlins won't hurt you!' His reassurance however didn't prevent me from visualising a flying parachute ignited from one of those sparks from the slow revving engines.

My premise of course was groundless; in the first place, those sparks were 'dead' and had anyway been present but invisible during all our previous daylight jumps and secondly the plane is dozens of yards away before the chute develops, well clear of any sparks or other danger.

The night jump was a 'quick stick' and when the instructor gave the order to hook up, we all rose and affixed our 'safety pins' to the static line. Then at 'Action stations!' we crowded down towards the door, each man clinging tightly to the envelope on the back of the preceding man.

I had my arms firmly clasped round the parachute on the back of my brother, who was also undergoing his parachute course, and with whom I had already performed the previous three descents. At the instructions 'Number one go -two, three, four, five, six, seven, eight' we surged forwards and flung ourselves out of the door to be whipped apart once again by the tearing slipstream.

In a moment it seemed I was hanging in velvety black space in utter silence but looking down, I was puzzled at the lightness of the scene and it seemed as though the ground was covered in snow. At once I realised that I was hanging directly above another chute, and I wondered what the text book had to say about that predicament!

As far as I could tell, we would land together with me on top and the other underneath me with broken limbs all round. As I cogitated on the problem it was solved suddenly – the chute below vanished, and I was rolling on the invisible ground.

Behind The Lines with The SBS: My Life in L Squadron during WW2

Des just awarded his SBS wings after completing a Parachuting course at Ramat David Airbase Palestine 1944. (Marshall Family Collection)

I had overlooked the fact that the other man would hit first and the light breeze would carry me a few yards in the second or so before I landed, but that is just what did in fact happen. As soon as I had collected my chute, I wandered over to the other man and found it to be my brother. We had made a good close exit indeed!

That night jump I think is one of the most memorable. For of all the descents we made, that one was the easiest. It was, as the instructor told us, like stepping into a box lined with black velvet. The apparent absence of wind during the fall added to its illusion as one seemed to be suspended in a cool comfortable void with no sound or movement to disturb one's serenity.

Even the landing was less strenuous, for the inability to see the ground meant that one was more relaxed (a point stressed throughout the course) and so that it literally hit one's feet and caused the necessary roll automatically.

We went back to our billets quite elated again, not even apprehensive at the thought of the morrow's jump. I don't think that in the case of parachute jumping, familiarity breeds contempt but I do really believe that the more jumps one does, the less foreboding about the thing, especially when the jumps are done in fairly rapid succession. I know that in the morning following our night exercise I felt very little of the 'butterflies in the tummy' sensation attendant on my previous effort.

We did two jumps that morning and our course came to an end the next day after one demonstration jump by the whole school. That was quite an impressive affair and one of the few occasions I remember actually seeing other chutes in the air while making a descent. The sky seemed full of floating canopies of white, amber, and camouflaged silk and gave me an idea of what it must feel like doing a concerted attack by chute.

Later that day we returned to Athlit, qualified parachutists and quite the proudest group of men in Palestine. As soon as we were settled back in our tents, needles and thread were produced, and we rapidly stitched large safety pins on to the backs of the special SBS wings we had bought for the occasion, so that we might appear next day with the beautiful silver and blue decorative suitably pinned on our right shoulders.

CHAPTER 35

BACK TO ATHLIT FOR MORE TRAINING

The following month was spent in active training in and around the camp.

This took the form of small arms firing at targets strung out in a small cove from a group of rocks on the shore, running the length of the beach carrying each other on our backs, mock attacks by one patrol upon another ensconced in a small redoubt formed by a knoll at the edge of the camp, and so on.

I remember how one of these mock attacks became quite violent on one occasion. The attacking party used phosphorous bombs as a smoke screen, throwing the missiles to within a few yards of the knoll, where the bursting phosphorous shot out in all directions, leaving its trademark of burns on the parched and stunted grass. This caused the defenders to keep their heads down, as a splash from a spot of this phosphorous would mean a spell in hospital at the very least, but we replied by pitching 'red devils' in the direction of the attack. These were small red plastic grenades made by the Italians, large quantities of which had been captured in the desert.

We didn't consider them very dangerous, as it was said that one would only be badly injured if a red devil burnt against one's body. There was however a small ball bearing in each grenade (I don't know its purpose) which would act like a bullet if it hit anyone. Luckily this didn't happen on the occasion in question, the only damage caused being splinters of plastic material which the attacking party and some of the defenders were busy picking out of their skin for the next few days. Yes, they took their mock battles seriously in SBS.

Another point of our training was the 'Mile swim'. This was a compulsory affair and each man had to make the attempt to swim across the widest point of the bay, approximately a mile in distance. It was a gruelling business, even in the still blue waters of the bay, but most of us managed to complete the course, and those that didn't were dragged aboard the accompanying Folboats and other Dinghies and brought ignominiously ashore.

Inadvertently the officer in charge of our section at that time, who organised the event, did not take part himself, sitting comfortably in a folboat shouting disparaging remarks at the stragglers! I managed to finish the course somehow, but I didn't enjoy it. I like swimming for pleasure, not by order.

This same officer organised several quite interesting schemes for our further training and although most of them entailed a considerable amount of footslogging, I must say that I enjoyed most of them.

Once, by previous arrangement with the inmates, we made a night attack on a Jewish settlement in the hills near Haifa, and each man stealthily crossed the usual barbed wire, crept between the buildings towards the 'target' – a water tower, and each man was as stealthily stalked and captured in silence by the alert defenders. The attack was over in a few minutes, and we all adjourned with our Jewish hosts to a sumptuous feed in their communal dining hall.

I am not over keen on the Palestine 'townie' Jews but I never found anything but prompt hospitality and friendliness from the members of the numerous settlements that dot the countryside, where they gleaned a difficult but adequate living from the impoverished soil, helping each other in every activity, working, each man for the good of the whole.

The following day we attacked and captured an entire garrison of a Palestine Police Post near our camp. We all entered from different directions, and my party effected our entry by using the apparently least hopeful method. We took a 15cwt (hundredweight) lorry from our camp, one without a hood, and the driver raced down the road towards the PPP. On the back of the truck four of us knelt, clinging to the side of the body, until we steered off the road, across the grass and alongside the barbed wire fence surrounding the PPP. Here our truck slowed for a few moments, and we leapt over and into the compound. We had timed it to arrive as the swinging searchlights on the tower had passed the point and we were inside the perimeter in darkness while our truck roared away down the road to mislead the defenders into thinking it was merely passing on its lawful way.

As soon as we hit the rough grass of the compound, we raced forward to the shelter of a building. Here we found a darkened window with an iron grille over it and climbing onto each other's backs we clambered up to this grille so from there it was an easy matter to reach the roof. Once there we raced across the flat roof, down into the central parade ground, and marched straight in a mess room where we found half a dozen, half-dressed and very surprised policemen. We took them prisoner at the point of our guns and then moved stealthily along the corridor to where we knew the armoury to be located. Here we found our comrades in charge and in a few minutes, it was clear that the whole PPP had been taken.

Back to Athlit for more training

The Palestine police had of course been warned of the proposed attack (it wouldn't do to make it without notice in Palestine – too many deaths would undoubtedly have been caused) and they were very generous in their admission of defeat, but their commanding officer was very disturbed at the ease in which the attack had succeeded. We heard later that he re-organised the defences thereover and dared our officer to try again. This was not possible as we moved quite soon, but I doubt if we could have pulled it off again as easily! I wonder what happened to that PPP when the Jewish trouble started after the war?

Before we left the area our energetic captain had a couple more schemes to work out of his system. I think they are worth reporting as it will serve to give some idea of the training we underwent. It may interest someone who reads this record.

The first scheme was this: We were taken into the hinterland on a lorry to a crossroad on the inland side of the Carmel Range. This was to be our rendezvous, and from it we were then driven across country for some miles and each man was dropped about a mile from the next man with instructions to make his way back to the original starting point. No maps were issued, and we were warned that our officer and several other types would wait in the area of the RV to try to intercept and capture each man before he reached his goal.

I was dumped by the side of a track running across a small black valley surrounded on all sides by hills. I had kept my eye on the sun and decided that my return course lay at right angles to the track in a north westerly direction. It was about 11.00 am when I started, and as we had been supplied with no food or water (these had to be acquired off the land) I moved as quickly as I could through the hilly country hoping to find some sort of habitation where I could obtain my lunch.

After a couple of hours, I came across a small Arab farm where the surprised and rather suspicious farmer and his family gave me food and water, but these were not helpful in directing me to the place I had wanted to reach. This was not surprising as I did not know its name and couldn't describe it eloquently in my 'Army Arabic', but while I was doing my best, another one of our patrol arrived. I was pleased to see him but told him that he must have come off his course. He had been dropped before me and should have, in my opinion, moved roughly north, whereas by crossing my course he must have travelled north-east. He didn't agree and told me I was going in the wrong direction, but after tossing a coin my course won and we set off together.

It is almost impossible in the country of England to travel for four hours in one direction and not find a hamlet or village of some description, but that is what happened to us. We climbed up and down hills all the afternoon without finding a single building, until about 4.00 pm we came on a road which happened to point in the general direction of our objective.

This proved to be correct, for after another hour's steady going we came over the crest of a hill and saw our crossroads in the distance. We also saw, nearer at hand, a Jewish settlement, and decided to make for this point and get some tea.

As we moved off down the road, we saw our truck in the distance moving towards us. We immediately dived off the road and hid in the undergrowth. After a few minutes' wait we heard the truck slow down and stop about 50 yards away. Not daring to breathe, for fear of capture, we waited in the heath and watched. We saw several of our erstwhile companions and hugged ourselves with glee as we assumed they had been captured. After a few minutes the truck turned round and moved off and we followed, keeping off the road until we reached the settlement and had the tea we expected.

By 6.00 pm we were ready to return, so keeping a careful eye on the road we made our way right back to the crossroads without being caught. Happily waiting for the defenders to return and be amazed at our cunning we sat and smoked by the wayside, but after a half hour we decided that something must have gone wrong and that we might as well return to Haifa.

Hailing the first Army truck that passed we were soon sitting comfortably before two glasses of tea in a café in the town triumphantly discussing how we had outwitted our 'clever officer', and then after a notable interval we scrounged another lift on another lorry and were delivered back at Athlit by 8.00pm.

We expected to be greeted with some awe, having made our way through the 'Enemy line' unscathed, but our reception was far from awe full in that sense anyway!! The sergeant of our patrol saw us walking back to the tent and bellowed out 'where the bloody hell have you two been? You'd better go and see Lofty (our officer) he's doing his nut!'

Wondering what the shemozzle was about we hurried over to the officers' lines where we found Lofty in a state bordering on homicide.

'What the devil do you two mean by it hey?' he thundered. 'Everyone else was back at the RV by four as instructed and although we hung around looking for you for two hours, we couldn't locate hair or hind of you.'

'Four o'clock?' I asked. 'I didn't hear you say anything about four o'clock did you sir?'

'No,' he answered.

We told Lofty what we had done, and how cleverly we had evaded his patrol. 'You think it clever, do you?' he asked. 'Just how clever you don't know. When I got back to Haifa I called at the PPP thinking you might have got mixed up with the Stern gang[26] or some bloody shower like that and we had half the PPP in the country searching for you while you've been boozing in a Haifa pub. You'll hear more of this Marshall'.

Back to Athlit for more training

But we didn't....

Our glory at being the only ones to get back to the starting point without capture faded from sight, but we carried a different kind of glory some days after- as the only two men who could get the Palestine Police in a stew!

The best local scheme Lofty devised was where we set off at midnight to walk to Azzib, our original camp, which lay about 50-60 miles north. We moved out of camp and up towards the coast road, but when we were nearly at the road Lofty turned left off the track on the open railway line, running parallel with the road.

If one has never marched along a railway, one cannot appreciate the horrors of the undertaking. The sleepers are never evenly spaced, and it is impossible to develop a regular stride, as although for three or four paces one may find a firm footing on a sleeper, it invariably happens the next sleeper is too near or too far away to react in the same stride. This is a very wearying method of progress, and one which sapped our energy far more quickly than would have been the case, had we been marching along the road.

The 12 miles or so march to Haifa, which could normally have been accomplished in something under three hours took us nearer four and a half hours due to the strain of staggering along the tracks. No doubt this was designed by our officer to test our strength, and I am sure he found it an adequate test.

At length we reached the edge of the sleeping town and made our way down into the harbour, where we circled round the edge of the harbour to the southern end, where the mole began, and found ourselves at the boathouse maintained and occupied by our 'Boat men'. It was still dark, although the sky above Carmel to the east was lightening, but we prepared and ate our breakfast and were allowed to have a couple of hours' sleep before the rest of the day's exercise.

The sun was well up when we roused from our makeshift beds of tarpaulin and netting in the steamy atmosphere of the shed housing boats under repair, and after another brew of tea we set about the next item on the agenda. This was a visit to a captured Italian steamer which I believe was used to ferry goods about the harbour and neighbourhood. It was a fairly small ship, not much longer than the ferry boats plying between Portsmouth and the Isle of Wight and we all crowded down into the engine room where we met the Italian engineer who had been captured and stayed with his ship, renouncing Mussolini at once, as did all Italians when once taken prisoner!

This man who spoke reasonable English showed us the vulnerable parts of the engines and we stood around discussing the best type of bomb which might be placed in the tangle of pipes and pistons in order to put the engines out of action.

I wondered if our next move would be to find a derelict ship and blow it up, but we didn't have any such luck! This visit was merely by way of a diversion on the part of our officer, and one which might prove useful in the future if ever the patrol was within striking distance of an enemy ship. The engineer suggested that we might be interested in crawling along the propeller shaft in order to find its weak points, but after a glance at the greasy dark evil smelling tunnel, we politely declined his offer. We finished the trip with a cursory glance round the rest of the ship and then amidst a multitude of '*Arrivederci*' we left on our next pursuit of bloodiness.

We knew our destination was Azzib, still more than 40 miles north, and we none of us looked forward to the remainder of the trip and were bemoaning our lot at having such a keen type for an officer. We were pleasantly surprised then, when instead of moving straight back to the road, we went back to the boathouse, and after a bit of preliminary wrangling, Lofty persuaded one of the boatmen to take us to sea in his Dory.

This Dory was an unrigged, motor powered vessel about 20ft in length, broad in the beam and high in the bows and stern, both of which were pointed. We piled into the boat, nine of us and the boatmen, and set off out of the harbour. As we passed the concrete tower at the seaward side of the harbour, marking the entrance through the boom, we grinned at the notice which someone had painted in bold lettering on its wall. It read, in letters two feet high 'They also serve who only wait – the keepers of this BLOODY (In red) gate!'[27]

The ack ack gunners standing in the summit of the tower waved and made rude signs at us as we passed and were answered with equally vulgar remarks from the crew. Once clear of the harbour we took a course which lay diagonally across the long 'L' shaped bay formed by that piece of Palestine where it forms a 'badge' on the map, our destination being a point just south of the ancient Arab town of Acre.

The day, as are all days in June on that coast, was fine, and we had a pleasant enough cruise for half an hour or so, resting our hapless limbs in preparation for what we knew must come. Lofty must have decided that this would just not do, for long before we could even see our destination, he suddenly ordered the boatmen to make for the shore.

The awkward Dory swung round clumsily across the wavelets, and in a few minutes we were approaching the long shelving sandy beach. The Dory's draft was not very great, but nor was the shelving of the beach very sharp, in that, in order to avoid fouling the propeller, the boatman had to heave to whilst still some dozens of yards from the shore.

We should have anticipated some such foul trick on our officer's part, but nevertheless it came as a nasty shock to have to leap over the side into two or three feet of water, albeit we had removed our slacks, boots and socks and had them slung around our necks, we still received a nasty wetting, and before we had staggered up through the surf, which was quite appreciable here, we all were pretty well soaked.

It was still mid-afternoon, however, and the sun was hot, so after drying our shirts in the warm air, we replaced our comparatively dry boots and slacks and socks and marched off moodily along the sandy beach. To anyone who has travelled along that coast, this stretch of beach between Acre and Haifa will be familiar. It was quite desolate, and the sand which started the beach became a small strip of arid desert for some distance. Inland, the dunes were only interrupted at odd intervals by withered diseased palm trees, almost devoid of foliage and leaning at grotesque angles and forming fantastic shapes as they struggled against the certain doom which threatened from the creeping sand.

From all appearances we might have been marching along the edge of the Sahara Desert, with only the sea on our left to make for relief from the beastliness of the scene.

The sand where we walked was dry and being well above the edge of the sea had become fine and powdery, so that marching was a difficult process even worse than our march on the railway lines the preceding night.

Dusk was falling by the time we marched the end of the bay, and we turned inland onto the road before actually reaching Acre, so that we bypassed the town on the landward side. Soon, we came upon a small solitary building at the side of the road and finding it to be a café of sorts run by an Arab, we were permitted to sit down for a while and have refreshment in the form of a horribly chemical '*Gagooza*' [a name for lemonade].

After a short lunch we started off on what we thought would be the start leg of our journey, hoping to reach Azzib that night, but Lofty had either had enough himself or didn't want to arrive during the dark hours, for after a couple of hours going, he called a halt.

He told us that we would make a night of it here, as we moved off the road into some trees marking the edge of a field of root crops and cooked our supper on our 'Tommy cookers' and after a good deal of cursing at our folly in being dragged into this life, climbed into our sleeping bags and forgot our sore feet and aching limbs in sleep. The fact that we lay on hard lumpy earth didn't detract one iota from the ease in which we all dropped off into deep slumber.

Lofty had us all up and about before dawn next day, so that we had our breakfast, packed our kit and were on the way before the paling sky in the east announced that the sun would soon be showing itself.

It was not more than a few miles walk into Azzib, and the air was just acquiring the trade winds as the sand heat was felt when we marched up the last 100 yards to the gate of our original camp and I saw that the old EPIP tent had been removed so that the half dozen huts on the crest of the hill had reign over the surrounding slopes.

Behind The Lines with The SBS: My Life in L Squadron during WW2

For the rest of the day, we were entertained in and around the RE stores, using up large amounts of a variety of explosives, making 'beehives' of '808 plastic' to drive small deep holes in the ground, cutting sections of old rails with primed guncotton and setting fire to the dry bracken of the hillside with the explosion of Lewes bombs. After dark we were sent off on a scheme of Lofty's. We were to attack in groups and cut out sections of the main north-south railway line running along the coast a mile or so to our west. We did not, of course, carry real explosives- Lofty could not trust some of our number not to take him at his word and blow out whole sections of track, but we carried lumps of guncotton to fix to the rails as evidence of our having achieved the objective.

Half of the party went off first- these were to act as sentries guarding the rail while we the attackers left soon after nightfall in twos and threes to attempt to make our way through the guards and sabotage the track.

It was a scheme which should have only taken an hour or less, but Lofty had it laid to last the whole evening. We had our own ideas about that, and decided that we would play fair just so far and no further. We soon reached the rail at a point about midway between the limits laid down by Lofty, affixed our charges and retired into the surrounding bush. Then we moved along the rail, quietly waiting till the patrolling sentries came along and passed, then we scouted around until we made contact with the rest of the attackers.

When we had all assembled in the spot, each group having fixed its charges, we waited by the side of the rail until the first sentry came along in his patrol, and we called softly to him. He recognised our voices, and coming down to our hide, he was told that we had fixed the charges, but didn't say where. 'Good' he said, 'I am about fed up with loafing about up there, let's have a drag.'

We told him not to show any lights by puffing our cigarettes, and then we moved along until the next sentry came in sight. This man joined us with alacrity having heard of our success and we did the same with the other sentries until the whole track was clear of all sentries except one – Lofty!

Then we had carefully avoided in our strolling up and down the track collecting our comrades, so that we all left the immediate area, retired into the surrounding bush well out of sight and sound, and sitting down comfortably against trees, we lit up our cigarettes and sat there chuckling at the idea of one solitary officer defending a railway line which had already been destroyed!

It was perfectly fair in a way, for the attackers really had attacked notwithstanding the sentries, who in this turn had really attempted to intercept us; their failure to do so being only due to the length of the track they had to cover being too great for so small a number, and the fact that the surrounding countryside provided good cover right up to the railway embankment.

Back to Athlit for more training

The only thing we did not carry out was to waste a lot of time reconnoitring and scouting before attacking, and that we did not consider necessary, so that we felt it was a joint punishment to leave Lofty on his own for a while, squatting hopefully on a deserted track.

After half an hour's 'Loaf' the sentries crept back to their positions, and we attackers treated Lofty, and informed him that the attack had been carried out, and the line destroyed. He was, I think, a little surprised that we had all managed to assemble after eluding the sentries and demanded to be shown the fixed charges. This we willingly did, leading him along the track showing him the expertly fixed blocks of guncotton, and picking the sentries on our way!

That scheme was in my opinion a success, for we won, and Lofty lost although he didn't know it!

CHAPTER 36

MOCK ATTACK ON CYPRUS

The last piece of training we had in the Middle East was a fairly large scale exercise with the whole of L Squadron taking part. It was an attack on Cyprus, and the old hands in the squadron wisely nodded their heads when they heard of the scheme.

'It's summertime' they said, 'Looks like a dummy run for the annual outing to another island.' They didn't say which island, but most of us had our own guess at the final objective. It was not a difficult guess, for the SBS had already made two sorties to Crete, and it was always at the back of our minds that we would have to go there once again, especially as the Germans were known to be withdrawing numbers of troops from the area, presumably to help defend the west wall against the invasion which was obviously coming soon.

For our practice attack on Cyprus, we went first of all to what of a lot of us considered our second home- Beirut. Here each patrol was accommodated aboard an HDML, one of those small launches from which we had made most of our attacks in the Dodecanese a few months previously. The one my brother and I and our patrol went aboard, was a new one, fresh out from the UK, and the crew were also new, but just as friendly and obliging as our old shipmates willing to give up some of their own small comforts to see that we were treated as guests, and not the nuisances we must have been, with our heaps of kit, rubber dinghies, folboats and so on.

The small flotilla sailed out of Beirut harbour late in the afternoon of our arrival. We moved together through the gathering dusk away from the coast of Lebanon, but after some hours we noticed that our ship had left the others astern, and that they had turned north, while we moved a little north of west. About 10.00 pm, after being alone for some hours, we were warned to be ready for the landing, and coming up on deck we found a dark mass of land to the east. It was the north-western end of Cyprus, and we were in Morphou Bay.

As the HDML stood to, with her engines just holding her steady against the current, our Jock corporal (who was in charge) went ashore with a couple of matelots and the 'Jimmy' (first officer) in the ship's dinghy. They took with them a strong line, which was paid out from the ship as the dinghy moved shoreward. Soon afterwards one of the matelots returned with the 'Jimmy' and told us they had made the line fast ashore, and our patrol with its kit were to go ashore in the dinghy taking our course along the line.

We had never before landed in this way, and it was a trial to discover whether it would alleviate the usual difficulties in landing a group of men in separate boats from a drifting ship. The difficulties were not imaginary, for it usually meant that at least three boatloads had to be landed and they sometimes landed hundreds of yards apart so that valuable time was lost, and unnecessary noise made in gathering the patrol together.

No doubt the new method did do away with some difficulties, for it meant we all landed together, but the discomforts attached to this new method did more than make up for the time saved. In fact, no time was saved, for we were all so wretchedly wet with the dripping wet line being hauled across us and our kit as we pulled ashore that we hardly noticed the real soaking that was our lot when we reached the shore. The loaded dinghy had so deep a draft that we had to scramble over the side while still some yards away from the beach, and stumble ashore through considerable surf. The soaking meant that we were in no fit state to take on a long march, for you just can't march in soaking wet shirts and trousers.

Fortunately we had, from our recent experience, come to expect some such landing, and we had removed our socks and shoes, so that we only had to slip off our pants and shirts, slide into dry ones from our packs, dry our legs and feet and put on our socks and shoes.

This did not take a great deal of time, but had we landed in rubber dinghies or folboats it would not have been necessary to do more than roll up our pants and remove our boots and socks, taking only a moment to replace them after landing.

When the patrol was fully clad once more, we set off through the bracken at the seashore. The ML by now had pulled away from the shore and was no longer visible through the gloom. The night was very dark and stumbling through the bushes and potholes of the marshland we made very heavy weather of the 'going'.

Eventually, after about an hour's march, we struck a road going south-east and after a short rest under cover we moved off along this easier path. In a few minutes we came upon a small hamlet wrapped in darkness. We debated as to the wisdom of going through, but as it appeared so deserted, decided to risk discovery. We made the opposite end of the village without being challenged but we did notice that one place, which looked like a wine shop, had lights showing through slits in shutters, and we wondered how many eyes observed our passage.

Behind The Lines with The SBS: My Life in L Squadron during WW2

That we had been observed and that intelligence had been sent ahead became obvious at the end of another hour's march, for as we neared the outskirts of a village called Morphou, we were challenged and arrested by a huge Cypriot policeman riding a horse. The whole thing was a farce, for had the invasion been real we certainly would not have been caught by a lone policeman and even had that unlikely event taken place that same policeman would not have lasted the night to report our arrival.

As it was, we were only playing at soldiers and could obviously not take any active steps to resist arrest, so, we were marched off to the police station and interrogated by members of some form of field security. We then ate the remains of our haversack rations and turned in for the night on the floor of the charge room.

In a fit of mischief, I engaged the station sergeant in conversation and while talking to the old boy I lifted his truncheon out of his holster and laid it on the table behind him. When we finished talking, I walked around behind him to my sleeping bag and lifted the truncheon from the table and slid it into my bag. I kept it for the whole of my stay on the island, returning it to one of the FS characters at Kyrenia just before we left the island, with the advice that he admonish the police about their carelessness in leaving lethal weapons in exposed places where they were available to invading troops!

After a night in the 'cooler' we were packed aboard a three tonner and told that as we were out of the exercise, we were to be delivered to Nicosia transit camp, there to await the end of the scheme.

On our arrival at the camp, we were cordially welcomed by the camp Adjutant, given a 'casual' payment, that is an extra small week's wages and told that we might come or go as we please until the exercise is at an end. This suited us all very well and we repaired to the town to taste of its flesh pots.

We stayed in the camp for several days, until all the invading force had been finally rounded up. Very little took place of note except that my brother and I had a further taste of a Cypriot jail. It was on our last night in the town, and we were naturally celebrating with a friend from the marine patrol.

Drunkedly he'd had had a little a little more than we had, or possibly his capacity was less, with the result that by the end of the evening he was virtually incapable. We were half carrying him towards the edge of the town and suddenly a 'Garry' – similar to the horse drawn cabs of Cairo– came trotting along. We hailed the cabbie and asked him to transport us to the camp, a matter of some 5 miles outside the town. He refused, and as a punishment for his churlish attitude we overturned his cab.

Unfortunately for us, this happened to be almost directly opposite the police station and in a matter of seconds we were whisked into custody and deposited into the charge room. Things looked a little black for a while and we could visualise being left to cool our heels on the island while the rest of the squadron returned to Palestine.

While we were discussing the unpleasant fate facing us an inspector walked into the charge room and was told of our misdeed. He was a very nice inspector however and after hearing our own account of the story he grinned sympathetically, told us we were bad lads and ordered coffee all round.

Things looked a little brighter and while we sat drinking the coffee the inspector asked us all about ourselves and what sort of work we were engaged upon. We told him as much as was consistent with security and he was very interested, saying how lucky some of us were to have such a satisfying job in the war while he had to be content with such mundane tasks as keeping the peace and watching that not too many rowdy soldiers upset too many cabs in his province.

The evening ended very satisfactorily for us as the inspector suggested that if we reimburse the cabby with a pound, he might take a lenient view of the case. This we did, drawing up just enough money between the three of us to satisfy the cabby and our friend the inspector who then kindly put us in a police car and had us driven back to the camp. I had heard many unkind things said about Cypriots and have said a few myself but that inspector was one of the island's gentlemen and I feel that it is only because of his leniency that we did not find ourselves on a court martial.

Things were a bit tricky in Cyprus at that time and trouble with the civilian population was usually rewarded with severe penalties.

The following day we were all loaded once more on the ubiquitous three tonners and driven off to Kyrenia where we found the MLs waiting in the harbour. We took fond farewells of our friends the security people and set off for Beirut.

The HDML our patrol was travelling in took part in some gunnery exercises on the way home, firing at floating targets laid down by the flotilla commander, Adrian Seligman. Our own boat was equipped with a Bofors gun, mounted forrard, in addition to several machine guns and an Oerlikon aft.

The Bofors was a new fitting and had taken the place of 3-inch gun, the latter being the original standard equipment, and the din in the tiny mess deck had to be heard to be believed when the Bofors was letting fly.

We found that night however that its noise was not the only hardship caused by the gun. The sea came up during the night and it was soon apparent that the down blast of the gun had burst much of the caulking in the deck planks. The water came streaming into the mess deck every time the ML put her nose in the sea, and we of the SBS were the immediate sufferers for such were the limitations of space in these craft that we had to sleep on the mess deck, and it was soon impossible to keep dry in the two or three inches of sea water swilling about the floor.

Behind The Lines with The SBS: My Life in L Squadron during WW2

My brother and I soon gave it up and took our sodden sleeping bags up into the wheelhouse where we spent the rest of the night yarning with the very young First Officer Lieutenant Hadfield. During conversation with him it transpired that he had been a seaman on the *King George V* battleship in the Home Fleet before taking his commission and had in fact known our third brother Stan, who was also serving on that ship in the C in C's staff.

As a footnote to this small incident it is possibly worth recording that after the war this officer while serving at Pompey met and married a Wren whom he then discovered was our cousin Daphne. The arm of coincidence seems to have infinite length.

At dawn the next morning we returned to the mess deck for breakfast and looking round discovered that our number was one short. It was another of our marines and on searching the boat we found him wrapped in a gas-cape lashed firmly to the top of an ammunition locker on the upper deck groaning that he only wanted to die! He had spent the night in this position fully exposed to gale and sea and suffering the awful pangs of seasick. His condition, though sad, gave rise to much ribald comment as he was one who, ashore, was loud in his scorn of those who were not seafarers. Of course, in his recovery he explained that he was used to big ships which 'didn't try and do bloody somersaults' but only rolled or pitched majestically.

Top Left. Des and Bill's brother Stan who served in the Royal Navy during WW2. (Marshall Family Collection)

CHAPTER 37

TO MERSA MATRUH

After our return to Athlit in Palestine we led a quiet life for a few weeks interrupted with spells of mad excitement engineered by some of the foolhardy and hare-brained schemes devised by our patrol commander.

At the end of this period, we had a couple of days' leave in Haifa then left by train en-masse for the south. This journey lasted several days and took us right down into Egypt and then up to the coast again on the road through the salty marshes, past the ghastly relics of El Alamein – with its mine-lined tracks marked in faded signs and the broken hulks of burned out tanks scattered to the southern horizon, then through El Dabaa until we finally came to a stop at Mersa Matruh. This by now famous town by the sea was practically deserted, its only inhabitants being a few members of various Army units and a few Arabs who had managed to find enough shelter from the remains of their erstwhile houses to start life once more in some sort of home.

Mersa was too far away from any centre to be important enough – yet – for any official efforts to be made to rehabilitate its original citizens or attempt to rebuild the ruins of their

Des enjoying a bit of R&R in Beirut. (Courtesy of Ian Layzell)

homes. It was noticeable that the most damage had taken place in the native quarters of the town. The more fashionable avenue of shore wooden houses – relics of the pre-war days when Mersa was another Monaco - were apparently still in good order but we didn't investigate as it was reported that many mines and booby traps had still to be cleared and it was not worth losing a limb or life to explore some pre-war princeling's parlour.

Possibly the most striking thing about Mersa was the Italian military cemetery. This was full of well- made, well- kept graves of soldiers, sailors and airmen of Mussolini. The fallen men's comrades had seen to it that their friends did not go in want of memorials to their virtue and valour. Each grave had some souvenir or memento of the occupant military trade or rank. For example, on one grave of an artillery signaller was, at the head, a miniature Army wireless set and stretching above it a small wireless mast connected by a model Windom aerial to a similar mast at the grave's foot. A wooden cross with the man's name, rank and number and a sentimental verse decorated the head of the grave and to complete the picture a rusty pair of earphones draped the top member of the cross.

There were many other equally detailed and romantic epitaphs to the fallen – so many in fact that at first glance one might have mistaken the cemetery for a military dump with the litter of helmets, broken rifles, equipment of all sorts and models of guns, aeroplanes and ships mounted on the serried ranks of graves.

We were housed in a primitive barracks close to the shore of the small cove which formed the harbour at Mersa Matruh. These barracks had last been occupied by Italian troops and were full of mural depictions of the Italian soldier's nostalgia for his home and pleasure. Primitive these barracks were indeed. I almost wonder now if barracks they were or stables.

The block I shared with the rest of the squadron was a long low single-storey building divided into compartments each about 12ft square, with one door leading from a covered walk into each compartment and each with two small windows, unglazed, high under the roof. The rooms were of course quite bare of furniture or fittings, nor was there provision for any form of lighting. Into these comfortless cells we moved our sleeping bags, mosquito nets and rucksacks, four men to each room, and there we stayed for a week or so.

The officers fared a little better for they occupied a three storey building which I imagine was the regimental HQ of the military unit whose home it had been originally. Also, in this building we had our mess room and stores.

Our days at Mersa Matruh were spent in training. We carried out assault courses, explosive courses, and the inevitable training in wireless and cipher work.

Our spare time was spent swimming or wandering through the town to the newly opened and quite inadequate NAAFI. Swimming was a popular pastime until someone reported that in the fighting around the town during the Battle

To Mersa Matruh

Des, Paddy Hills, Jim Webster and Tom Humphreys (half hidden) Mersa Matruh June 1944. The following month Des will begin his operation on Crete. (Marshall Family Collection)

of Mersa so many Germans had been killed that their comrades had not time to bury them all and had accordingly disposed of the bodies in the water of the harbour and the adjacent lagoon. We had evidence of this one evening in the NAAFI, which backed on to our lagoon. Someone was staring at the water and called our attention to an object floating on its surface. We all crowded close to the shore to see and found to our horror that the object was a very long dead German whose body had probably been trapped in sand or mud and then released by moving current and now rose to the surface to remind us that he had been there longer than us –much longer!

Swimming died a noticeable death as a pastime after that episode.

The roads through Mersa Matruh were full of reminders of war. On one occasion we were walking home one evening from the NAAFI when someone spotted a gleam under a hedge at one side of the road. The light was reflected from the top of a German helmet which rested on a small wooden stick marking the lonely, isolated grave of a soldier who must have died in the collapsed slit trench behind the hedge and had been buried there.

During one of our assault courses our bomb happy patrol commander had the brilliant idea of our splitting up into pairs and making an approach to a given spot keeping under cover the while. This was innocent enough in all conscience but to make it interesting he installed himself behind the sand dune which was our objective and provided himself with a Bren gun and full magazine. There he sat and if he saw a movement as someone approached the objective he loosed off a few automatic rounds low over the offender's head. Several of our patrol objected to this one sided game and slipped off to collect their own small arms and the course developed into our battle royal with bursts of Bren fire interrupted by the vicious spitting of Schmeissers or the snap of Carbine shots. This annoyed 'Lofty' the officer whose fire became longer and lower so that the 'game' might have ended in bloodshed had not an irate naval officer walked out from the building known as 'Admiralty House' and threatened to turn the guns of the MLs in the harbour on our position if we 'didn't stop the bloody row!' I think it was with relief that both sides give up the sport and returned to lunch.

Our time at MM drew towards its close and the pending operation loomed near. We all had a pretty good idea where we were going and no one was too happy at the prospect. It was commonly agreed that we were destined for Crete, a perennial favourite of Jellicoe's and we all agreed that it was a case of taking the pitcher too often to the well.

Eventually the signallers were sent for – eight of us all together – and were told that an operation was pending as if we weren't already fully cognisant of the fact. We were told that to keep numbers down to a minimum and reduce the risk of losing more than was absolutely necessary (this cheered us) only one signaller would go with each patrol and further that, only three targets were to be engaged and therefore that two patrols would be combined into one large attack and the others would engage the two enemy targets.

Then the eight signallers were put in a sweepstake and the three lucky names drawn. The first name drawn out of the hat was mine and so great was the shock that I took no further interest in the proceedings until I realised that three of us were standing apart from the others who looked on us in an interested but mournful way – as one would regard an acquaintance who has just informed one that he intended to take his own life.

Having dismissed the remaining signallers our officer then briefed us, or to use his own phrase 'Put us in the picture'. It happened that our targets were to be three oil and ammo dumps. One dump was in the west end of Crete, the second in the middle of the island and the third in the eastern section.[28]

The marine patrol, with whom I would go, and who were a bloodthirsty bunch of young thugs, were to carry out the central attack but before that four of us were to be landed on the island to carry out a recce of the target a week or so before the actual attack. The four comprised the officer, Captain Dick Harden, his bodyguard Marine Nobby Clark, the Interpreter Stephenson who had been with me in Stampalia, and myself with my set.

Capt. Dick Harden. (Courtesy of the SAS Archives)

After the briefing the next four days at Mersa were spent in busy preparations, the rest of my party with collecting plastic explosive, time pencil, primers and the rest of their infernal machinery. My time was fully taken in choosing and checking the best wireless set available, swotting up on cipher and codes, collecting a 'clone – horse' (a small compact battery charging engine) batteries, crystal, petrol and oil for the engine and ammunition clips for my Colt.45 automatic. When I had all my belongings gathered together, they presented a formidable pile and I gloomily thought of the difficulties of transporting this lot across the mountains of Crete – hoping our intelligence people had made some suitable arrangements regarding transport on the island. I thought this was a forlorn hope – I was wrong.

CHAPTER 38

TO CRETE VIA TOBRUK

Finally, the day came, and we moved our paraphernalia down to the small jetty at Mersa Matruh and on to the waiting Fairmile ML345. This was the first time I had travelled on the larger petrol engine boats, and I found it a pleasant change from the smaller slower HDML to which I had become accustomed in the Dodecanese islands. As usual there was no accommodation for we three soldiers –Stephenson, Clark and myself, but we had not far to go and the weather was hot and still, so we stacked our equipment in the engine room hatch, lay down beside it to bask in the sunshine on our short cruise. How deceptive the scene was! As soon as we left our little harbour we found the launch rolling horribly so that laying down was in fact the only comfortable (or least uncomfortable) way of travelling. The trouble was that as always, when possible, the boat sailed so close to the coast as possible so that what little seaway there was, was rebounding in the crest and we were rolling on the cross currents caused by the backwash. Still the day was lovely and the sea breeze just enough to take the vicious edge off the sun's blazing heat so that we enjoyed this first leg of our journey from Mersa to Tobruk.

The day was drawing to a close when we entered Tobruk harbour. The sights that greeted us amazed me. I had imagined from the account I had read that Tobruk was destroyed and its harbour hardly in use. Yet on the rising ground beyond the harbour we could see a town of white houses, wireless masts on the eastern side of the harbour giving every appearance of a thriving port. But the harbour itself is what most impressed me. Over the wide expanse of water were scattered ships of every kind – large liners, warships, dirty tramp steamers and native sailing boats. It was only when we came up to the floating jetty that we saw that the whole scene was merely a façade- a shell which served only to hide the utter devastation which had been wreaked by bombing and shelling by both sides during the incessant battles for this key military point.

The houses were roofless and as we drew near and had a clearer view we could see as the individual buildings became separated that the few almost complete structures only concealed many devastated ruins behind. The ships

To Crete via Tobruk

in the harbour area were mostly hulks and deserted with their backs resting on the harbour bottom – only the upper part of the hulls and their superstructure shining above the water.

Across from our jetty was a large Italian troopship – formerly one of the Duce's liners looking for all the world as though it were lying out in the harbour waiting for the tide, but we could see that its boats were smashed, its hull rusted and broken and its superstructure hanging in ruined shreds over the dead body of the ship.

Surprisingly, Tobruk, like Mersa Matruh, was still virtually deserted although more than eighteen months had gone since the last shell screamed through the streets and the last bomb found its billet in the harbour.

As soon as we had tied up the three of us set off to explore the town. It was a sorry exploration – practically no building remained complete, and it was a disconsolate trio who eventually found their way to the building outside the town in the desert which had been adapted into a NAAFI. We spent the evening there drinking the only beverage available – Guinness stout. It was with relief however that we eventually returned to the cheerfully crowded discomfort of the ML's mess deck and went to bed in our sleeping bags laid on the deck.

The following day passed slowly in that miserable ghost town and an hour or two before light faded we set out of the harbour on our 200 mile dash northward to Crete – aiming to reach the large area patrolled by E. boats after dark – but not so late that the ML could not be caught in daylight in the same area on its return trip.

An hour or so after leaving the harbour the low coastline of Africa dropped below the horizon and we were alone on a blue sea gently rolling to the steady swell. After a meal in the mess deck, I borrowed the bunk of one of the duty watch and turned in for a few hours' sleep.

Surprisingly, now that the die was cast and we were irretrievably committed to the operation, I felt no fear and merely a sort of fatalism. We could not turn back and worrying about the future was fruitless, so I slept.

The next thing I knew was when Stephenson shook me to tell me that we were approaching the island and that we should prepare our kit for landing. I climbed to the upper deck and at once I was struck by the beauty of the scene. I have seen many tropical and sub-tropical nights at sea but never I think, one to match the enchanted night as we approached the island of legend – Crete.

The sea was calm and still, while overhead the night sky presented a deep purple dome flickered with stars. The stars were brighter near the encircling horizon but almost overhead they faded into nothing in the glorious light of a huge full moon – seemingly near enough to be touched by the tip of our gently swaying mast.

Behind The Lines with The SBS: My Life in L Squadron during WW2

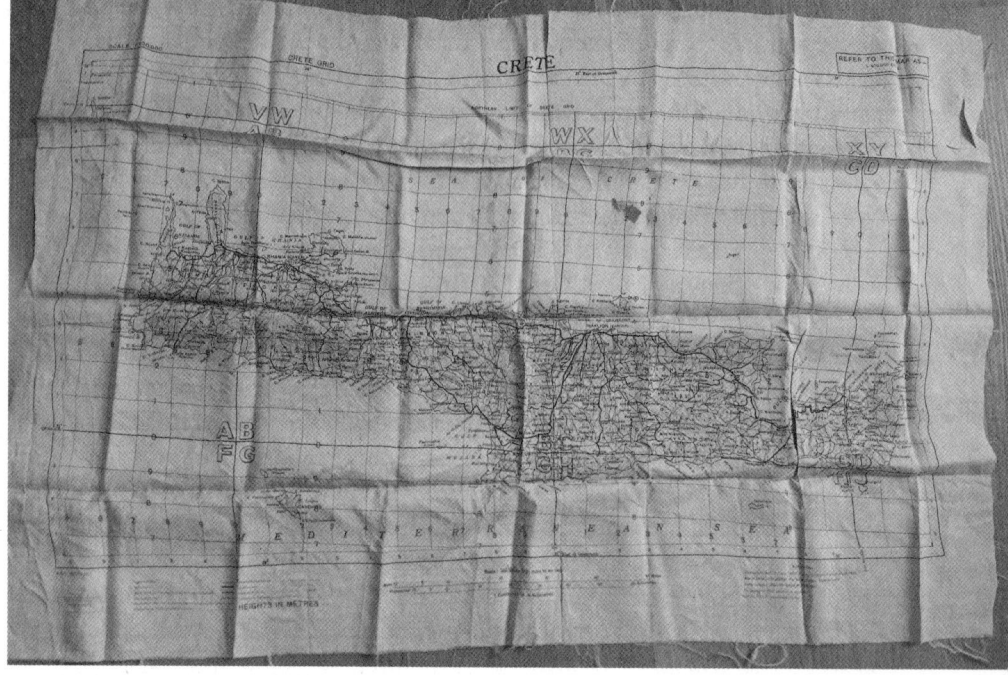

Des' silk map of Crete. (Marshall Family Collection)

Clear in the moonlight we could see silhouetted to the north the great humping mass of the island with its central point clearly marked by Mount Ida soaring behind the mountainous coast ahead of us. The beauty of the scene struck me with all its intensity but as I stared, I felt again the qualms which had been sublimated on our departure from Tobruk.

Beautiful as the moon looked, I thought it's a menace to us this night for surely if any enemy watch stood in these distant cliffs, he could not fail to observe the dark shape of our boat as it made its approach. Yet we made the approach in peace and no warning flash heralded the whine of a shell to challenge us and no machine gun rattled its denial of our right to enter this enemy fortress. So, in a silence broken only by the subdued murmur of our motor, we made our kit ready and the sailors unlashed the dinghy in which we were to land. We inflated a rubber dinghy in which we would load our luggage and heaved it over side – towing it on a line until it would be time to disembark.

While we were thus preparing, we drew nearer still to the land and when I next looked around, I saw to the west that the land had broken and we were passing a small island separated from the main island by a mile or so of water. The mountains loomed high above us, and we could see in the moonlight the vague outline of trees and shrubs dotting their lower slopes. Presently we passed a small headland to the east of us and could clearly see the gleam of a beach at the landward side of a small bay.

In a few more minutes our ML had stopped its engines and we lay to a matter of 50 yards from the beach. In the pale light on the beach, I picked out a number of forms and the thought again came to me that there might well be Germans waiting to receive a welcome bunch of prisoners of war – but I need not have worried. While we were making our preparations on board the Navy had received and answered a signal light from the shore – giving us assurance that our reception committee was the right one.

As soon as we stopped the dinghy was put over side and Dick Harden and Clark went off with two sailors while Stephenson and I loaded the other dinghy with all our paraphernalia. In a few minutes the dinghy was back, and we went ashore towing our other boat with us.

Many hands came forward to help our boat through the shallows and when I stepped onto the beach,[29] I found a party of a dozen bearded ragged Cretans busy unloading our stows. I was surprised to find that instead of talking in whispers they were speaking rapidly and loudly laughing and cursing as the mood took them – contemptuous of the Germans when my imagination told me that one might be lurking in the bushes.

While our stows were being checked ashore I looked around and found Dick Harden speaking in English to what looked like a Cretan, albeit a blonde one, and I was introduced to Captain Hugh Fraser, a member of Force 133 who had been living on the island for some months with the *andartes*, the local name for partisans. Fraser was a slight man with a fair beard and hair dressed in the style of a Cretan peasant and addressed by the *andartes* as '*Leftheri*' – a local nickname which had been affectionately bestowed upon this self-effacing man by his tough companions.[30]

Beyond the group I saw several small donkeys tended by a youth. At once I realised my gloomy forebodings about the transportation of my heavy wireless gear were unfounded. Here was the necessary means of moving it across the island without having to manhandle it ourselves. Once again, I was to be proved wrong.

In a matter of minutes our gear was all landed and our boat's dinghy left towing our rubber dinghy behind. While we were sorting ourselves out on the beach, I heard the motor of the ML's engines as she started up and saw the dark shape of her moving quietly out of the bay. Much as I would like to have been aboard, I realised that these sailors had taken a considerable risk in getting us this far and were now in even greater danger. They must reach an area reaching miles out to sea before dawn otherwise they would almost certainly be spotted by planes and attacked by E-boats. Their armament was so light and their construction so thin that they could never hope to out match one of the larger, faster, enemy vessels.

I noticed at this point that something of an altercation was taking place between Harden and Fraser. The latter's loud voice was demanding to know what bloody fool had the bright idea of landing us in uniform without the necessary change of kit which would make us at least part of the local picture. His concern was not so much for our safety as for his friends. Apparently, he said, if any stranger saw us wandering about the island in uniform word would almost certainly go round that allies had landed, and such word would soon reach German ears with the result of an intensified search being made of the neighbourhood and possibly revealing not only us (who didn't matter) but the *andartes* (who did!). Anyway, he argued, nothing could be done just then but asserted we must find some kit as soon as possible. We felt rather stupid about the whole affair although of course it was none of our doing.

Incidentally the accusation of being dressed in uniform was true only in the broadest sense. I wore no hat, a blue shirt and a pair of 'operational' slacks. These latter were a strong trill with all sorts of concealed places. Inside the waistband was sewn a silk map of Crete, a steel hacksaw moulded in a rubber container was hidden down the fly and in each turn up was a small sewn pocket containing gold sovereigns and a tiny compass – all designed to be used in the event of capture and escape. Footwear was hardly uniform – we wore suede desert boots with crepe soles. They were comfortable but proved unpractical in the rocky mountains of Crete.

The *andartes* soon had my gear loaded onto the donkeys who were fitted with a workmanlike harness, primitive but effective. It consisted of a thing looking for all the world like a trestle. This was placed across the animal's back and the gear tied on each side – the driver ensuring that the weight was evenly balanced on either side. When this was done, a long strap like a girth was placed over the whole cumbersome affair and drawn tight beneath the animal's belly – so tight did they draw these girths that it was quite funny to see how the small creatures' legs lifted off the ground as the men strained the strap into its last notch.

All this landing and preparation took very little time so that in less than thirty minutes after disembarking our little convoy of men and animals set off. Heading was a short, ragged Cretan followed by Fraser, Harden, Clark, myself, and Stephenson with the other men and donkeys bringing up the rear.[31]

We crossed the beach and moved through rough gorse growing at the edge of the sand towards the dark shape of the hills to the landward. In a very short space of time, we were climbing through small trees along a track leading into the hills. Every so often we came into a clearing from which we could look down and see the Mediterranean bathed in moonlight and for quite some time we could still see the dark shape of our ML moving south across the path of the moon. All movement of the sea was lost as we climbed above it and it looked like a sheet of silver in the glaring light with a frill of surf where the water met the rocks at the headland across the bay.

The track took us ever higher up the side of a fairly steep hill until we cleared the scrubby trees and marched forward across the bare hillside, following the track alongside a small dry wadi below us. After about an hour's climbing, we stopped beside a waterhole where an underground stream came to the surface. We filled our water bottles from the pure icy cold water and our *andarte* friends' gave us from small bottles, some of their own island's spirit drink. It was warming and exhilarating and after the rest and drink I felt I could climb for hours, never thinking I should have to do just that!

Once again, we set off at a fairly smart pace, climbing ever higher into the mountains. For long periods as we moved round the shoulder of the hill, we lost sight of the sea and the marching became more difficult as the hill obscured the moonlight and in the darkness we could not see where our feet fell.

After another two stops we came out once more into the moonlight above the first hill we had negotiated and looked out and down at the sea. It was amazing to me to observe how greatly the limit of the horizon had extended. We could see many miles into the southern sea although of course by now our boat had disappeared. The moon had also passed well on its way and was dropped into the west so that the shadows in those silent mountains became darker and longer, deceiving our eyes with the distances.

We had really had little sleep on the journey to Crete and our tiredness was now beginning to tell. Each time we stopped I fell to the ground ready to sleep but after a few minutes' rest we had to rise and move on once more. As Fraser explained, we must reach our hide on the mountain top before dawn as the Germans might well decide to make a drive through the lower slopes to try to pick up the odd *andarte* – the mountain tops were safe as the Germans no longer dared to attack the known hides of the Cretan partisans – they had suffered too many casualties in hunting the lion in his den!

Finally, after what seemed many weary hours of climbing, we topped the last slope and found ourselves on a small flat saddle between two mountains. This was obviously the southern end of a pass, and it was here we were to stop on the first leg of our journey.[32]

The sky was lightening towards the east by the time we spread our sleeping bags on the ground besides a small rocky mound and climbing into the bags we slipped at once into a deep fatigued sleep.

Some hours later I awoke to find the sun high in a deep blue clear sky. The *andartes* were clustered together around a fire against the hillside brewing something in a pot. We washed and didn't shave and rolling up our bags we wandered over to where the smell of cooking woke up our appetites and reminded us that it was twelve hours or more since we had last eaten.

We ourselves had bought a few rations with us – not much as our personal kit and rations had always to be kept to the absolute minimum in order that we might carry the more operational gear. One great boon and comfort we had each allowed ourselves was a pound of tea we had stuffed into our rucksacks. We spent something like four weeks on the island and we made our four pounds of tea last until the last day. This was done by saving some used tea from each brew, drying it out and adding it to a smaller than usual amount of fresh tea in the next pot. It was tea but only just!

We shared the *andartes'* breakfast of stewed goat meat, adding some of our small stash of corned beef and it tasted wonderful.

The rest of the day we spent in sorting out our kit and caching it in a secret cave hidden by bushes a few dozen feet down the mountain side. Hugh Fraser had been appalled at the amount of gear, wireless sets and so on, which we had brought with us. It transpired that he had a British wireless operator with him in his main headquarters across the other side of the island (where we were going). This man had a complete set of equipment, wireless sets, charging engines and fuel for the latter so that my own equipment would not be necessary – all I would need would be my crystals for calling Cairo and my cipher books and charts. The remainder of the stuff would remain hidden here at our first stop until we returned to this place at the end of the operation. The wisdom of this decision was clear when we found that we would not be allowed to use the donkeys further in the journey – the rest of the way we would carry all our gear ourselves – a very dismal prospect but one which would have been formidable had we had to carry the wireless gear as well.

That night we set off again on our journey. Our party had shrunk in size to half a dozen, we four SBS men, Fraser and our Cretan guide. Our path was easy at first through the pass and we made good time in the comparatively level ground between the steep walls of a ravine at the north side of the ground on which we had camped. We started the march an hour or two before midnight so that when we came into more populated areas we would be reasonably sure of avoiding any contact with late travellers. This was a remote danger for in that island of trigger-happy Cretan-hating Germans nobody made a practice of wandering at large after dark, except our friends the *andartes* in their predatory expeditions.

Very soon we started our descent to the central plain and that part of the journey was one of the most difficult and uncomfortable of all our marches. As it was downhill, so to speak, it should have been fairly easy but anyone who has marched across mountains carrying heavy packs will agree that this is a fallacy.

To Crete via Tobruk

The track here was formed by the dried bed of a mountain stream, obviously a conduit for the melting snows and rain of the wintry mountain top. Its floor was narrow and formed of loose stones so that we could walk only in single file, our feet slipping and sliding on the rubble as we strove to balance our heavy packs.

At some points the track almost levelled out then suddenly dropped vertically in what must in winter be a waterfall. Where this happened, the warning was passed back by the guide and each of us had to check our sliding, slipping progress to avoid plunging over the small precipice and we had here to un-sling our packs, lower them to the man in front at the bottom of the fall and then climb down the face before recovering our rucksacks to continue the climb down.

Once again, we were blessed by the brilliant moonlight, although for most of the way down the mountain side we were in shadow from the thick shrubs growing high on each side of the dry watercourse. Also in the early part of our march the moon was hidden by the bulk of the huge mountain to the east of us.

Our first stop was made on a wide ledge overlooking the valley and here we sat down to relieve our aching leg muscles and take a drink from our water bottles. As we sat there, I looked down at the plain bathed in moonlight far below. I could see fields fairly well cultivated, starting in a terrace formation from the foot of our mountain and gradually levelling out as the slope diminished into the flat plain. A few buildings which I took to be farms could be seen scattered about in the moonlight and far across the valley, where the ground rose again, I could see the gleam of white houses of a village.

We continued our staggering painful progress down through the shale and rubble and eventually we stopped again at the foot of the mountain. After a short rest we moved across the fields, keeping to the borders. Walking on the level was almost as difficult to me as our precipitous descent because my leg muscles, which had become used to catching my leg weight in turn on the slope, now started trembling violently with the reaction.

During the first part of our journey, I remember having thoughts about everything connected with this operation, what sort of food we would get, where we would hide, whether the operation would be successful and worst of all, would I be killed or maimed? It never occurred to me then or at any other time that I could be taken prisoner, but it happened to some. As the march progressed my mind changed however, I realised my feet were sore, that my legs ached, then what a weight my pack was and how the bergen rucksack frame gouged into my back and finally my whole back became an aching automaton and I thought no more, only cursing at the next step and then the next with no thought but with the present moment of pain and fatigue. I suppose the others felt the same, but they did not show any sign so that I felt alone in my musing.

After about an hour we reached the far side of the Plain and found ourselves for the first time on a road. This road appeared to run roughly north eastwards and skirted a steep rocky cliff at the point at which we reached it. From this rock sprang a clear cold stream and we refreshed ourselves once more before moving on.

I was surprised to find when we started again that we were to follow the road. It seemed a foolhardy risk to move abroad at night on open roads on an occupied island, but I suppose really the danger was remote as the Germans themselves did not like travelling these roads after dark for fear of ambush.

Very soon we reached the village I had seen from the mountain and the inevitable village dogs started their vocal denial of our rights of entry. It was not a long village but as we marched through the deserted winding street the howling and barking was passed from one canine throat to the other, following us until we were out of earshot once more.

It was some four or five hours since we left our mountain hide and I was feeling very tired as we plodded onwards across the island. I hoped at every bend in the road that the moonlight would show us whatever destination we were heading for, but I was continuously disappointed.

At one point as we were marching along a section of road which traversed the side of a hill, with terraced groves stretching above on our right hand and dropping to a riverbed on the left, I really thought we must have arrived at our destination. The guide suddenly left the road, and we followed him down into an olive grove where he stopped. He joined in conversation with Hugh Fraser and then abruptly left us. By now I could not have cared what happened, so fatigued was I and sat down beside a tree and fell fast asleep to have a series of terrifying nightmares. Almost immediately it seemed Dick Harden shook me. I staggered, protesting, to my feet, almost unable to lift the apparently unbearable bulk of my pack off the ground and stumbled after the others and we were on our way again.

This time however, we had not far to go. After rounding a bend in the hill, we left the road and moved to the right across a piece of flat open country. Soon we reached a clump of bushes on the left and broke through these to find ourselves on a narrow track going along the side of a ravine. In the darkness I could not see the bottom of the valley to our right and overhead the bushes grew thick and tangled, cutting out the sky. My story nearly ended there for the man in front of me was too far ahead for me to see and in the darkness, I slipped and fell. It was a small section of broken track I had stepped on and my foot fell on empty air. Luckily, I fell forward and landed on my chest on the far side but unluckily Stephenson was right behind me and using me as a stepping stone trod on my pack and the pair of us lay sprawling until the others came and with Stephenson's help hauled me out of the hole.

CHAPTER 39

FIRST HIDE OUT ON CRETE

Our journey came to an end soon after and we found ourselves in what looked like a shallow cave on the edge of a precipice at the end of the track. Our guide said farewell and climbing thankfully into my sleeping bag, I slept once more.

By the time we stopped marching I had lost track of time but in fact it was only an hour or so before dawn that we reached our hide.

The sun was high and hot when I woke and found Nobby brewing up tea on a Tommy Cooker. I had slept for 6 hours, and it was now after 10.00 am. After we had drunk our tea and eaten some bread left by our hosts, we looked around us.

Our hide was not nearly as secure as had appeared in the dark. It was in fact not a cave, but a man-made arbour of branches and leaves built on a ledge overlooking a roughly cultivated orchard growing down the sides of a narrow valley. The tops of the valley walls were high above us but anyone moving across the opposite hill could not fail to see our small encampment. It was a very pleasant and cool refuge however in the hot sunlight and I would have been quite happy to stay there until the end of the war without having the prospect of that dreadful journey back to the coast. I thanked God for the rest and prayed for it to be long.

As the warm sunlight seeped into my aching limbs I lay and thought of the horrors of that march, when my feet were sore and bleeding, my legs and body creaking with strain and the sweat underneath the pack sticking the rough harness through my soaking shirt into my shrinking flesh.

We had marched across the mountains of Palestine, climbed the rocky islands of the Dodecanese and trained hard for months but no training had fitted us for the hilly country we had come across nor the vicious pace that had been set.

During the afternoon a fat cheery Cretan who introduced himself as Giorgio 'something-akis' came and gave us to understand that this was his 'garden' and while he was delighted to have us as guests, he would be even happier when we took our dangerous presence elsewhere. He did produce a loaf of bread and a piece of goat's milk cheese which we welcomed with flowing gratitude.

Behind The Lines with The SBS: My Life in L Squadron during WW2

In the evening a newcomer appeared. He was dressed in black shirt and breeches with striding goatskin boots and had a ruddy complexion, blue eyes and blonde hair. His voice was even more unexpected. He introduced himself in a broad Yorkshire accent as Hugh Fraser's wireless operator[33] and presented us with a parcel of clothing which he ruefully told us had been purchased by the Cretans with some of his and Fraser's small stock of sovereigns.

He handed out the clothes and we took our choice. It was indeed a poor choice at best. My lot was a cheap thin check shirt badly sewn and finished and a pair of thick brown serge breeches – in appearance, a cross between jodhpurs and western trousers. These too were so badly stitched that in the first wearing the legs split side ends up from the bottoms. I pulled my Army socks outside the tight fitting ends and with my now very battered and shabby desert boots I must say it gave me a very passable imitation of a Cretan. I am dark and had grown a moustache prior to the trip and as I had not shaved for two days my scruffy appearance all helped the deception. For headgear I was given a Sariki, a sort of shawl cum headscarf made of black crocheted coarse cotton. This was folded into a triangle, the point laid over the head towards the forehead and the long ends rolled up to the head and brought round and tucked into each other in front. The lacy bits hanging out of the Sariki did not in any way detract from the villainous appearance that the whole set up presented. I was to wear this costume for the whole of my stay on the island with the exception of one memorable night.

We stayed for several days in this idyllic spot, lounging in the shade of the arbour, smoking and talking or sleeping, occasionally wandering down through the thick bushes in the side of the valley to the gurgling stream running its length. The latter forays however were discouraged by our hosts who visited us every day, bringing food and news. They did not like our exposing ourselves to the vulgar gaze of any passer-by for fear of talk getting back to the Germans of strangers in the vicinity. In the parochial life of this part of Crete everyone of course knew his neighbours both near and distant and our presence would therefore be an outstanding topic of conversation as strangers.

We eked out our meagre rations with what scraps of food the *andartes* could spare from their own pitiful stores, supplemented occasionally by chunks of goat's meat bought by Fraser with his dwindling bank of sovereigns. The food sent over to us was usually coarse bread and locally made cheese with the occasional choice morsels of goat flesh. It was insufficient and unvaried but we had no cause to complain as we were, after all, interlopers and knew full well what a struggle these poor peasants had even in peacetime to find enough to eat. Under the German occupation they kept barely above starvation level as, of course, the Germans took the best and most of all things.

First Hide out on Crete

One thing seemed plentiful, at least among our *andarte* friends, and that was the fiery drink I mentioned earlier and they kept us supplied with a small but enlivening ration of the latter, for which we were truly thankful.

During this period, I do not recall being scared or worried at all – merely bored. In fact, since landing on the island the fears I had entertained beforehand had entirely disappeared. The bogeyman of the German which had loomed so large in my imaginings of life on the island did not seem real now that I was close to it. The bogey of course was real enough to Fraser and his partisan friends, no less than to the ordinary country folk, but to us in our sheltered existence in that quiet arbour it seemed inconceivable that any bullet headed German would bother to disturb our tranquillity.

I think what first dispelled my anxieties were the fatigue and tiredness of our march to this spot. When your mind is numbed by plodding relentlessly forward on sore aching feet and your sweaty body creaking under the weight and discomfort of a loaded rucksack you do not find room for fear. It is there, soon enough, when danger suddenly threatens but one's mind does not seem able to cope with the existence of pain from one cause at the same time as fear of an enemy as yet unencountered. By the same token I have found that when tired, apparently to the point of exhaustion, one suddenly finds fleetness of foot and speed of thought when unexpectedly confronted with immediate danger. The one circumstance seems always to be cancelled by the other.

The tranquillity we felt in our arbour was baseless. Although we did not see any more of Giorgio the owner of the garden, Hugh Fraser or Yorkie, one of whom visited us each evening, brought daily news that the old man's protests at our presence were growing stronger. He feared of course for his own safety if we were found on his land and felt we should be more securely hidden in the *andarte* headquarters.

Eventually Fraser capitulated to the old Cretan, more for anxiety over Giorgio's ability to hold his tongue than to satisfy the old man's claims. It was quite on the cards that Giorgio would air his grievance abroad and bring down just that disaster he was so anxious to avoid.

So one dark night we shouldered our rucksacks once more and followed Yorkie and an *andarte* guide out of our refuge and back along that narrow track to the screen of bushes at the end of the 'garden'. I remembered not to find the broken piece of the track and reached level ground without mishap. We re-traced our footsteps to the road and marched silently along its border for a few hundred yards. Then we crossed to the west side and leaving the road moved down through trees covering a steep slope. As we left the road we heard the rumble of a powerful motor and seconds later a large German transport vehicle followed by a staff car roared by a few feet from our shelter in the trees. Thankful that we had missed trouble so closely we continued down the slope to the bed of a river.

This river, probably in winter one of respectable size, was now only a shallow stream a few feet wide and we forded it without difficulty. Its bed lay in a deep narrow valley with a steep mountain running on its western bank. We followed the stream alongside this wall of rock for a time until the wall ended, and we found another gorge breaking into the mountainside at right angles to the stream. Our guide led us up through thick bushes along the side of this gorge until the track turned back on itself and we found ourselves climbing upwards along the side of the hill towards the river once more. At last, the bushes ended and we came out on a flat, broad ridge at the mouth of the gorge overlooking the river.

The ground fell away steeply below us to the river then rose again to the road which we could see about half a mile away in the dim light. On our left rose the bulk of the mountain but we found there on the inner side of the ridge a large cave, its entrance screened by bushes and dimly lit by a fire burning in its inner regions.

Skoteini 'The Dark One'. Located between the villages Argyropouli and Archontiki. It was the HQ of Hugh Fraser and the Andartes in the region. A chapel has since been built into the cave entrance. Source: (Hugh Fraser General Report. SOE Greece 859) (Photo Courtesy of Chris White)

CHAPTER 40

SECOND CAVE HIDEOUT & RECCE OF TARGET

Yorkie parted the bushes and we followed him into the entrance of the cave. It was at least 15ft high inside and about the same wide. The inside wall of the cave was about 20ft beyond the entrance and just near this wall burned a fire with a pot boiling on its flames, supported by rocks. Seated round the fire was a group of some dozen *andartes* squatting together smoking and talking in low tones. Hugh Fraser sat on a rock near the entrance of the cave talking to Marko, the leader of this group of *andartes*.[34]

They all looked up with interest at our arrival and Fraser introduced us in the local dialect. We were at once made welcome and soon we were sharing the meal prepared by the *andartes*. As we sat eating and talking, we were surprised by the sudden arrival over our heads of swarms of bats who flew into the entrance, across the cave and disappeared through a narrow fissure at the far end of the cave. While we stayed at that hide it was a nightly sport for us to stand at the entrance of the cave armed with long branches and attack these bats as they flew out in their twilight sortie and again meet them on their return an hour or so later. Needless to say, we had no success and came to share in the common belief that bats are fitted with a form of natural radar which makes it possible for them to avoid all obstructions which come in their flight path.

There was not room in the cave for all of us to spread our sleeping bags out under its roof so that we four newcomers spent the nights sleeping out on the hillside just above to the west of the cave – screened from observation by bushes which grew thickly all-round the narrow level stretch of our dormitory.

Now that we were with Fraser at his headquarters, I was able to use his operator's wireless set to keep my call schedules to Cairo. There was very little news for us to send and we received only acknowledgements from Cairo of our signals- they had no orders for us yet.

On the day after our arrival at the HQ, Harden and Stephenson went off with Marko to reconnoitre the objective. It was a few miles to the east of us and they set off some hours after night fall in order to get to the area late enough to miss meeting any Germans who might be working in the vicinity. We saw them go, wishing them good luck and wondering if we would see them again.

Our fears were unfounded, for Stephenson and Harden returned during the early hours of the morning and we all left our virtuous couches to listen to their report and very disappointing it was – at least from an operational point of view.

They had arrived above the target without being stopped and after watching the movements of the German sentries had separated and moved slowly and carefully round the outside of the perimeter. It was a petrol dump but it soon became obvious that to both Stephenson and Harden this was becoming or had become past tense. All the bays visible were empty and for all they knew the hidden bays were also cleared of petrol. The German guard was now obviously nominal, possibly guarding the one or two military vehicles still standing within the perimeter. Neither of our people saw more than two sentries. This was proof positive that the dump was no longer used. The Germans in this *andarte* ridden island would never leave two men only to protect the perimeter of a real dump.

So, it seemed that all our preparations and efforts had been for nothing. Of course, ours was only one of three targets to be attacked and providing the other two dumps had not also been moved, then at least the objective as a whole would not be a failure. It was small comfort to the fire eating Harden however and he at once set about searching for new targets. The result of his search was a signal I sent to Cairo on his return asking if we might have permission to blow a bridge forming a vital viaduct on the main east-west road along the northern coast of the island.[35]

Although this signal was acknowledged and understood by Cairo for some reason HQ never gave us a reply on the subject and without the necessary permission, we could not take the responsibility of such large scale sabotage. It may have been that HQ had a later invasion in mind when the loss of the bridge might be an embarrassment to our own advancing forces but whatever the reasons, they did not give an answer.

There were only a few days left until the time of concerted attack and Dick Harden and Fraser were in frequent conference with the Cretans trying to earmark a suitable target for our small force. Harden had included in his signal instructions that the balance of our patrol should not land now that our main target had dissolved and we four would carry out the attack on any target which might present itself on the day.

So, we passed our days in and around the cave reading, smoking (when we could get cigarettes), eating (when we could get anything to eat) and sleeping often. I spent a good deal of my time in the company of Fraser's wireless operator, helping the Yorkshireman to do his chores around the set, charging

Second cave hideout & Recce of target

Signals message Des sent to Cairo requesting permission to blow up the bridge near Koufi on Crete. (Marshall Family Collection)

the batteries and maintaining the small charging motor. I found that the latter was in an inner cave, the entrance of which was a narrow slit in the rock at the back of the main cave. This narrow tunnel – so narrow as to permit only one person's passage at a time and that only possible by moving sideways – led into the hillside for some ten feet or so. Beyond it was a high vaulted cave, the far end of which I never explored but whose sides were not more than 8ft apart. It was as dark as the pit inside and when we entered there the air was made hideous with the squealing of multitudes of bats that were suspended from the roof in their thousands and who resented our intrusion on their sleeping quarters. The air inside also stank foul with petrol fumes and once having started the motor to charge the batteries we hastened out of the inner cave to the fresh air of the main chamber, leaving the bats to enjoy the noisy chugging of the motor – the sound of which was inaudible from outside.

Occasionally we made our way up the steep side of the mountain to a rocky ridge near its summit. From here we could look across the country to the north where the sea gleamed bright and blue in the sunshine beyond the hills. We could also watch a section of the main road running along the island and sometimes saw German and Italian Army vehicles charging along about their lawful occasions.

When up on this point it was necessary to keep well concealed, for the hills around had many shepherds tending their flocks and in the terrace valleys below we could see men working in the vineyards and olive groves. We could watch them but they must never see us for the old reason that the average Cretan is an egregious creature who knows who is who and where his neighbours should be and if he saw strangers in a strange spot the news would soon be broadcast.

Our waiting days were enlivened by two incidents, one of pleasant memory and one not so pleasant.

Earlier in this story I mentioned Manoli Kanakakis – the Cretan boy who had escaped with Stephenson from the island and who had eventually joined us when we were on our way up to the Dodecanese. Manoli's village was not very far from our hide and Stephenson, after much badgering, persuaded Harden to allow him to visit the boy's mother and pay his respects. Stephenson was enough of the diplomat to be trusted not to spill any beans and in any case Manoli's family were not likely to spread any news as they kept much to themselves, their son's escape making them suspects by the Germans.

At all events Stephenson went off one night accompanied by a Cretan guide insisted upon by Fraser and returned in the small hours to tell us of the wonderful reception he had received from the family and with the added news that we were all invited to pay them a visit and enjoy their hospitality.

Harden did not much like the idea – nor really was it a wise move but eventually we prevailed on him and we went. In fact I was not keen on the thought that we would be jeopardising our chance of getting off the island by this walking into what might well be a German party but the boredom of the past week or so overcame any anxiety and I joined with the others in persuading Dick Harden to give his blessing and come with us to the house.

Two nights after Stephenson's visit we set out – once again not too early, nor too late- and with Fraser as guide we made our way down the hill across the river and out to the road across the valley.

It was a dark night – our erstwhile friend the moon having now died the death and we crept along the verge of the road in absolute silence. The journey was not long but in my anxious mind I felt less and less safe with every step that took us further from the comparative security of our cave.

Second cave hideout & Recce of target

We came to a bend in the road and suddenly Stephenson, who was in front, caught Fraser by the sleeve and stopped him. We soon heard what had alarmed him. It was the sound of several feet and muttered voices beyond the curve and we shrank quietly into the bushes bordering the road.

For all our care we must have given some notice of a presence for immediately the approaching sounds ceased and we crouched, sweating, in the shadows waiting for the next move. I found that I was holding my Colt automatic at the ready and put up my left hand to cock the jacket – stopping short as I thought of the noisy click with which it might reveal our position. I saw in the shadows that the others were also gripping their pistols – the only weapons we were carrying that night.

For minutes no sounds were heard and I strained my ears to catch any whisper which might betray our protagonists. Suddenly a voice broke the silence. It was on a high pitched note which revealed the caller's nervousness and thankfully I realised it was speaking Greek. At once Stephenson called out in reply and gesturing to us to follow, he moved out onto the road.

We moved forward to the road and found ourselves at once in the centre of a group of Cretans from the village ahead. They were good citizens doing their normal work by day – obeying the orders of the German garrison and leading a peaceful existence but at night they sloughed off their mantel of subservience and crept out into the hills to plan the sabotage, murder and final overthrow of the occupying troops. Most Cretans of good health and strength were *andartes* at heart and lived this sort of double life – serving the Germans by day and robbing and murdering them by night.

This particular group had heard our approach and had thought, as we did, that they were being met by a patrol of Germans. They told us as we stood talking quietly by the roadside that they had made preparations to kill us until they realised no German patrol would have gone to ground as we did. On the contrary, a group of enemy troops meeting *andartes* abroad after a curfew would have opened fire at once on the Cretans. The fact that we froze into silence had saved us.

We parted after a few minutes' talk together, shaking hands all round and our friends moved - more quietly this time – towards the west while we continued our journey eastward to the village.

A mile or so further on, the road dipped and turned suddenly down through a copse and on emerging from this we found ourselves at the end of a village. Stephenson told us we had arrived and led the way to a house close by on the left. It was the usual small, whitewashed, square cottage type of building with a door and one window in the wall facing the road. No lights showed anywhere – either in this or any other home in the village.

While the rest of us moved into the trees by the side of the house Stephenson approached the door of the house and knocked. In a moment he had disappeared inside only to reappear at once and lead us into the house. As soon as we were inside the lamps were re-lit and we could see something of our hostess and her home. The lamps were primitive - merely a wad of wool twisted into a wick floating in a saucer of olive oil. Surprisingly however, although there were no more than two or three, the light from the burning wicks was sufficient to see comfortably and clearly every detail of the small but comfortable cottage room.

As on the outside, the inner face of the walls were whitewashed, but so covered were these walls with all manner of ornaments and impediments that little of the walls themselves could be seen. The walls were covered with pictures and photographs, hung with rough woollen rugs, brass plaques and the like. The furniture was sparse but comfortable and we sat ourselves down on an upholstered bench between the curtained window and a table to one side of the door. The whole place was spotlessly clean and bright, and we felt almost out of place in the comparative luxury after our primitive existence since arriving on the island.

Manoli's mother greeted us when we entered and also there was a girl of about fifteen and a much younger boy, Manoli's brother and sister. Of his father we saw nothing, and I believe Stephenson told us he was dead so that this small

The village Koufi, Crete. Manoli's family home centre of pic. The Cretan *andartes* destroyed the telegraph poles on the evening, 22 July, in the nearby Village Episkopi. (Marshall Family Collection)

family fended for itself under the rigours of the occupation. They were a shy but friendly group and made us welcome at once.

I do not like to think of the way they must have sacrificed themselves in order to provide the meal we proceeded to enjoy but in view of the terrible hardships and shortages which existed on Crete it really was a magnificent spread.

As we could not for obvious reasons stay for very long, we started the meal at once. We had our dish of casseroled goat meat beautifully cooked and garnished with olives, aubergines and a variety of other unidentified vegetables. With this we were given white soft bread that melted in the mouth and a side of omelettes. This main course was followed by a dish of tiny white grapes – rather bitter but nevertheless delicious. The whole meal was washed down with an excellent young wine, which continued to be served after we had finished eating. It was to us a royal banquet.

It was not of course possible for us to converse with our hostess although Stephenson carried on a continual conversation with her, assisted occasionally by the taciturn Fraser. The latter was justifiably nervous at first – he was responsible for us after all, and he knew better than we what danger there was not only for us but more so for the kindly folk in our presence at this house. As the wine flowed however, Fraser relaxed as we all did, and it was a very happy group of strangers who sat in that small Cretan homestead on that summer evening.

Towards the end of the evening a very odd coincidence took place and one which set the seal of success on the outing for all of us. It was the arrival of Manoli himself. He had landed on the island with the group who were preparing the attack in the extreme west of the island; they had already reconnoitred their target and all was ready, so Manoli had sought and obtained permission from the officer in charge of his party to make the trek to his own village to visit the mother who had not seen him since his escape almost a year earlier. The journey was a long one, taking up almost half the length of Crete and he had been on the move for several days and nights. He could not stay longer than this one evening as he must at once start on the return journey along the island back to his party to be there in good time for the operation. The coincidence was that we and Manoli who had all been on the island for almost two weeks should have decided to come together on this particular evening to his mother's house. It certainly made the evening a real success and where his family had been pleased to entertain us as the absent Manoli's friends, they were now delighted to shower every hospitality on us now that their son was returned to them.

The evening drew to its close eventually and we regretfully took our leave of Manoli and his family in the very small hours of the next morning.

We left the house as quietly as possible – having learned that a German garrison lived in a house at the other end of the village street - and crept silently upwards on the road through the trees. None of us was quite in full possession of his wits by now – so generous had the Kanakakis family been with their wine - and it was the knowledge that we were in fact tiddly that caused our excessive caution as we slithered like stage villains in the shadow of trees and bushes. Fraser had a tendency strangely enough to be aggressive and muttered dark things about what he could or would do to any German patrol who were unfortunate enough to meet him tonight.

Nobby, the youngest of the party, had a tendency to giggle and Stephenson made great play of silencing him, with a long wagging finger of one hand waving beneath Nobby's nose while Stephenson's other hand was held to his pressed lips in gestures of silence. Harden and myself were I think too tired to show our stupor in anyway other than to stumble drunkenly forward in the darkness, happy but tired.

That we were not quite in *'compos mentis'* was proved in no uncertain manner. Fraser, who was our guide, led us we thought surely enough along the road back toward our cave. After a while he stopped and drew into the trees at the side of the road. We gathered round and he told us that he was not quite certain about it all but he believed – yes he was almost sure - that he had passed the spot where we should have turned off the road to cross the river. Well, that was simple enough we assured him, all we had to do was return until he located the right spot and there we were!

So, we about turned and marched – rather more soberly this time – back along the road. Several times we stopped and suggested a possible place but each time Fraser shook his head. At last we decided we must have come back too far and turned about once more.

By now a grey mist was swirling up towards us from the valley on our right and with it went our chance of finding the correct spot to cross. Finally, we decided we could not spend the night wandering about the road, and we left it to move down into the valley of the river.

In the trees and shrubs cloaked in mist it was as dark as the pit and we stumbled and bumped constantly against unseen objects – bruising and scratching ourselves and tearing our cheap clothing. At one point the ground fell sharply, almost vertically down towards the river and we tumbled in a group some dozens of yards before we fetched up sharply on a lower terrace.

The night was far advanced by now and, quite sober, we were becoming anxious about finding shelter before the morning light exposed us to any early patrols which the Germans were in the habit of sending out. Fraser told us that he just did not know where we were and that he could not guarantee our finding our way back to the cave before daylight.

Second cave hideout & Recce of target

Our plight could have become desperate but we were saved by a quaint tradition of Cretan shepherds, in the form of a chapel that suddenly loomed out of the mist in front of us. These chapels were to be found all over the lower hills of the island, usually roughly built of local stone – held together by home-made mortar and stood about 15ft high. They were usually dedicated to some local saint and the only furniture found inside would be a crude statue portraying the saint in classical Byzantine style. This one was roughly circular in shape and no more than 10ft diameter. The entrance was low and led into a dark evil smelling interior. We did not object to the smell however and laid ourselves wearily on the earthen floor to sleep among the deep layers of goat and sheep droppings. The shepherds who prayed in the chapels were not averse to using its shelter for their charges as well as themselves.

It was full light when we awoke and, the mist having lifted, we found the inside of the chapel bathed in sunlight streaming through a small unglazed opening high in the rough wall.

The problem arose now as to what we should do. To stay in the chapel meant a day without food and possible discovery by any wandering Cretan working in those low hills while to leave and make our way back to the cave would also be to court observation and the usual possibility of unwitting betrayal. We discussed the point for some while and eventually it was decided by all of us to risk the journey back to the cave now while it was yet early.

So, we left the shelter of the chapel and descended quickly to the riverbed. The banks of the river were pretty thickly shrouded in bushes and trees which provided us with cover. We followed the riverbed for some distance until Fraser picked up a landmark and we found ourselves only a matter of half a mile from the ravine in which our cave was situated.

We scrambled quickly up to the cave without meeting any strangers and thankfully settled down once more into the monotonous but comparatively safe existence in that shelter. We were lucky to have made our journey to Manoli's village and back without trouble and in retrospect it appeared to have been an unnecessary risk to take but we all agreed it had been worth the chance we had taken. Anyway, no trouble had come to us so we forgot the incident – looking forward once more to the prospect of the fast approaching day of the job for which we had come to Crete.

CHAPTER 41

THE RUSSIAN COOK AND THE POTENTIAL POISONING OPERATION

The other incident which enlivened the days was one which does not in my opinion reflect very much credit upon us or our companions. One day a partisan hurried into the cave and held a long and earnest conversation with Fraser. Stephenson listened in and as he scratched his face, I could see that even that stoic was moved to something like excitement at the *andarte's* words.

When the conversation was finished Fraser told us the story. It appeared that on the edge of a large village to the north of us was a house which was occupied by a German garrison. There were twelve soldiers in that garrison, and they were served, as so many Germans were, by a Russian prisoner of war who did all the chores for the troops – their cooking, washing and cleaning. The *andarte* had met this Russian while the latter was drawing water some distance from the house and in some way the Russian and the Cretan held conversation with each other. Neither spoke the other's language but apparently, they each had a smattering of very poor German and used this hated tongue to convey to each other their common hatred of the people whose natural language it was.

The Cretan was convinced by the Russian that the latter would do anything to help destroy Germans and effect his own escape. The first he would do in order to qualify for the *andarte's* help in the second. The *andarte* had said no more but came to Fraser with the suggestion that here was an opportunity to kill a dozen Germans without risking wholesale massacre of *andartes* in an attack on the garrison.

Fraser asked his ideas and having digested them he passed them on to us. It was too obvious of course. The Cretan had proposed that we provide the Russian with poison with which to lace the Germans' food and when they had succumbed, the Russian would walk away to be escorted to the shelter of the

The Russian cook and the potential poisoning operation

andarte HQ. We none of us liked the idea, although the other Cretans jumped on the scheme as a brilliant proposition. Stephenson perhaps disliked it least, but he had more reason to hate Germans than most of us. We talked it over for hours, weighing the possibilities against each other. If we helped the Russian to do this thing it would be an inhuman breach of all war convention. But war was not conventional – the Germans themselves had demonstrated that here in Crete. They had descended one day on the village of Rhodakino – near our landing place – and commandeered everything that took their fancy from wine to women. Most of the menfolk of the village were fishermen or shepherds and so were away from home at the time. One had however returned during the raid and found his daughter had been raped by a group of German soldiers. He went out into the village like an avenging angel and with his bare hands had attacked and killed three soldiers one after the other before taking his son and moving into the safety of the hills.

The response was quick and final. The troops burnt the village to the ground, bayoneting three women and children who had not perished by fire. The menfolk returned to the village to find a cemetery – this was an example of German war conventions.

So, this argument did not impress the Cretans during our discussions in the use of poison. Another objection was that if we destroyed the Germans then would not their compatriots descend on the village and take similar reprisal as they had done at Rhodakino. The reply was that if the evidence was clearly left that the Russian prisoner of war was responsible even the Germans could find no excuse to sack the village. And so the argument proceeded all that day with us weakening in the face of the enthusiasm of the others.

Ultimately, we gave in and Fraser provided a phial of poison the nature of which I do not remember and handed it to the Cretan to take to his Russian friend. The man left, darkness fell, and we saw him no more that night. We passed a night and day of conscience probing discussion and thought, trying to convince ourselves of the justice of the action. It was no use, at least for me. To shoot an enemy in the heat of battle, to bomb him from aeroplanes, to blast him with mortars or even attack and kill him from ambush, these things, though unjustifiable at any time, at least were commonplace in war. But to use poison seemed to me then and still does, the lowest and most despicable way to dispose of your adversary. True, ours were not the hands that administered the death, but we provided the poison and approved the act, and my conscience could not accept the rightness of the act whatever the circumstances.

We waited anxiously for the following night to fall and after darkness we looked constantly out of the cave for signs of the Cretan returning. At last, we heard the rustling of footsteps on the track and in a moment the partisan walked into the firelight followed by a short nondescript figure in a shabby grey uniform.

The Russian was certainly unattractive. He was in a dirty, shabby, German uniform without badges or regimental marks of any kind. It was too large for him as he was no more than five feet tall. Although his body was slight, he had a plump pink face which was topped by a completely bald pate. His face was not as I imagined Russians to be, that is, Mongolian in cast. Rather could it have been the rough rugged countenance of the East Anglian farmer. It was nevertheless ugly, and he made no sort of impression on us at all in the beginning. On being addressed however his face split in a huge grin and at once he was transformed from a sulky Asiatic into a cheery European.

The Russian had a name of course, but I forget what it was. We christened him Joe, after the father of his country, and Joe he remained whilst he stayed with us. He could speak no word of Greek nor English and as I was the only person who had any German, I acted the part of interpreter and he and I held long painful conversations in an atrocious tongue with accents that would have shamed a low class Berliner.

Joe told me that he had carried out the murderous task of poisoning his captors very successfully. It had started the previous evening when our *andarte* had delivered the small bottle to him secretly before he prepared the Germans' supper. He had, he told me, given them the usual sort of stewed meat with that beastly German Army invention *Knäckebrot* – a very poor imitation of the sort of crisp wheaten biscuit that Englishwomen sometimes eat to provide sustenance without increasing their weight. The Germans had finished their meal and called for coffee. This was ready for them, and Joe took it into their room after pouring the contents of his poison bottle into the coffee can. German *ersatz* coffee has such a vile taste that it easily concealed the flavour of the poison, and the doomed men drank up without complaint – one even asked for a second mugful, Joe told me happily. He had no idea of the length of time the poison required to act in and he cleared up the dishes nervously waiting for the first signs of trouble.

Apparently, it took an unusually long time to work for the Germans retired to bed still in good health. Joe by now was in a great state of nerves and wondered whether to wait and see or try to escape before the thing proved to be a damp squib. He stayed in however and his patience was rewarded by a squeal of agony from a German bunk. The howl woke the others, and, in a few minutes, they too were stricken. Joe described the following proceedings with all the graphic detail that a limited vocabulary allowed and he made me feel sick.

I told Fraser of the success of the thing and hoped to leave it at that, but he insisted on the details, so I tackled Joe once more. For the sake of brevity, I will merely say that of the dozen men in that garrison, eight died during the night

The Russian cook and the potential poisoning operation

and the others the following morning. One had had the strength to telephone to the nearest German military medical centre and report and the morning brought an MO and a couple of orderlies.

They did their best, but the potent liquid had done its work on the poor devils and not one lived to see another dawn. Joe had left the house soon after the first alarm and was anxious to leave for other pastures, but his *andarte* guide took a morbid interest in the proceedings and they stayed nearby to watch until the German doctor arrived, when they had gone to ground.

After getting all the horrid details from Joe I tried to find out if he had any feelings of conscience or regret at the action but his enthusiasm for the whole affair proved that such feelings did not exist in this savage little beast. This increased my revulsion, but I was impelled to try to ascertain the motives and reasons of this cold blooded little killer.

So, during the evening I talked to him again and got his story in some sort of form. Joe was in fact a farmer who toiled the land on the banks of the Volga near to Astrakahn on the Caspian Sea. His was not a collective farm – no, just a piece of ground that was not good enough to be taken over by the State and for some years he had been left alone to toil on his plot of land with his wife. They had no family – much to his regret – and when the war came it became abundantly clear to Joe that they never would. He was well into his forties then and along with all his neighbours he had been pitchforked into the red Army as an artilleryman and put against the Germans in the summer of 1942. His war had not lasted long for in a month or so of bitter fighting his battery had been overrun and he had been captured and much to his surprise not murdered by the Germans, although he did see their tanks running over the bodies of wounded Russian gunners and had watched the following infantry machine–gunning the disarmed Russian prisoners.

Joe together with a few hundred of his compatriots had then had an indescribably wretched time for the best part of two years. They had been marched – with short periods of transport - right across Russia to Germany from one camp to another. Then without pause they were again marched forth into Europe, finally coming to a halt in France, where the Germans had dumped them in a filthy decrepit collection of huts in a desolate valley. He arrived in France early in 1943, one of a much depleted group of Russian PoW's. Most of his comrades had died of exposure, starvation, exhaustion and brutal treatment on their stupendous journey. Their food had been less than the minimum to maintain life and when I asked how he survived he shrugged and explained that when the food was distributed some of his comrades were dying and too weak to eat so he and the other few survivors had augmented their rations with those of their dying companions who logically enough did not need the food.

I looked and felt disgusted with this confession, but Joe did not seem guilt burdened as he continued his story. It appeared that the Germans now revealed their reason for keeping a few Russians. They offered these starving, naked and exhausted men food, clothing and the comparative comfort of Army life if they would accept the gracious Fuhrer's uniform and swear allegiance to the Reich. Not that the Russians would ever be asked to fight – No, they merely wanted loyal camp followers who would go to the garrisons in the newly acquired colonies of Greece, Crete, Yugoslavia etc. and serve the brave German soldiers who were stationed in those countries.

Joe told me that he had of course refused, although many of his weaker willed compatriots had succumbed to the temptation and left for unknown parts. He had remained with the other Russian heroes in France in that appalling camp until the winter, watching the others die around him in the squalor. With the winter rains however came floods and soon their camp was under water. The Germans could not move them, keeping them in the waterlogged compound under the eyes of machine gun towers. Even their few belongings were several feet deep in water and after several days of living, sleeping and working soaked to the skin, Joe and those of comrades who could walk offered their allegiance to the Reich and so he came to Crete, where he had been stationed for nearly a year.

Although Joe did not show any signs of the hard treatment he claimed to have received, we were inclined to accept his story – so detailed was it and as he had had some months at a reasonable living standard it was feasible that he could have replenished the flesh he must have lost since his capture. We also knew that most German garrisons on Crete had Russian servants so his story may well have been true.

He told us that whatever was to be his fate he was happy at having destroyed some of his hated enemies and looked forward, so he said, to joining the allies and fighting once more against the Germans. He could never return to Russia apparently as his country's leaders regarded POWs as deserters and having served - though unwillingly - with the enemy he would assuredly be executed if he ever fell into the hands of the Red Army. He had regrets of course, as he would not see his wife again, but he was philosophical about this as he realised she must believe him to be dead and by now probably mourned him no longer.

So, our little group was re-enforced by one more and a very willing worker Joe proved to be. He accepted chores without question – eagerly offering to do all our small household tasks - and for all his cold bloodedness he soon became popular in the few days we remained at that cave.

CHAPTER 42

THE AMBUSH

At last, the long awaited day came upon us as we had been on Crete a little over a fortnight, although it seemed very much longer, and we were glad that we were finally to do some small thing to justify our presence and earn the hospitality shown to us by our hosts.

Harden and Fraser had decided that the most we could hope to do would be to carry out an ambush and it was arranged that our small party of four, Harden, Stephenson, Nobby and myself, should leave the cave after dark and position ourselves at some vantage point where it was most likely that a target would present itself.

To ensure that some traffic would appear in the road in the following dawn we organised the *andarte* band into a communication sabotaging party. We equipped them with our entire stock of Cordtex explosive fuse and they provided themselves with axes and saws. This party was to roam the countryside between Retimo and the west, cutting down and destroying all the telephone poles they could during the night. This would be certain to call out German patrols on the road and it was one of these that we hoped to attack. The object of Cordtex was swift demolition. It was wrapped tightly round a telegraph pole, fused and fired. The resulting flash was sufficient we knew to cut the average pole cleanly in two, bringing down the upper part of the pole and the wires, which would then be chopped up and destroyed; when this Cordtex was all used up then the axes and saws would be employed.

During our last day we carefully cleaned, oiled and inspected our weapons. I had a Marlin automatic – rather like a Tommy gun but heavier to carry although firing a smaller round. Nobby had a German Schmeisser, Stephenson a Tommy gun and Harden and Fraser American Carbines.

For the purpose of the attack, we all donned our so called uniforms once more – so that in the event of capture we could claim PoW rights and not be shot at offhand, we hoped!

As soon as darkness fell, we ate a final meal of goat flesh and bread and following Fraser we moved out of the cave, down across the riverbed and on to the road.

We marched silently and swiftly towards Manoli's village but about a mile before we reached it, we turned off across the fields for some distance and soon reached another parallel road which wound its way northwards through the hills towards the coast. At one place we came across the bridge that Harden had seen on his original recce and inspected it to see if we could have done any considerable damage. It would not have been possible with our small store of plastic to have done more than dislodge a few feet of the concrete parapet, although we found that the Germans had already drilled holes underneath ready to receive demolition charges should the occasion ever arise when they needed to blow the bridge.

We crossed to the other side of the ravine on this bridge and walked along the road in the shadow of some trees. Suddenly, as we approached a bend, we heard the rumbling of heavy motors. We stopped and climbing from the road up into the trees we took up position ready to attack whatever transport would come round the corner. Nothing came, although the noise continued. It sounded

View underneath the bridge near Koufi. Note the holes on the bridge wall. Could these be the same as those made in preparation to blow the bridge by the German occupiers. (Marshall Family Collection)

The Ambush

like a heavy tank lumbering up the hilly road but although we stayed silent for some while no target came into sight.

We were puzzled and more than a little worried until Fraser gave an exclamation 'of course' he said, 'it's those bloody Junker transports flying out of Suda Bay'. He told us that the Germans used heavy transport planes at night to carry their troops back and forth to the Greek mainland and as we were now very near the coast the airfield was not more than a few miles beyond the hill in front. The character of the country and the trees had distorted the sound of the aircraft engines so that on the still night air they had sounded close and lower than really was the case.

Relieved, we moved back on the road and continued our journey. As we walked the ground rose and turning a corner we found ourselves following the road round a spur of hills at the eastern end of a valley. The road continued past this spur, passed into a redoubt and returned westwards onto the northern arm of the redoubt. When we had reached the middle of this arm Harden and Fraser stopped here and discussed the position, finally deciding that this was a good spot to spend the night and lay our ambush for the following dawn.

We left the road and climbed above it into some thick bushes and trees, finally coming out onto a low cliff some fifteen feet above the road. This cliff was well covered with thick shrubs, and we curled ourselves under convenient bushes to spend the night. After all the waiting and preparation for the great day I had lost the sense of excitement and fear which its prospect had engendered and after a while I fell soundly asleep.

I was woken by Nobby and sat up cold and shivering in the damp air of early dawn. It was not quite full dawn but the sky over the eastern hills was swiftly lightening and as we watched we saw the first bars of sunlight shafting obliquely through two hills on our left, lighting the valley below sufficiently for us to see the details of its topography.

Our small cliff was well placed on a slight bend on the road so that we could see a considerable distance to our right, as far as the next bend westwards of our position and also, we could clearly observe the road where it fell away to the left into the horseshoe formed by the redoubt in the hills. Directly opposite us and lower, the road came out of the horseshoe and disappeared round the opposite spur. Beyond the road on our left the ground rose steeply upward between the shadows of the hills while to the right the valley fell steeply in a ravine which opened out into what was almost a plain bounded on the north by the coastal hills and on the landward side steep mountains arose among which we knew lay our cave home.

As it was obvious the Germans would send out patrols at first light to examine the broken wires of communication, Harden lost no time in deploying his small force. I was placed on the left side of the cliff looking almost straight down the road of which we had come the previous night with Nobby immediately on my right. Harden lay in the centre with Stephenson on his right while Fraser's position commanded the western approach of the road. We were invisible from each other, hidden as we were in the thick undergrowth, so it was arranged that signals would be passed by touch. Harden would pass the signal when he had selected his target, and we were not to attack until he had fired the first shot.

So, we lay waiting and the time seemed to crawl by on leaden feet. Now that we were about to carry out the attack, I found that instead of shivering as I had on wakening, I was now hot and my hands gripping the sub-machine gun become wet with perspiration. I do not remember being frightened – our raid had been so fool proof up to now that I did not believe or even think of the possibility of being caught or killed. No – I was keyed up with tension but had no fear at that point. Nevertheless, when I first heard the engine in the distance my heart thumped painfully, and I wriggled myself deeper into the dead leaves under the bushes.

The noise was soon distinguishable as that of a motorcycle, and it was approaching from the west, that is up the road which lay on the other side of the cliff away from me. I tensed myself even more and waited for the signal of Nobby's foot against my leg. It never came and in a moment with a roar and cloud of dust the motor bike dashed by under my nose.

As it roared down towards the horseshoe, I saw it driven by a German soldier and that another soldier, who might have been an Italian, rode the pillion. They both carried rifles across their shoulders, and they were not apparently examining the countryside. Rather did they give the impression of going to a specific destination in a great hurry. The driver wore the unmistakably German Afrika Korps type cap with its exaggerated peak but the pillion rider no cap at all and his black curly hair looked most unlike that of the *Herrenvolk*. Both men were dressed in faded khaki drill, and each wore an overcoat.

In a few moments we watched the motorcycle disappear beyond the bend round the hill opposite to our perch. The noise echoing round the valley walls died away and peace again settled on the land. I found myself clutching feverishly at my gun and could feel my toes curled into two sweating balls in my desert boots. Slowly I relaxed and looked around me. The others still lay quietly on my right – by twisting my neck backwards I could see Nobby's left trouser leg sticking out of a bush a yard away from my foot. No words were passed, and I wondered what sort of target would prove to be acceptable to Dick Harden. The motorcyclists were not I supposed good enough for him and on reflection it became obvious that we could attack only one target before we made our escape so that it was not worthwhile to destroy a pair of harmless soldiers when bigger game might present itself.

The Ambush

The sun climbed higher above the hill, and I began to feel its warmth seeping down through the tangle of vegetation over my head. The air was deadly silent after the racket of the motorcycle. No breeze stirred the scrub on the valley floor below and though I looked as far as I could see beyond my bushes, I could not see any form of life on the roads or hillsides.

I suppose a quarter of an hour passed in silence as I lay fidgeting uncomfortably in that undergrowth. Then my ears picked up a noise – hard to distinguish at first then gradually across the valley it came more clearly – the sound of men's feet marching ruggedly. No clear cut tramp of disciplined troops but more like the shuffling noise of a crowd of workmen returning from their labours.

At last, we saw them. Round the shoulder of the hill opposite – from the direction in which the motorcycle had vanished. I picked out the first of a group of soldiers. I did not count them but there must have been at least a score of them marching steadily but out of step up the slope round the horseshoe towards our hideout. This was obviously a mixed group of Italian and German troops led by a burly German NCO striding along at their head.

They were all dressed in drill – the Germans in Khaki – some wearing Afrika Korps caps with the usual forage cap- and the Italians – mainly hatless in the coarse light blue drill of their desert troops.

As I crouched tense against the earth I studied their approach. I saw that three or four men carried light machine guns across their shoulders while the remaining Germans had rifles or Schmeissers. The Italians all seemed to be equipped with their standard Carbines with the spike bayonet hinged to the muzzle.

This I thought must be our target. We could wipe out a force of this size without their ever being able to fire a shot. Resolutely but with a pounding heart I aimed my gun at the soldiers at the far end – following their approach with the muzzle of my weapon, waiting for the kick from Nobby to inform me that Harden would attack. No kick came and slowly the enemy troops approached our hide. I could hear them now talking and laughing together with no hint of the imminent danger entering their heads. Closer they came and still no signal to fire.

Eventually they were right under our cliff and the soldiers passed out of my vision. Suddenly an order was given and to my horror the patrol came to a halt directly below us! This was too much! I sweated with anxiety and excitement and tried to stick my body into the ground. I felt certain that the enemy had spotted us from afar and had fooled us with their nonchalance long enough to surround and attack us but apparently, I was wrong. They stopped and most of them squatted down on the sloping foot of our cliff, lighting cigarettes and taking swigs from their water bottles.

I was praying that they would get up and move on when to my utter horror one left the rest and started climbing the slope towards me. I shifted my position slightly to keep under the muzzle of my gun but to my relief he disappeared a matter of three yards away to the left and subsequent sounds indicated that he had left his comrades to answer the call of nature.

After ten minutes or so the group rose and forming some semblance of order, they moved off again on the road to the west. They were now out of my line of vision altogether, but I could hear their tramping feet for some while afterwards.

Once more, I relaxed and began to hope that we should see no more targets – the suspense was killing me. Was this man Harden never going to attack? I wondered, would we lay here all day in the baking sun just watching the movements of the enemy until such time they spotted us and we lost the advantage of carefully laid ambush?

I need not have worried. Hardly had the noise of the marching soldiers died away when a new sound travelled across the valley. Again, it was the noise of an engine but this time a heavier vehicle than a motorcycle was approaching.

It appeared around the bend opposite, and I saw at once that this was the obvious target for us. Not even the choosy Harden would overlook this I felt.

It was an open German staff car with four occupants. We could not see their rank, but it seemed to me they could not be anything but officers and accordingly fair targets for our bullets.

The car came round the horseshoe, and I heard the driver change gear to take the steeper slope as he turned towards our hide. It was travelling quite slowly as it neared us, probably no more than 20 miles an hour. When it was a matter of 200 yards away, I felt Nobby's foot kick my leg.

This was it! - I thought. I wiped my hand on my sleeves and took a firmer grip of the gun, waiting for the first shot from Harden.

The car came closer and suddenly it seemed to be moving quite fast. It reached me and I could clearly see its occupants. Before I could study them, it was directly beneath me and I heard the crack of shots from Hardens carbine. I pressed the trigger and the Marlin jumped in my hands as it sprayed bullets down towards the vehicle. The car kept moving however and in a split second it passed beyond my sight. The others kept firing for what seemed an age but was probably no more than five seconds. Then I saw Nobby leap to his feet and shout. I looked up at him and saw him raise his gun and fire away from me. Then he disappeared into the bushes to his right and jumping to my feet I followed him.

We found Harden, Fraser and Stephenson running down the slope to the road. I scrambled down after them and saw how successful the ambush had been. The driver must have been killed in the first few shots and had fallen on

The Ambush

his side so that he was now lying across his dead comrade in the front seat. In falling he must have pulled the wheel with him and crashed the car into our cliff. One man in the back was lying crumpled in his seat but the fourth occupant was gone. Nobby was still up on the cliff, and I heard him fire another burst from his gun. I looked up and saw that the missing German had apparently leapt out of the car and was now running up the road to the west.

At Nobby's firing the fleeing German flung himself to the ground but rose again and at once raised his arms. We shouted at him again and slowly he walked back to the wrecked car. When he reached us, I saw for the first time a man in terror of his life. His eyes were staring, his mouth was open, and the sweat streamed from his forehead. He kept his arms stretched to their fullest extremes above his head and I could see that his whole body was shaking. The poor devil – I felt sorry for him and realising he thought this was an ambush by *andartes* who gave no quarter – I told him in German, 'Do not be afraid – we are British'.

He glanced at the car and at once he seemed to forget our existence. He moved to the back seat and looked at his comrade. He raised his head and looking at me said 'he is not dead but wounded'.

This man's fear was quite gone now, and he reached in and half lifted, half dragged his comrade out of the car. Under our direction he laid him on the slope some 20 yards away from the car round the bend of the road.

Harden and Fraser examined the car and its remaining occupants. They found to their disappointment that the men were not officers, and the highest rank was that of the driver's companion who was a Gefreiter. There was a collection of signals equipment on the floor of the back seat – a couple of drums of field telephone cable, some telephones and the usual gear of a signals troop. Strapped to a central pillar were three rifles and slung on these was a belt with a holster containing a Walther automatic.

We left all this heavy gear which was worthless to us – taking only the automatic pistol which was handy to carry and examined the wounded man. The two men in the front seat were very obviously beyond all human help so we left them in the car.

To ensure the total destruction of the vehicle Nobby placed a Lewes bomb under the bonnet and Harden inserted another bomb in the petrol tank.

The German who was unhurt quite ignored us and was gently cutting away his wounded comrade's trousers from the hip. We saw from the mess that the wounded man had been hit several times in the right groin. His body lay inert, and his face was literally grey and shining with moisture. That he had lost a great deal of blood was all too obvious and equally obvious was the fact that he would not live very much longer. However, to ensure that he did not end his life in agony Harden took from his own first aid kit a syrette of morphine and thrust the needle into the dying man's shoulder. He looked at the other man and said carefully '*morphium*'. The German nodded and Harden handed him two small tablets of morphine and at his direction I told the German haltingly that they must be given to his comrade in one hour if he had not died or been rescued in that time.

I was surprised at the attitude of the German who was unhurt. I had expected fear, hatred or at best interest but once he realised he was not to be shot out of hand, he showed complete indifference to us – giving all his attention to his wounded comrade. We told him that the car would blow up in a few minutes and he just shrugged and turned his back on us.

We had moved away from the car just around the buttress formed by our erstwhile hide and suddenly there was a terrific explosion and we could see pieces of wreckage flying past us down the road as the car disintegrated.

Harden gave the German a sheet of signals pad and we scattered several more sheets around the area of the ambush leaving one in the dying German's jacket. On each sheet I had, under Harden's direction, written in block capitals,

'THIS ATTACK WAS CARRIED OUT BY BRITISH COMMANDOS WHO FOUGHT IN THE BATTLE OF CRETE. ANYBODY FOUND CARRYING OUT REPRISALS ON THE CIVIL POPULATION WILL BE GUILTY AS A WAR CRIMINAL AND WILL BE PUNISHED ACCORDINGLY'

The object of this is obvious, but it was a forlorn hope. We realised that whatever evidence we might leave to the contrary, the Germans would take their vengeance out of the innocent in default of the guilty. We knew it and the Cretans knew it also so that now that the job was done, we were in greater danger than ever of betrayal by the sorely tried *andartes* and their passive compatriots. It behoved us to leave the island as quickly as ever possible and this was our intention of course.

We immediately took the first steps in this direction. The ambush was complete – Germans were killed, their vehicle destroyed – and incidentally a perfectly good stretch of road blocked by the wreckage, and we had disrupted the enemy's communications.

CHAPTER 43

THE BUGOUT

After a glance around Harden gave the order and we set off at once along the road down the horseshoe towards the hills to the east. We reached the bend in a few minutes and here left the road and started climbing rapidly up through some trees towards the saddle above us.

From the first shots of the ambush until the moment we moved off down the road no more than ten minutes elapsed. It occurred to me as I pointed up the hill behind Stephenson that the infantry patrol would not have got very far since they left just a few minutes before the car arrived. It was unlikely that they would have heard the sound of our firing – hilly country muffles and distorts sounds to such an extent. But they could not fail to have heard the explosion as the car blew up and might well retrace their steps to investigate.

We stopped for a second at the top of the hill and looked down over the trees to the scene of our action. To our combined horror we saw, coming round a bend half a mile beyond the wreckage of the car, the patrol of German and Italian infantry. We did not stop to see what happened – it was too obvious.

They would reach the German we left who would tell them which direction we took, and the hunt would be up with our having barely any start on them. The thought put springs in our heels and we fairly raced over those hills. Fraser led us on a zig-zag course down through streams, up rocky slopes, into woods of stunted trees and across meadows surrounded by low loose stone walls. We took the latter in our stride, vaulting over where possible and flinging ourselves bodily over stone walls which were too high to vault.

We slowed down after the first mile to a steady trot but even so, I began to wish I had stayed at home. My heart hammered my chest and felt as though it would explode with the pressure of the air I was forcing it to consume, and my legs wobbled dangerously every time my feet landed on a loose stone.

Although I did not take time off and admire the view, twice as we traced our course I noticed fallen telegraph poles and tangled wires. One had a cleanly cut stump showing while the other showed the ragged evidence of axe strokes. Our partisans had been busy during the night!

We kept on the move for about an hour and suddenly I found that I was beginning to recognise the country. It was as we descended the steep side of a ravine and then followed the course of a stream that I noticed that we had returned to the 'Garden' in which lay our first refuge – the arbour in which we spent our first night in the district. I thought grimly that Giorgio would be pleased to see us now that we had become hot, so to speak.

Soon we scrambled up to the familiar little ledge and cradled low behind the screen of bushes and twigs. It was obvious that we could not stay here long – it was too open, and the enemy patrols could not be far behind. Fraser decided to leave us for a while and make a reconnaissance alone. He was anxious to get us back to the cave without delay but could not risk us running into any patrols that might already be on the roads. The only hope was the communications being disrupted. As they were, our pursuers would have to foot it to Rethymno (recorded as Retimo in the original morse code document) to give the alarm and if they had wasted time in hunting us through the hills before sending a runner to the town, then so much further grace was given us to reach safety.

Fraser went alone as he was the only one in civilian clothes and left us to ponder our future in that lovely little arbour. The morning was well advanced by now and it was very hot. We were all extremely thirsty but could not risk 'exposing' ourselves by going down to the stream that gurgled so tantalisingly at the foot of the ravine below us.

After an hour Fraser[36] returned and told us that as far as he could find out no general alarm had yet been given and we must risk being observed in our uniform. At all costs he must get us back to the cave and plan a future move so we clambered to our feet and set off once more.

We followed a new track this time – a longer and more circuitous route than that of our first journey to the cave. Fraser took us south and west over the hills – keeping in trees wherever possible and at all times clear of roads and habitation. Fortunately, he brought a water bottle with him, and we managed to slake a thirst which by now had become intolerable.

Finally, we found ourselves overlooking the cave and soon scrambled down the track into the safety of its regions.

We found a good number of *andartes* waiting for our return. They were loud in their acclamation of our valiant action and no less vociferous about their own nocturnal activities. As we knew, they had succeeded in destroying virtually all telephone communications in the area and had wreaked so great a havoc that it would probably be weeks before the Germans finally repaired the damage. With all the joyful glee with which the *andartes* shouted, each in an effort to be heard above the others, it was obvious from their frequent glances out of the cave and their repeated questions as to our pursuit that they were all in a highly nervous state. They were not alone in this of course.

The Bugout

We were, each of us, fatigued and hungry yet no one made a move to prepare any food. I doubt if it would have been eaten as, speaking for myself, I knew I was famished but had no appetite. Nevertheless, I was waiting for something and only realised this vaguely, but the tension and excitement was too great to enjoy food.

By mid-day all the stragglers had returned, and each new arrival brought gloomy news of German activity on the roads to the north. This worried us but by now the fatigue and excitement took its toll and most of us in the shade of the bushes near the cave slept, leaving the future to take care of itself.

Towards the end of the afternoon, I was awakened by Stephenson and together we moved into the cave where we found the others crowded at the entrance staring across the river at the road opposite. There was good reason to stare. Moving south along the road was a German TCV and as it passed away from us, we could see that it was fully loaded with troops in battle order. Soon after the lorry had disappeared another came into our view and followed in its wake. These were the first of several TCV'S which passed along the road at intervals of five or ten minutes, and we soon guessed their purpose.

The road ran roughly north and south across the island. We were near the northern coast, and it seemed certain that the Germans were sending troops down the road to the south coast, each lorry stopping a few miles before the preceding vehicle. Probably the troops could then be deployed and commence hunting the country at each side of the road. Thus, as our route back to the coast would be parallel to and comparatively near the road it was likely that if our journey was too long delayed we would almost certainly run into one or more of the searching patrols.

Our future was decided at once. We could not stay here any longer. Eventually a lorry would stop near the cave and a search would soon reveal its existence to the enemy. By the same token, the longer we waited the more widespread would become the search to the south of us and the greater the chance of being intercepted on the way to the coast.

Fraser acted immediately. He dispersed the *andartes* to their homes and hides, retaining only two to act as guides. He arranged for everything that was not portable to be securely hidden and then we methodically removed what traces we could of occupation from the cave and its environs. The charging engine and fuel in the inner cave were fairly safe from detection unless the Germans used local guides who knew the cave and its almost secret inner chamber. If they were found – well it would be too bad. Fraser would be informed on the grapevine and would know not to return to this hide.

Having eaten a hurried snack and filled our water bottles we formed up ready to move off. In the party were Fraser, Harden, Stephenson, Nobby, Fraser's wireless operator, Joe the Russian and myself escorted by two *andartes*. Fraser was mournful at our prospects. We rightly argued that we were too many to hope to avoid observation and too few to hope to avoid defeat if we were attacked. Still there was no cure for we had to go and go in a group, so off we went.

There was more than an hour left of daylight as we went, and we were very grateful for it as the speed set by the *andartes* was not one we could possibly have held if we had to travel that unknown country in darkness. We followed no tracks – simply went straight up the hill behind us, across its top to another and greater hill then eventually into the mountains beyond.

I suppose we must have put some 2 miles between us and the cave before darkness fell – 2 miles on the map that is. Probably more like 5 miles if the distance covered by our feet had been levelled out.

In a very short time, my old enemies were back with me – a sore back, aching feet and shortness of breath wind.

Things were worse this time than our original journey for we had landed after weeks of training in the best of condition and well fed. Now we were doing the same journey but over a new and rougher route, after idling in a cave for three weeks or so and eating only what we could get from our generous but poorly provisioned hosts. Little wonder that we found this new march strenuous and intolerable but tolerate we had to, or fall into the Germans' hands with the best hope a year or two in a PoW camp or worst an unpleasant death at the hands of the Gestapo who had published their intentions if they ever caught any of our unit.

When night came it was with almost total darkness. The moon which had been full when we reached the island had waned and all we could hope for was the slim melon slice of the new moon late in the night. So our progress at this stage was slow and painful. To help matters we passed over the shoulder of a mountain and found a road, almost no more than a donkey track leading in the direction we wanted. We made good time while this track lasted but after a few miles it swung sharply eastwards and we had to leave it once more for the stony hillside.

The night was warm, and we sweated like horses. Being a bad marcher, I had consumed most of my water by now and was nearly expiring from thirst when we topped another rise and found ourselves following a gentle slope into a vineyard. We stopped here and I gorged myself on the cool bitter little grapes which were ripening on the vines. I was surprised to find a vineyard up here and apparently miles from any village, but Fraser said that it was probably tended by the men of the valley to the east and that the grapes grew best in the hill vineyards.

After a short rest we carried on again towards the mountains looming darkly to the south. We were in a small plateau, and I guessed about halfway across the island. This small plateau was probably the same that spread out and down into the central plain to the east which we had crossed on our way north, so long ago, it seemed.

We reached the foot of the mountains in another hour and finding a small stream here we stopped again. This was the last time I saw Fraser for he told us he must leave us and strike westward across the island to meet a parachute drop of supplies being made in a dropping zone some miles away that night. After giving instructions to his operator as to their next rendezvous he shook hands, and we watched his slim form in its dirty black shirt and breeches and stinking sheepskin boots climbing up the slope to our right.

Fraser took one of the *andartes* with him and after he had gone Harden held a council with the remaining Cretan and us. We decided that we could not face the mountains that night and that we would camp there in the trees, starting at first light on our way up the steep cliffs ahead of us. The Cretan was not happy at the idea of moving in the daylight, but we over-ruled him – in our unvoiced, we said we would rather he bagged than stumble up that frowning wall of rock in darkness. So, we slept.

True to his promise the *andarte* woke us at dawn and after eating the few bits we possessed we dragged our protesting bodies forward to the assault of the mountain. It was horrifying in prospect, but the horror increased in the actuality. Never have I had a more painful or unpleasant morning as that on the northern slopes on that escarpment.

In daylight we saw that it was impossible to scale the cliffs ahead of us so we moved westwards along the face of the mountain until we found a place that provided a likely means of ascent. It was the dry bed of a stream but so precipitous that it appeared to me that the stream must have been more of a waterfall in the winter.

Anyway, with protesting limbs and mutinous minds we started the climb. Every step was an effort as with each one we had to hoist our bodies a yard higher up that cruel track of stones. As Stephenson said afterwards, 'it was like climbing up a bloody cinema screen!' The sun became unbearably hot overhead and as we looked up its glare was directly in our eyes above the next ridge.

Those ridges! I have, in the course of the war, climbed unwillingly up many hills and rock faces but never have been so heartbroken by the appearance of one false crest after another. The trouble was of course partly due to our inactivity of the past few weeks. Usually when called upon to assault mountains we were prepared by weeks of intensive physical training of marches, swimming and climbing and even the worst of the Mediterranean's bumps did not present much horror to men as fit as we became after that training. But we were completely out of training with little or no exercise and insufficient nourishment and these mountains made us realise the value of training for the job!

Behind The Lines with The SBS: My Life in L Squadron during WW2

As the morning wore on, we crawled up the slopes like crippled flies on a windowpane and after a couple of hours Nobby Clark, normally the fittest of men, began to complain of exhaustion. It was something we all suffered from, and we all voiced our distress at intervals of gasping but Nobby really looked ill with feverish eyes and a hanging jaw as he staggered panting from one stone to the next. Stephenson and I were last in the little convoy and when Nobby suddenly stumbled and fell sideways against the cliff face we dragged our own protesting frames over to help him. He lay against the rocks with his eyes closed and his head fallen on his chest. We raised his head and saw the white strained features and sunken eyes.

Stephenson, who knew more about these things, shook Nobby roughly and shouted at him to brace up. The lad opened his eyes listlessly and said 'It's no good, you push on, I've had it, it's malaria I think.'

We knew he had had that body racking disease in the Far East when serving with the Marines and it was quite likely that being in a weakened state, as he was, that he was at the beginning of a relapse.

'Don't be a bloody fool Nobby,' said Stephenson. 'You've got to make it – come on, you're holding us up.'

Nobby muttered a foul word and tried to drag himself upright but failed. Stephenson looked at me and scowled. He most of all dreaded the prospect of being taken again by the Nazis and it was obvious that as we couldn't leave Nobby behind we should have to stick with him and face being put in the bag.

I said 'What about Benzedrine Steve? Would that do any good?'

'God knows, but it's an idea' he replied and dived into his rucksack for the little bit we all carried.

He forced Nobby to raise his head and open his mouth and thrust two tablets of the stimulant between Nobby's teeth. Nobby started gulping and Stephenson then gave him the last of his precious water.

Again, Stephenson showed his old companion's wisdom – the rest of us had emptied our water bottles by that time and were now all suffering the desperate pangs of thirst.

Nobby lay back but he had his eyes open now. Stephenson grabbed his shoulder and motioned to me to do the same. We dragged Nobby into a sitting position and then rolled him forward so that he crouched against the rocky path.

Then the pair of us heaved on him until, protesting, he started once more to move slowly upwards. By this time Harden and the Cretan were some distance higher than us. They had stopped but on seeing our ministrations they moved on. It would do no one any good for us all to be caught in one place and it might be possible for them to get help back to Nobby once they had reached the top of the mountain.

The Bugout

Moving even slower than before we continued to climb. Suddenly, miraculously, Stephenson and I noticed Nobby going strongly ahead of us, taking good strides up through the rocks and obviously recovered from his exhaustion. Stephenson grinned ruefully at me and said, 'Want some Benzedrine?'

'No thanks' I panted 'I know what the after effects are!'

'Me too' he grinned, and we resumed our climb.

The sun was past its zenith when we saw Harden stop and look down at us from a crest. He had reached the top and within a few minutes we had climbed over the last few boulders to find him and the Cretan standing by a well in a small grove of trees.

CHAPTER 44

WIRELESS PROBLEMS

Ah, the blessedness of that water! It was cool, fresh and life giving. Forgetting all the rules about drinking too much on the march we drowned our parched insides on the heavenly stuff. Then we lay down in the shade of the few trees and relaxed, letting the tension and fatigue drain away from our bodies.

Harden was too wise to let us rest too long, however. He knew that the longer we stayed there the more reluctant we would become to resume the journey. Although we were relatively safe here, he felt rightly that true sanctuary lay only at our destination at the headquarters of the mountain dwelling partisans.

Accordingly, he strode over to us and unsmilingly lashed us with his tongue until we crept away wearily to our feet ready to resume the journey. As we stood for a moment preparing ourselves, adjusting packs and so on I looked around us. We were on a narrow plateau with what appeared to be a sheer drop behind us – the way we came looked impassable from this angle. Looking down along our route I could see the green and brown plain far below, misty in the sun's glare.

To the south, the way our journey lay, was a gradual slope with a few mountain peaks just clearing the horizons crest and, on both sides, east and west were higher mountains so that we stood in the seat of a chair with the back and sides before us and the distant floor behind us.

Our guide led us off to the east towards the dark brows of the escarpment there and after an hour's fairly easy going we came up to the black rock face towering bleakly above us. My heart sank. Not another wall to climb! I prayed!

Our luck was in – we were on a donkey trail crossing the mountain from north to south and instead of going further east over the higher range we turned south to follow the track towards the coast.

The trail followed the line of the mountains to the east, and we soon cornered the shoulder and lost sight of the plain which we crossed the previous night. Now we were hemmed in with hills all round, but the trail unnervingly found the cracks and crevices between the rocks as we moved steadily upward on the rising ground.

Wireless Problems

Late in the afternoon when we were feeling exhausted again from the unbroken routine of walking, walking and still more walking we broke out from the black rocks of the hills and found in front a smooth round hillock rising gently from the rugged countryside. At its top were some roughly made sheep pens and we could see men gathered round the structures staring in our direction.

Our Cretan guide, tireless as they all seemed, increased his pace, grinning at us and pointing ahead. We had, it appeared arrived.

When we reached the men on the hill they greeted us warmly. Lifting off our packs, shaking hands, laughing and jabbering madly all at one time. Their leader Marko was a short man. Nearly as broad as he was long with very dark skin and thick black hair bursting out from a filthy black cap and a huge Cretan moustache obscuring the lower half of his face. He was dressed in a German uniform jacket, British Army breeches and sheepskin boots and appeared to be as dirty as any Cretan I had yet met. He gave us a hearty welcome to his den– the sheep pens- and he offered us to eat delicious new bread and fresh sheep's milk.

We squatted down with relief, took the food and drink and relaxed. It looked as if we were to be made at home here and primitive though it all was, we didn't care – we should be on our way home in a day or so – we thought!

It was dark by the time we settled in our new temporary home so after chatting awhile with our new friends we moved into the shelter of one of the pens which had been roofed over with branches and sacking and made ready for the night. I was so tired after the exertions of the last twenty-four hours or so that I slept like a log – disturbed only by the fact that Marko was sleeping on the ground with his head level with my feet so that his feet were only inches from my nose. The fact that he never removed his boots or socks to wash was only too evident but apart from making a mental note to avoid this position, should we spend more nights in the pen, I slept.

The following morning, we set about making our arrangements to be picked off the island, so I went in search of my wireless. When we first arrived on the island weeks before Hugh Fraser had decided that my signals equipment was too heavy to have to haul across the island and had handed it over entirely to this particular group of *andartes*. It had consisted of a radio set, a charging motor, two batteries, a four gallon Jerry can of petrol and a can of oil.

After much explaining of what I wanted to the *andartes* who seemed strangely unable to grasp the point, I finally made the mud clear and a small party of them disappeared into the mountain fortress to recover my gear.

It must have been hidden some considerable distance from our camp for it was several hours before they returned. Fretful hours, for by now we were all anxious to be taken off the island before the German net closed in – as it inevitably could – given sufficient time.

At last they arrived wreathed in triumphant smiles with the gear – or most of it – loaded on the back of a pair of donkeys. The can of oil had completely disappeared and although Stephenson in his best Cretan dialect explained carefully what it had been like not a single man there admitted to having ever seen the can let alone hidden it!

The jerrycan was also empty of petrol and similarly the *andartes* denied any knowledge of its contents. One man who declared he had carried it on arrival even explained – with a demolishing reasonableness that it could never have had any petrol otherwise he could never have been strong enough to carry the full can.

It seemed a matter of small consequence however as I had originally taken the precaution of filling both the fuel tank and the oil sump of the charging motor before we handed it over on our arrival, so that even if the batteries were flat, it could still be some way of charging them for long enough before the motor died of starvation.

I rigged up the set, laid my aerial and connected the batteries in turn as I had supposed they were both flat. On examination I found that one of them was even bone dry – all the electrolyte having drained out through the air vents in the plugs when the battery was stood upside down. Only a Cretan could be so dim!

Displaying a masterly patience I disconnected the second battery – examined it and found it had at least its fair quote of electrolytes. So, I prepared to charge it and set up the motor for the purpose. For some reason the sticky fingered *andartes* had opened the petrol in its tank as this was still full but – destroying blow! – the sump was dry of oil. A tell-tale stain on the base showed that this too had leaked away when they had stored or carried the motor on its side.

Our plight seemed hopeless as unless I could get a message through to Cairo, they would probably write us off as we were so long delayed and had almost certainly by now corralled the boat which should have been making the trip on alternate days in the hopes of picking us up.

I stood staring at the set with a circle of *andartes* standing round jabbering at the tops of their voices and worst of all grinning amiably at me as though the failure to raise a spark of life from the set was a huge joke.

Harden and the others made usual sort of infuriating suggestions that are always made by the layman to the expert whose magic equipment has failed him. I explained carefully and restrainedly that without a charge in the batteries I could not work the set and without oil in the motor I could not charge the batteries. I even apologised for never having taken a course in telepathy so that I could not transfer a message by thought and without this any hope of contacting Cairo were doomed to failure.

Stephenson then made the bright suggestion that the Cretans may have some oil somewhere but on making enquiries this proved negative. Then our *andarte* showed signs of excitement and jabbered at Stephenson who shook his

Wireless Problems

hand and said, 'This character says he can get hold of some olive oil but I don't suppose that would help would it?' It seemed pretty useless, but I grasped at the straw and asked him to get the oil and we could try it.

After a while the *andarte* returned, and I duly filled the sump with a pint of the watery looking olive oil. I had never heard of it being used in this role but anything seemed better than just praying!

Having connected the battery I swung the engine into action and after sweating at it for what seemed hours it fired and continued to putter protestingly. Even so I knew this could not last and after a quarter of an hour the whole of the motor was nearly red hot. I switched it off and let it cool for a similar period and then repeated the dose.

At the end of a long and arduous day at this disheartening job and using up all the olive oil in southern Crete as it appeared to me, I had induced some life into the battery.

Then came the great moment. I rigged the set again, connected the battery, switched on, turned the aerial and tapped out my emergency call sign to Cairo. Joy of joys they heard me! As soon as I had their ok I tapped out the signal already prepared by Harden and didn't stop until it was complete. Cairo again acknowledged and asked if I could receive a coms signal. I replied that I was not able to and said I would listen out in four hours' time for the reply and closed down. By this time the battery strength had weakened again, and I was afraid that I would not be able to operate again.

After running our charging motor again in the same way for the full four hours I again had enough life in the battery to listen out for Cairo and managed to take their signal. By the time I closed down it was after midnight, but I settled down and transcribed the message which told us that the boat would pick us up the following night at midnight.

The relief in our minds was reflected in our behaviours and four thoroughly exhausted but happy men scrambled down once more to sleep in the sheep pen – Marko's feet notwithstanding.

The sun was high over the mountains to the east when I woke. I lay on the dusty floor of the sheep pen watching the strip of sunlight narrowing at the entrance and looked around me. Stephenson was still asleep next to me but Nobby, Harden and the *andarte* were missing. As I lay there listening to the sounds of their movements and voices outside I felt reasonably content at the thought that tomorrow I should wake in Tobruk harbour after we had been collected by the Fairmile.

Nobby stuck his head under the skins which formed the roof of the pen and said, 'Come on, rise and shine we've got a visitor.'

I climbed out of the pen, waking Stephenson as I moved, and walked out into the heat of the sunlight. I was still drowsy after the late night and excitement of the previous day and the steady warmth of the sun did nothing to wake me up. As I stood there yawning and scratching my head, I noticed that the *andartes* were standing in a group a few yards away.

In the middle of the group was our visitor. He was a Greek priest whom I learned had heard of our presence and had made the journey specially to see us from his monastery some miles to the east of our camp.

He was a large man and looked magnificent in his flowing robes as he sat on what looked like the smallest donkey on the island. His face was encircled by a luxurious black glistening beard and crowned with long flowing hair of the same quality. His hair supported a tall black hat and his skin was dark brown and as smooth as a woman's. As I approached, I noticed that his eyes were bright blue and twinkled with good humour.

As he sat on his donkey he looked enormous, and his size accentuated the smallness of his steed. Yet in no sense did he appear ridiculous in the comparison. Such was his presence and personality that ridicule was the furthest thing from the mind when one met this fine man.

The priest dismounted as I approached and then the sense of the ridiculous did creep in, for in spite of his height on the donkey and his great girth his legs were very short so that he was in fact not much taller than most of the Cretans standing around. Still, he lost some of his presence as he moved among us.

Stephenson appeared then and was greeted gravely by the priest who recognised him from his earlier wanderings in the mountains. He introduced us all and translated the priest's remarks that he admired our courage and so on in attempting to attack the Germans in so small a force. He went on to say that he and his countrymen were themselves ready to lay down their lives to purge the island of its tyrannical masters. It rather spoiled the whole thing because this was so much the sort of vain boastfulness which one heard all over the island by people who in fact did precious little to make life unbearable for the German troops.

The priest stayed with us for the morning and took his share of breakfast – warm sheep's milk to wash down new bread and a coarse local cheese. He left at midday saying he must set off for his home in order to be clear of the mountains by dark but before he parted, he gravely blessed us all and wished us God speed and an early return to help them liberate their island.

After he had gone, we laughed at his stagey clergyman act but nevertheless I for one was impressed by the man as he obviously did his best to live up to the part expected from him.

CHAPTER 45

EXFILTRATION FROM CRETE

We spent the afternoon cleaning up and making ready the gear for transporting down to the beach that night and when all was ready, we waited. This was necessary for although we had not done anything very exerting for a day or two the shortage of good solid food was making itself felt and we were, none of us, as strong or fit as when we first landed in Crete. A long haul down the mountainside during darkness would call for all we had in reserve.

By nightfall all was ready and a long line of men set off from the small plateau and started to make its way down the mountainside. There must have been thirty odd men with we four British men, the now two Russians who had appeared again with their escort and practically the whole gang of *andartes*. Four donkeys were also among those present to carry our heavier gear.

During the first hours' descent things were very difficult for it was pitch dark and the track we were following was steep in places and broken so that a badly placed foot would have resulted in at best a twisted or sprained ankle if not a fall. However, the moon that had lighted our way up that path nearly a month earlier appeared round the mountains in due course and our passage became easier.

We stopped once on the journey down to drink at the brook where we had halted on our way in and by 11.00 pm we were among the heavy scent of the sage bush which lay thickly on the ground behind the beach.

Harden called a halt there and we gathered round him. He arranged that the whole party should stay among the shelter of the bush and the trees while he and I went forward on to the landward edge of the beach to await the arrival of the boat. Standing on the edge of the beach we stared across the faintly gleaming sand at the dark line of the sea. It was only possible to identify the edge of the sea by the slight glitter of the surf. The sea stretching beyond was dark and anonymous. No line could be seen where the horizon would be and to me it appeared as though the sea continued upward over our heads like a dome of darkness hiding the enemy behind and what we hoped were friends in front. Harden and I stared into the darkness searching for the blink of light which would tell us our ship had arrived. We were still staring miserably with smarting eyes an hour and a half later, wondering whether the faint flicker of a torch a half mile away at sea had been missed by our two pairs of eyes.

At last Harden called a halt to the vigil and we returned unhappily to our party in the bush behind to tell them that for once the Navy had failed us. All of the men there had been watching the sea as closely as we had, and they all agreed that had the faintest flicker of light appeared it must have been spotted.

After a council of war, it was decided unsafe to stay on the coast during the following daylight hours, and in any case one might have another vain wait the next night unless we were in contact with Cairo. So, we retraced our bitter steps up the mountain once again to the *andarte* camp where we found the Force 133 wireless operator waiting with the four *andartes* who had remained behind. Their surprise at our return was as great as our disappointment but after mutual commiserations we settled down to spend another night, or as little of it that was left, on Crete.

As soon as it was possible the following day, we went through the heart breaking routine of forcing some life into our wireless batteries and once more I managed to get a feeble twitter out of the set – sufficient to get through to Cairo and hear from them that that bad weather had held the boat up. Their last feeble message was to say that the Navy would try again on the next night but one and then each alternate night thereafter for a week. This now cheered us considerably and we convinced ourselves that nothing could stop the Navy from doing it next time.

So, after yet another night and day on the mountain we once again trooped down the now familiar track to the beach. I remember wondering at the time where the Germans were and why they had missed finding us for so long. I spoke to Stephenson about it and he reported Marko as saying that the Germans would not venture into the mountains but had a post round the headland of our beach a place called Rhodakino and south to the west at a second village and would no doubt be looking out for a ship coming to take us off. This cheered me up no end and I almost began to wish the Navy would not come. It appeared from what Marko said that this stretch of the coast was the only suitable place for miles where we might be picked up and the Germans probably knew this as well as the *andartes*.

We reached our beach again and once again spent a fruitless two hours searching the blackness for a light. By two in the morning, it was clear that this was not going to be our night for leaving and we cursed the Navy and returned to our friends, feeling our welcome must be running out. This time Harden refused to return up the mountain and after a lot of argument the *andartes* agreed to find a hiding place for us inland from the beach but within easier reach of it than several hours' climb up and down the mountain.

Exfiltration from Crete

Consequently, we trudged through the bush away from the beach until we reached what appeared to be a jungle in the darkness. We forced our way through the thick bushes and stunted trees down into a deep ravine and made ourselves comfortable for the night under heavy thickets. Daylight hardly penetrated through the very dense growth of vegetation over and all round us and we felt relatively safe from observation.

Food was becoming a problem and we had, none of us, anything like a square meal for several days, existing for the most part on bread and water with the odd piece of stale cheese that one of the other *andartes* had produced from somewhere. Harden got Stephenson to make representations to the *andartes* who were after all our hosts and were the only source of supply we had available. Eventually after much talking and waving of arms a pair of them disappeared and returned an hour later with a dead goat. I learned later that this belonged to one of the dispossessed men of Rhodakino who was in our band, and he had salvaged a few goats when the Germans had sacked the village. Hence the fierce arguing that went on before he was persuaded to part up! Harden gave him one of a very small stack of sovereigns and the goat herd was nullified.

I watched the *andartes* as they prepared the goat for the pot. They stripped its coat, cut it in half down the middle and having carved up the one half flung it complete into a pot of water on a brushwood fire. The other half was stored for future use. I was a little squeamish at the idea that they had neither topped and tailed the animal nor removed any of its less pleasant innards but I felt when I smelt it cooking that I could after all manage to eat the wretched creature now, so ravenous was I.

I was never ready. When the goat was boiled and dished up into our mess cans I stared at the grey greasy mess and saw a piece of jawbone with a tooth or two still attached, an eye floating contemplatively on the surface and what I gave the benefit of the doubt to and called tripe.

Hungry though I was it took a considerable effort to place these revolting morsels in my mouth and then reduce them to a condition capable of normal digestion. I thought I would never feel able to look a goat in the face again after that meal but the following day when we had the other half of the animal, I was overjoyed to find my portion was mostly flesh and found every mouthful succulent and delicious.

The first night in the bracken we did not go down to the beach as we knew this was not one of the alternate nights on when the boat might be expected. The following night we all trooped there once again and waited.

Harden and I once again went onto the beach to watch although we knew we must be early by at least an hour. It was a very hot night and after a time I suggested jokingly that we all ought to go for a bathe in the flat calm sea to

Behind The Lines with The SBS: My Life in L Squadron during WW2

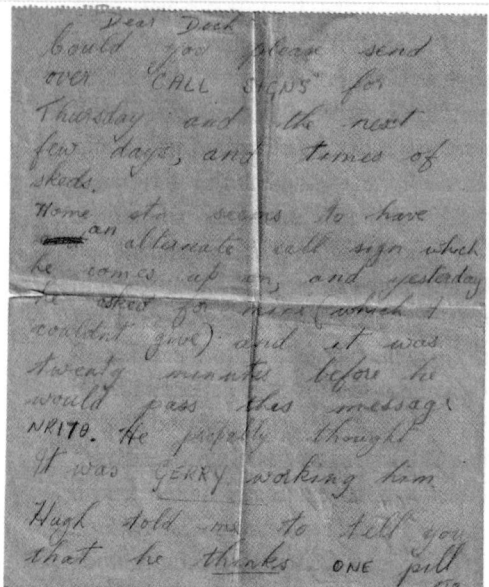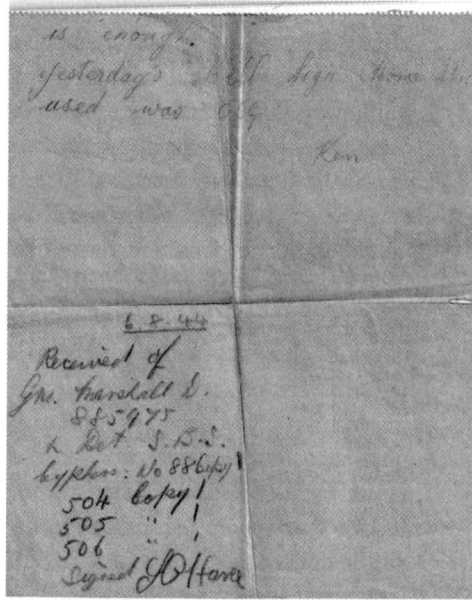

Above left and above right: Decoded ciphers relaying a message from Hugh Fraser to Dick Harden dated after the Patrol had left Crete. (Marshall Family Collection)

pass the time. To my surprise he agreed and said that he could see no reason why the whole party should not have a dip in turns.

I doubled back and told the others and so remote had the German threat become that the suggestion was welcomed by the other British boys and the two Russians. The Cretans could not understand it at all. They considered the whole idea foolhardiness and did their best to dissuade us. Not I think from the point of view of attracting the attention of the Germans, rather from the danger of wetting one's whole body at one time – a thing they could rarely be accused of doing!

So, for an hour, two men at a time rolled quietly in the surf luxuriating in the heavenly feeling of warm sea water covering the dirty dusty bodies which had gone for so long without a decent wash.

Then at midnight – the earliest at which we could expect the Fairmile, Harden gave us the word to be alert and we redressed and returned to our positions watching the sea with a dozen anxious eyes.

At last, it came. I did not see the first flicker clearly as it was to one side of us. My eyes picked up a reflected flash in the corner of the retina and I said nothing, thinking it was imaginary as so many other flashing lights had been on these bitter nights of disappointment on the beach. I turned my head hopelessly in the direction from which I had imagined the light and after a few moments there it was without any vestige of doubt. Harden too had seen it and said 'There it is! Reply at once.'

I raised the Army torch and aimed carefully at the spot where we had seen the light and flashed our letters 'N'. Immediately there was an answering 'T' and after a few minutes' wait we could hear the steady mutter of the motors as the boat approached our position.

After the extraction by ML of Des' patrol, they returned to base at Mersah Matruh, Egypt.

The combined raids on the German fuel dumps in Crete had seen dozens of German personnel killed and 165,000 gallons of petrol destroyed. SBS loses totalled just 2 taken prisoner, Captain John Lodwick (author of the filibusters) and Bombardier Nixon.

Both men later escaped when a prisoner train transferring them through Serbia was ambushed by guerrillas. Linking up with this group, they eventually managed to reach the Bulgarian capital Sofia and were later reunited with L Squadron 134 days after their capture.

George Jellicoe commented on Lodwick's return, 'Ah, you're back. Damned slow about it, weren't you?'

By mid-September L Squadron were on the move again. Leaving North Africa for the final time, they sailed out of the Suez, heading for a new base at Monte Sant Angelo, Northwest of Bari, Italy. Some of the other squadrons had already arrived and the LRDG were also now based there. SBS members who had once taken part in raids during the North African desert campaign were now becoming reacquainted with those previously dubbed the 'SAS taxi service'.

The Germans hold on Greece had weakened and there became an increasing need to 'Defend the Fatherland' since the Allied D-Day landings in France and the Red Armies advance from the East through Poland and Romania. Winston Churchill recognised the Allies had to move quickly to secure Greece's future from the communist Soviet advances.

Operation Manna, as plans for the liberation of Greece had been dubbed, were now under way and an estimated 5000 military personnel deemed necessary to make this feasible.

As a force was being built from all available personnel in the British garrisons across the Mediterranean, plans were being formulated.

These were; to send an advance party into Greece and secure an airfield for landing supplies and which could be used by the RAF.

From there, the RAF could provide the air cover required not only to support the liberating Allied force, but also destroy any enemy shipping used to extract German personnel from the islands of the Aegean. Every available German soldier would be needed to defend the Reich.

Behind The Lines with The SBS: My Life in L Squadron during WW2

On the 23rd September, Major Patterson and 58 members of L Squadron, boarded 6 Dakota Airplanes. From Italy, they flew across the Adriatic and parachuted into the Peloponnese with orders to secure the airfield at Araxos, south of Patras.

Des and Bill were part of that 58.

Met with no resistance, the SBS recovered their scattered supplies and immediately set about carrying out repairs to the runway with the help of local villagers.

Patrols were then sent out on the main road to Patras with orders to protect a bridge, but as was discovered, the bridge had been destroyed before their arrival.

Patrols also moved south towards the Port at Katakolon, from where the Allies hoped to land the Seaborne element of Bucket-force, as it had been named.

The next day on the 24th, Lt. Colonel Jellicoe landed at Araxos. More Dakotas filled with supplies had arrived and 8 Spitfires crewed by 2908 squadron were also there to provide air cover. At Katakolon, an RAF regiment under the command of squadron-Leader Wynne was disembarking along with a mix of other elements of Bucket-force including a section of No. 40 marine commando.

Jellicoe's sights were now set on Patras.

Occupied by up to 900 Germans and an ailing support of 1600 members of the collaborationist Greek security Battalion (GSB) holding the eastern side of the town, the SBS were vastly outnumbered.

It was suggested by Patterson that the GSB might be convinced to surrender their arms if the allied force could assure their protection from the Greek communist ELAS group who were growing in strength across Greece and were signalling their intent for a power grab.

Negotiations began with the GSB for their surrender and stretched across a number of days.

Meanwhile, with their numerical disadvantage, the SBS carried out probing attacks on Patras and its Port giving the impression to the defenders that they were a far superior force in size.

Finally by 1st October, Jellicoe's patience had been stretched too far and an ultimatum was made. The GSB must surrender their arms by 06:00 the following morning, if they wished to secure the protection of the Allies.

It came to everyone's shock and surprise when at 20:00 the very same evening, hundreds of members of the GSB began arriving at the assembly points to give up their weapons. By morning, the entire GSB force had surrendered and quickly it became a logistical problem on what exactly to do with them.

Their surrender though had created a great opportunity for the SBS.

With the east of town now defensively weakened, a combined force of SBS men and those of the RAF Regiment entered in Jeeps reaching the centre of Patras.

The Germans still unaware that the GSB had abandoned their positions were caught off guard but after some brutal fighting were able to drive the British force back.

More RAF Regiment platoon numbers were brought up and soon it became clear the game was up. Over the next 24 hours the Germans began pulling out.

Escaping from the Port while under heavy attack, a troop carrying ferry was sunk and the harassing Allies surrounded the area.

Here demolition charges left by the Jerries were diffused before any more damage could be inflicted.

With this particular battle now over it was celebration time in Patras. Jellicoe and an ELAS Brigade Commander entered Patras in a jeep, flying the Union Jack and Greek flag side by side while civilians headed out onto the streets and celebrated the liberators. Flowers, grapes, wine, hugs and kisses were adorned on the allied heroes.

These scenes were repeated town by town, as the now emboldened SBS continued to head east towards Athens. As their jeeps took the coastal road for Corinth, they fired on the German boats trying to make the canal and to safety. A 76mm gun captured in Patras was used by Maj. Patterson to bombard the confused enemy, who returned fire into the air believing they were being bombed.

Only demolitions to bridges and road conditions on route could slow the progress of the SBS before they reached Corinth on 7th October.

Exchanged fire with the Germans ensued across the canal at Corinth and soon another GSB had been captured. Using a sunken liner laying on its side as a makeshift bridge, the SBS crossed the canal and from here the force split. With three patrols under Charles Bimrose heading towards Thebes and another under Keith Balsillie using a caique to cross into Salamina Bay and on into Piraeus they pushed on.

Maj. Patterson's task now with his diminished numbers of men was to protect the landing strip at Megara which could allow more reinforcements to land and support the advancement. After many skirmishes, they soon arrived in the form of the 4th Parachute Battalion but unfortunately due to high winds, seventy-five percent of the landing force were injured in the drop. With the wounded attended by the local female populace, the rest of the battalion and SBS engaged with the enemy on the approach to Athens.

The liberation of Athens finally came when unopposed and lead by Lt. Colonel Jellicoe and Major Patterson on bicycles, the SBS entered the city in their jeeps.

Behind The Lines with The SBS: My Life in L Squadron during WW2

It was Friday 13th of October. An unlucky date for the Germans who had pulled out of the city just a few hours early.

The Officers and some lucky members of SBS made themselves comfortable at the Hotel Grand Bretagne while other members of the Squadron found themselves equally lucky to be looked after in the homes of local Greek woman.

The next day General Scobie, commander of III Corps arrived and made the hotel his Headquarters.

Meanwhile, wild celebrations across the city were had with thousands of Athenians pouring onto the streets to celebrate the end of over three years of occupation.

Greeting their liberators and expressing their gratitude, the SBS were showered with gifts from the few luxuries they possessed.

The SBS enjoyed the next few days in Athens, soaking up the warm affections of the local population before it was felt the time had come to move on.

It was decided that Lt. Colonel Jellicoe should be promoted to Brigadier and given command of 950 men in the advance north to chase the Germans out of Greece.

However, he would need some additions to his uniform to fulfil the official look of his new position. His sometime driver, John House was sent off to his landlady in Athens who quickly set about finding the correct shade of red material to be used for the tabs on his collar. With help from her neighbours, the material was found and the uniform adjusted. She was very excited to receive the equivalent of ten shillings paid to her, for it was the only money she had seen in years.

In a convoy of fifteen jeeps and four trucks, the 4th Parachute Battalion, RAF Regiments (which had now been named Pompforce) and fifty SBS men left Athens in the push north towards Lamia.

Many bridges had been destroyed on the route but no sign of the German military was found. All that could be seen were clear signs of the destruction left behind during their retreat, as wrecked buildings, booby traps and abandoned equipment were all around. It appeared the RAF Spitfires had been busy during the last few days.

Further pushes north were made with abandoned German tanks and vehicles that had seemingly run out of fuel found on the route, but advances were then delayed with a significant battle at Kozani against the well dug in Germans.

This was the occupiers' last attempt at holding Greece and the SBS found themselves pinned down by accurate fire from the German positions. Relief soon came though in the form of a Battery of 76mm field guns and some well landed motor bombs by the SBS.

Exfiltration from Crete

Eventually, Kozani was liberated and Pompforce continued to push north to Florina near the Greek/Yugoslavian border but it was here that the SBS were ordered to proceed no further.

Returning to Athens, here began the roots of many romantic liaisons between some SBS members and their future Greek wives, Bill Marshall and Les Stephenson being two of those who after the war married their Athenian sweethearts and later settled in Greece.

It wasn't long, though before things began to take a sour turn.

With the political group EAM signifying their intentions for a communist takeover of the country and it's armed Militia, ELAS refusing to lay down their arms, the SBS found themselves caught up in the middle of a power vacuum. Various groups of royalist, communist and democratic minded groups vied for power and the SBS found themselves the target of ELAS aggression.

Untrained in street fighting, the following months saw some of the largest numbers of casualties to SBS personnel in their short existence so far.

CHAPTER 46

ATHENS DECEMBER 1944

Evening in Athens in December 1944 was a time when it was fit only for ghosts to be abroad, for only the supernatural could be sure of moving unscathed from point to point in streets which were like steep sided gorges with rivulets of tracer flowing in both directions as darkness enlivened the trigger happy ambitions of the ELAS and the British troops to wipe each other out. At times the rivers of tracer became raging torrents as some sensitive eye was deluded by the shadows cast by the aerial flares into imagining an enemy's stealthy approach. Then the shattering roar of Bren fire would awaken the less sensitive outpost sentries on each side of the gunner to empty their own magazines at targets no less imaginary than that being decimated by the nervy one.

There was however an island of comparative peace and safety in the centre of the city. This area was encircled by a 'Perimeter' which was an imaginary line drawn by General Scobie[37] a few hundred yards radius from his own HQ. The perimeter was a line of houses usually commanding a view of a road junction and manned by members of SBS patrols, parachute regiments troops and odd infantry sections, supported from time to time by Sherman tanks who usually made their presence known each dawn by drawing up astride a defence point and shattering the uneasy peace of the early day by the roar of their six pounders and rattle of the machine guns.

Inside the perimeter and safe from the danger of sudden attack were all HQ. Included in this happy bunch of 'Base stanchions' were my brother Bill, myself and the remainder of L squadron signallers. We had been ensconced in a disused hotel nearby Scobie HQ since the time a few days earlier when we, together with our patrols, had fought our way from our original billet into the perimeter then being formed. Our own original billet had been in a school which was in the centre of the poor quarter of Athens and from which the ELAS uprising had started.

We felt we had been disloyally abandoned by our patrols when they were sent without us to form their defence points on the perimeter and the sales talk of the squadron commander, to the effect that we were too valuable to risk on the perimeter, in no way brightened our feeling of guilt and uselessness.

After being in this very dissatisfied state of mind for several days and thoroughly bored with having nothing to do but call daily at the Toc H canteen to draw cigarettes and sweets, three of us, Bill, Jock Stewart & I decided one day to have a party in the evening. Booze was scarce and most of the tavernas were closed anyway but a lucky chance led us through the streets to a small emporium where we heard voices behind the darkened doorway. We decided

Des, Bill and Peter Howard holding a bottle of wine. Patras, Greece. Oct. 1944. (Marshall Family Collection)

that even Greek company was better than none and knew from experience that where the Greeks were so would hard liquor be.

We knocked on the door and after the usual silence common to these nervous days, a timid head poked itself round the door and asked in Greek what we desired.

Bill answered *'Ouzo'* and a stream of Greek indicated that this was impossible but by dint of presence from three shoulders the door yielded and we found ourselves in what in this country would be a grocer's shop – a grocer's shop with a liquor licence however, for on the shelves and counter were a thirst making array of bottles of *Ouzo, Retsina, Mavrodaphne, Samos* and other local brews. (wines & spirits)

Bill demanded a bottle of *Ouzo* and after the usual haggling we found by pooling our resources of BMA money, cigarettes and chocolates we could raise sufficient to persuade the owner to part with a large bottle of *Ouzo*.

A further point of persuasion was the fact that we had between us two Colt.45 automatics and a Schmeisser. Bill repeatedly emphasised his point to the owner by tapping him gently on the chest with the muzzle of his Schmeisser. I think perhaps this was the thing which weighted the balance in our favour because the SBS had a fearful and quite unearned reputation of being heartless bandits, pirates, gunmen and what have you. No doubt the green padrone felt it better to sell a bottle of precious *Ouzo* than to wake up in the gutter with ventilating holes in his chest. A completely erroneous idea of course!

Bearing our prize back to the billet we three sat down and gloomily tucked into the *Ouzo* debating the while how we might persuade the squadron commander to put us in a billet on the perimeter with our patrol. Within a short space of time the bottle was empty, and we were full of *Ouzo*, courage and plans. We decided that if they wouldn't let us go to the perimeter, we would go out ourselves and find some excitement.

CHAPTER 47

ATHENS JANUARY 1945

On Thursday, 4 January 1945, a combined patrol of SBS & SAS was moving along a street in Athens, looking for any member of the Greek revolutionaries, ELAS. We had been shooting at each other for a month, ever since GHQ had been ordered to give aid to the civil power in putting down the attempted coup by ELAS to take over the government after we had cleared the Germans out of Greece.

Our Patrol, having cleared the houses in the street in question, came to a T junction, and as we turned into the lateral street we were fired upon by an ELAS machine gunner. Most of us were wounded but the worst hit was John House (one time driver of George Jellicoe in the desert). A bullet took away most of his jaw and he was in a very bad state.

Norman Moran, our medical orderly, bound him up as well as he could with a shell dressing and John and I were then helped by the survivors back to a Bren gun carrier fitted with stretchers, and were driven to the nearest dressing station. A funny side was that, as we were stumbling to the Bren carrier, John's head was lolling on my shoulder, with the result that my windproof jacket became saturated with his gore. Once at the dressing station they thought that I was the worst hit and set about giving me a blood transfusion, until I pointed out that my wounds were slight compared with John's – and they then dealt with him.

To pursue the comedy – after I had been dressed with a head bandage and a sling, I returned to SBS HQ in the city centre, carrying my Carbine and John's Schmeisser and, as I walked through the streets (looking like something out of a Hollywood war film) all the residents clapped and cheered – most embarrassing.

I heard that after the shoot-up a Sherman tank was whistled up and demolished the machine gunner (An ELAS female!) with its armament.

I never saw John from that day on and as we left Athens a week or so later, we heard no more about him. I think most of us thought he had died of his wounds, which were horrendous.

Behind The Lines with The SBS: My Life in L Squadron during WW2

Les Stephenson, Des and Bill in Athens, Greece. Jan. 1944. Note Des' head wound above his right eye. (Marshall Family Collection)

Authors Note

In October 1986 Des visited Perth, Western Australia, for a holiday including a visit to the Australian SAS Association and later the Australian SAS Association annual dinner. To his astonishment and delight, his old comrade and buddy John House and his wife were also there.

John's story is that after being patched up in Athens and Italy he was flown home to Croydon and put into East Grinstead Hospital, where he was under the Great McIndoe for the next three years.[38] During that time they transferred bone from his hips and skin from his stomach on to his jaw and slowly (and painfully) rebuilt his jaw until he looked almost his old original self. Each transfer of bone segment or skin took six weeks and involved his wrist being attached to a sliver of skin on his stomach or attached to his face for the whole period until the living tissue took root, so to speak.

By 1949 he was out of hospital – having married his nurse, Angela, in the best romantic tradition and, finding it difficult to settle down in the UK, they emigrated to Australia where John became a farmer. They retired from the farm in Dongara in 1980 and have now settled in a house near Perth where they appear to be very content with children and grandchildren scattered in different states in Australia.

CHAPTER 48

THE ISTRIAN OPERATION

The liberation of Athens and fighting ELAS was pretty much over by the end of January 1945 as far as The SBS & SAS was concerned

L Squadron were then taken back to Monopoli via Bari in Southern Italy awaiting transport for their next operation which was to take place in Istria (Northern Yugoslavia, now part of Croatia & Slovenia).

Tragically, Major Ian Patterson was killed when on a separate flight to Bari the Dakota plane he was traveling on crash landed after hitting an olive

Des' silk map of Northern Italy and Yugoslavia. (Marshall Family Collection)

tree. Poor weather conditions and navigation problems found the plane off its course. There was only one survivor.

Major Patterson was buried at Bari cemetery.

In January 1945, The German Army had retreated from south-eastern Italy and were heading northwards back to their fatherland.

So once again, the SBS were greeted as liberators by the Italian people, except that this time they were wined and dined by many of the locals.

Colonel Dinky Sutherland was now in command of the SBS Regiment and had ambitions to go to Istria, Northern Yugoslavia in pursuit of the retreating Germans.

Eighteen months previously Fitzroy Maclean, an SAS officer and former OC of M Squadron SBS, had been sent to Istria on a British Military mission as a Soldier/Diplomat (he had parachuted in) in order to assess which of the two Yugoslavian resistance groups had the better fighting qualities against the Germans. He had concluded that of the two groups i.e. the *Partisans* & the *Cetniks*, the *Partisans* were the best allies.

The *Partisans*, numbered over 150,000, were led by Josef Tito (an unknown to the British Government, but who after the war became President of Yugoslavia).

They were (mainly) made up of Yugoslav peasants, left wing and of communist leaning. However, although their political beliefs were generally contrary to the British, their track record in harassing the Germans was far better than the *Cetniks* (who mainly comprised of officers of the former Yugoslav Army and who occasionally sided with the Germans against the partisans). So, the British consensus was to side with the *Partisans*.

With Major Ambrose McGonigal now in charge, L Squadron SBS was sent to Istria, in order to pursue the Germans and were joined there by the LRDG (Long Range Desert Group) who became their land transport.

The LRDG's job in the North African Desert was long over and now, along with the SBS and SAS, they had been operating in Greece and Albania prior to Yugoslavia.

When Des & Bill arrived with L Squadron in Istria, intending to harass, ambush and raid the Germans, they found that the Partisans wanted to be seen by the Yugoslavians as the country's liberators. They were determined to continue their own harassing and defeating of the Germans rather than have 'foreign troops' i.e. the SAS, SBS and LRDG do it for them. As a result, the SBS and LRDG took on the role of reconnaissance (coast watching) and signalling. They travelled around the coastline and near the islands, signalling by morse and in cryptic code the movements and locations of the German Navy in the Adriatic Sea who were transporting German troops back to northern Europe. the RAF then bombed and strafed the German Navy at sea.

So, for twelve days in April 1945 Des and Bill remained busy with their radio sets writing ciphers and sending them by wireless. The LRDG, fondly

The Istrian Operation

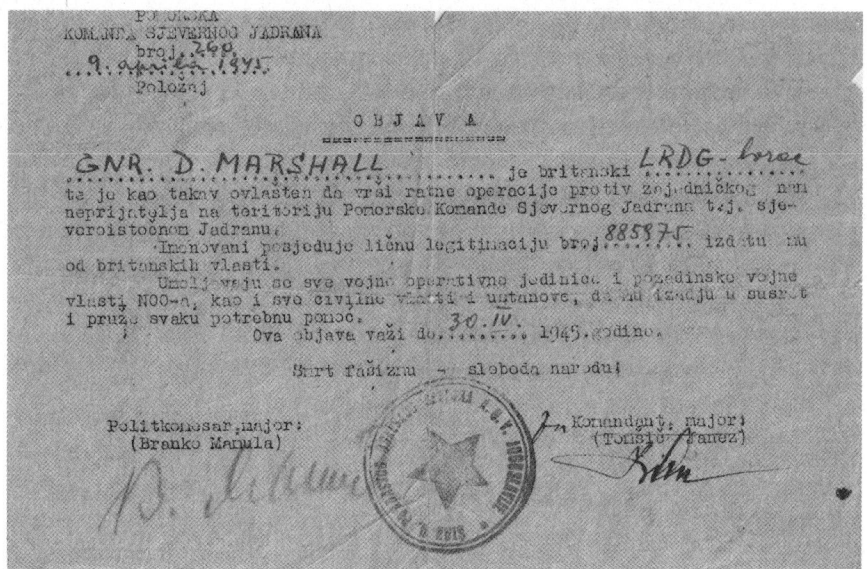

Authorisation 'Permit' document from the Northern Adriatic Command (The Partisans) to carry out operations in the Istrian Peninsula. note Des' rank as Gunner and unit incorrectly stated as LRDG. (Marshall Family Collection)

known as 'Taxi drivers' by SAS/SBS, also took part in the reconnaissance and surveillance in region.

The German Army were by now rapidly retreating from northern Yugoslavia and many were heading for the Brenner Pass in Austria, a conduit en route to southern Germany, intending to fight the oncoming British, American and Allied forces who had successfully invaded northwest Europe and southern Europe.

Where next for L Squadron SBS?

The final order received on 3 May 1945 from the L Squadron Sergeant Major Newlands was to prepare for a parachute operation on to the north side of the Brenner Pass in order to attack and slow down the retreating German troops.

A year previously Captain Philip Pinckney (SAS/SBS) had parachuted on to the Brenner Pass and blown up a railway tunnel used by the Germans. Sadly, he was captured later by the enemy and executed (of course this was yet another Nazi war crime).

Neither Bill nor Des had expected to survive their SBS lives during the Second World War and when they were told by SSM Newlands that they and their comrades need only take x2, twenty-four hour ration packs for this particular operation, they didn't rate their survival prospects as the operation sounded like a suicide mission!

Behind The Lines with The SBS: My Life in L Squadron during WW2

However, on 8 May 1945 as Des put it 'The Germans had the good taste to pack it in' i.e. the war in Europe had ended as the Germans surrendered on that day.

To their great relief, later in May 1945, Des and Bill were flown back to Rome and from there repatriated to England.

Above: Paddy Hills and Des on leave. Rome July, 1945. (Marshall Family Collection)

Left: Des at ''DE-MOB'' May 1946. (Marshall Family Collection)

CHAPTER 49

THE FINAL CHAPTER

As the SBS had evolved from the SAS in North Africa, they had no regimental barracks based in Britain, so in 1944 a temporary HQ had been established at Hylands House near Chelmsford, Essex.

By the end of September 1945 Des had arrived at Hylands House (in the meantime Bill had met and married a Greek lady named Despo and they were living in Athens).

During the Second World War all of the SAS and SBS troops had been selected from existing British Regiments and as Des had originally been a Gunner/Signaller in the Royal Artillery Regiment based in East London but serving across the UK and later the Middle East, he was eventually returned to the 85th Field Regiment RA in the East End of London in order to be "demobbed" i.e. honourably discharged from the Army.

Des was given a civilian suit and all his outstanding military pay and he then went back to his family home in Seven Kings, Essex. He was almost 24 years old.

Before the war Des had worked for Crittall Metal Windows Ltd in Holborn, London WC2, so naturally he re-applied for his job there and was accepted for employment there as an Estimator.

Earlier in this story we had made the reader aware that in 1940 Des had met a young woman called Joan Tingay, who became his girlfriend and whom he saw regularly when on leave and whilst stationed in the UK.

Joan had an important role in the British war effort as she worked in the City of London at the International Telephone Exchange as one of the supervisors. She had worked in London during the Blitz and had narrowly escaped on several occasions, being bombed whilst working at Faraday House. Joan lived with her family in Newbury Park, Essex and they had all witnessed the aerial dogfights between the RAF & German Luftwaffe over the Essex sky, including the shooting down of some RAF pilots who had bailed out over Newbury Park after the dogfights. On another occasion her family discovered a German incendiary bomb hanging in a tree by its parachute and which hadn't exploded, so the UXB team had to be called in to defuse the bomb.

Between 1943 and 1945 Des had few opportunities to see Joan as he was involved in secret work with the SBS in the Mediterranean, Palestine & southern Europe. Rarely did SBS get any leave and if they did it was taken in Beirut, Cyprus or in Turkish waters. But now in late 1945/early 1946, they were able to see each other on a regular basis. Before the end of 1945 they became officially engaged at St Botolph's Church in Bishopsgate and by the end of May 1946 they were married at St Peter & Paul's Church in Ilford, Essex.

They went to Dublin for their honeymoon in June 1946 and took the opportunity to eat as much food as they could including steak, eggs, cheese etc. all of which had been denied to them due to the food rationing in Britain during the Second World War (and which continued in Britain until 1954).

For the next five years they rented flats in the East End of London i.e. Leytonstone & Wanstead. Then in 1952 they put the deposit on a house in Newbury Park, Essex and took out a twenty-year mortgage.

As they both had witnessed so much death and destruction during the six years of the war, they were keen to have a family and over the next fifteen years had five children.

Meantime, although the SAS had been officially disbanded it was reconstituted in 1947 as the 21st SAS Regiment TA (comprising surviving

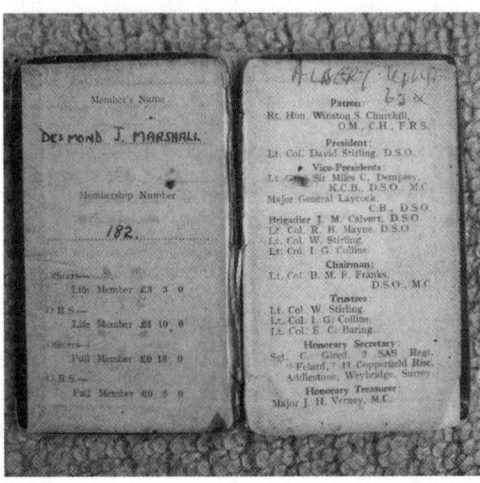

Above left: Des' SAS Regimental Association members booklet. (Marshall Family Collection)

Above right: Des' SAS Regiment membership number truly shows he was one of the Originals. (Marshall Family Collection)

The Final Chapter

members of the 2nd and 1st SAS Regiments from the Second World War) and had a new home in the Artists Rifles Drill Hall near Euston station.

Also, the SAS Association was formed and encouraged the Second World War members to take part in reunions and other activities.

Des & Bill became Association members and Des' membership number was 182. They both attended SAS/SBS reunions in London and met up with their former Second World War comrades, who now lived in the South of England, the Midlands & Scotland.

Around this time the Intelligence Corps (TA) were recruiting as the 'Cold War' in Europe was getting into full swing and the Intelligence Corps were offering former Second World War soldiers with relevant intelligence experience immediate promotion to the rank of Sergeant with NCO's pay.

Both Des and Bill, who were getting bored with civilian life and keen to earn more money in order to finance their mortgages, signed up with the I Corps. (Bill and Despo had returned to the UK from Athens several years earlier).

Des entered The Intelligence Corps (Reserve) in the early 50's and was immediately promoted to Sergeant. (Marshall Family Collection)

Behind The Lines with The SBS: My Life in L Squadron during WW2

By 1954, Des was commissioned as a Second Lieutenant in the I Corps and continued to serve in the Territorial Army and Army Emergency Reserve for the next twelve years. He was transferred from the I Corps to the Royal Engineers and promoted to the rank of Captain and finally to the Royal Corps of Transport as their 'Movements Officer'.

Des top left with other Officers of The Intelligence Corps. (Marshall Family Collection)

Des' Military Medals. (Marshall Family Collection)

The Final Chapter

By 1966 Des had reached the age of 45 and retired from the Army. He went into the Army list as a Major.

Des' war medals and post war medals bear testament to his extensive military service of eighteen years.

In 1979 the Greek Government contacted the British SAS Association as they wanted to invite the Second World War SBS members to a free holiday in Greece and Crete. Des and Joan were among the approximately thirty people who went along where they visited many of the places that their operations had taken place and saw displays of Greek Special Forces troops carrying out parachuting and amphibious military exercises.

Des retired from civilian employment in 1982 and then had seventeen years of happy retirement with his beloved wife Joan. He attended many SAS/SBS

Des and Bill pose with Military Plaques in the garden at 51 Ladysmith Avenue, Newbury Park. (Marshall Family Collection)

Behind The Lines with The SBS: My Life in L Squadron during WW2

Des enjoying a pint at an SAS reunion lunch with Bill Right, Wally Mackenzie left and Des' son Jerry (centre right). (Marshall Family Collection)

Manoli Kanakakis left at an SAS reunion lunch. (Marshall Family Collection)

The Final Chapter

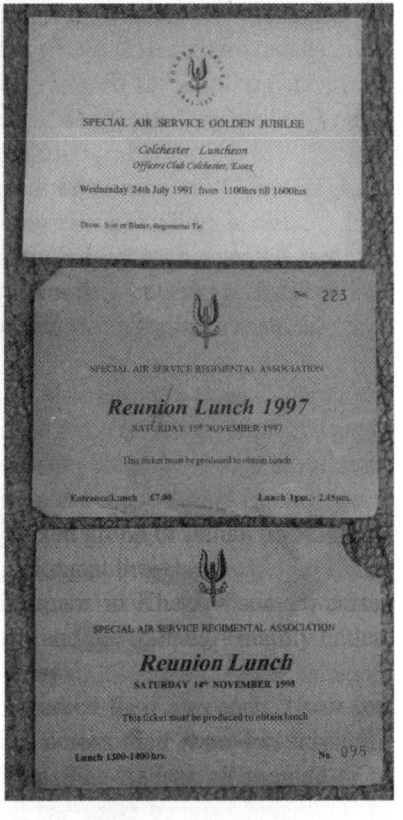

Des attended many SAS Association reunion lunches. Sadly 1998 was the last he attended before he passed away a year later. (Marshall Family Collection)

reunions in London, Colchester and Hereford during that time, the last of which was at the Duke of Yorks Barracks in November 1998.

Sadly, in August 1999 he passed away (he died of stomach cancer).

Joan reached the grand old age of 100 years in August 2021 and received a birthday card of congratulations from Queen Elizabeth II. She was also awarded a medal for her 'essential' service work in the Second World War working as a supervisor in the International Telephone Exchange in London during the Blitz of 1940.

Sadly, in January 2022 Joan passed away (she died of old age).

Des and Joan more than replaced themselves, not only did they have five children, but also twelve grandchildren and eleven great grandchildren.

MAY THEY REST IN PEACE.

Eighty Years Later……………

Twenty-five members of the Marshall family from the UK and Western Australia met up in Crete between 21 August 2024 and 6 September 2024, for our holiday get together and to commemorate a quarter century since Des had passed away by visiting one of the main islands of his SBS operations in the Second World War.

Whilst there we visited the village of Koufi where Manoli Kanakakis had lived and discovered his now 'unoccupied' house. In the courtyard there is a dusty Morris Minor 1000 with an SAS badge stuck on the back window of the car. We met his niece, Katerina (who lives next door) and paid our respects to Manoli at the local cemetery in Koufi where he was buried in 2005.

We also had two liquid lunches (on different days) in the Koufi open air Taverna and BBQ café Amadolakkos.

Behind The Lines with The SBS: My Life in L Squadron during WW2

Left to right, Grandson Robert and Sons Jerry, Iain, and Nick outside Manoli's family home August 2024. Previously visited by Des Marshall 80 years earlier. (Marshall Family Collection)

Manoli Kanakakis 1924-13/5/2005 His last resting place. Note the SAS insignia engraved on the headstone. (Marshall Family Collection)

The Final Chapter

Manoli Kanakakis gets several mentions in this book written about my Dad's (Des Marshall) life in L Sqn 1st SBS, based on his handwritten memoirs.

I had met Manoli several times in the latter part of the 20th century at SAS Reunions in the Duke of Yorks Drill Hall in Chelsea. He was always seen in a tight knit group of SBS Second World War members. Over those years I had the privilege of meeting about a dozen of these SBS Second World War veterans, as well as about a half dozen SAS Second World War veterans.

Manoli was always seated in a wheel chair as during his Cretan SBS operations he had been shot in the back and legs from a machine gun and from that time onwards he was a paraplegic.

Whilst in North-west Crete we also visited the museum of '*The Cretan Runner*' in Asi Gonia and met Nikos Psychoundakis who is the museum curator there and son of George Psychoundakis (the actual Cretan Runner). There is a book of the same name and it features the true story of the capture of Major General Heinrich Kreipe by the British SOE and Cretan *andartes*, which is the subject of the book and film '*Ill Met By Moonlight*'.

We also visited the Cretan '*Monument to the Fallen*' memorial high up in the mountains at Anogia (central Crete). The Anogia memorial is dedicated to the Cretan men and women who had been rounded up and shot during the German invasion and occupation of Crete and had their Cretan villages burnt to the ground by the Germans. The Germans did this as a reprisal against the local population under Hitler's orders as the Cretans and British had killed German soldiers in action. I believe Hitler's order was described as "The Fuhrerbefehle".

The 2024 holiday in Crete was the second time in my life that I had visited Crete. The first time was in the summer of 1969 (fifty-five years ago) when I had hitch–hiked/backpacked across Europe & Mediterranean islands.

The Cretans who live in the mountains are a tough and rugged lot by all accounts and it is clear to see from the statues that commemorate the *andartes* what fierce fighters they were against the German Wehrmacht. It is also clear from Des' book that German soldiers rarely if ever went in the Cretan mountains, because they knew if they did that they most likely wouldn't be coming down to the coasts again! We saw bullet holes in the helmets of German FallschirmJäger (Paratroopers) in *The Cretan Runner museum*, which clearly illustrates what effective snipers the Cretan's were with their own rifles and captured German rifles and machine guns.

It's clear that in spite of the German war crimes committed on Crete, the current Cretan generation show no animosity to the German tourists who visit. Nikos Psychoundakis, who is now in his early sixties, studied his working trade in Berlin in the 1980s and learnt to speak German there. Nikos' fluency in German is better than his English, so he and I conversed in German after the museum tour and whilst drinking the local Raki (spirits) I translated to my family what I think Nikos was saying to me. All in all it was a fantastic and memorable holiday for me and my family.

Footnote

During my life I have met John House of 1st SAS several times (the first time was in Australia in 1986).

In 1964 on my first ever trip to Germany at the age of almost 17, I met Hans Haep near Dusseldorf. Hans had been one of the German sailors captured by the SBS during the Second World War and whom Des and Bill transported from the Greek islands to Palestine from where he was further transported to a British PoW camp.

The stories of these two gentlemen will be described in our next book…………..

Nick Marshall

Des and Joan. Greatly missed. (Marshall Family Collection)

GLOSSARY

808 Plastic	Plastic Explosive
AB64	British Army Paybook
Ack Ack	Anti-Aircraft Guns
Afrika Korps	German expeditionary Force in North Africa
Ak Dum	Anglo/Indian Army slang. At once/Hurry
Aldis Lamp	Signal Lamp/Morse Lamp
Andartes	Cretan Resistance
Balmoral	Scottish Cap
Beaufort Scale	An empirical measure for describing wind intensity based on observed sea conditions
Binnacle	Housing for a ships compass and lamp
BMA	British Military Administration
Bofors Gun	40mm (diameter) Artillery Piece used for Ack Ack, 1930 Swedish Design
Brassard	An armband or cloth worn on the upper arm denoting rank or insignia
Breda	Italian Light machine-gun
Breeches Buoy	Rope based rescue device used for extraction from wrecked vessels
Bren Gun	British light machine-gun
BSM	Battery Sergeant Major
Bulwarks	Extension of a ships side above sea level
Bugout	Escape/Extraction from an ambush location
Caching	Hiding something i.e. weapons/boats/parachutes
Cadre	A small training unit
Caique	Greek fishing boat

Behind The Lines with The SBS: My Life in L Squadron during WW2

Calpaks	Kalpaks, Armenian/Kurd fighters formed by Terence Bruce Mitford
Carbine	long gun with a shortened barrel
Caulking	Flexible materiel used to seal air leaks/cracks on ship planks
Cetniks	Yugoslav Royalist guerrilla force
Cipher	One Time Pad (for coding)
Clone Horse	a small compact charging engine
Colt	Small arms weapon revolver or automatic (with magazine)
C in C	Commander in Chief
CO	Commanding Officer
Coracle	Small round shaped boat
Cordtex	Plastic explosive coil
Crystals	Used for changing radio signal frequencies
CWT	Hundred weight
Davis Escape Apparatus	Early type of oxygen rebreather
Dodecanese	10 islands off Greece (Eastern Mediterranean Near Turkish coastline)
Dory	Small boat with pointed ends and high sides
DOW 5	Telephone cable
Duce	Il Duce (Benito Mussolini. Italian Dictator)
DZ	Drop Zone
E Boat	Fast German patrol boat
ELAS	Greek Communist movement
Encode	Convert into coded form
EPIP	Eight Man Tent
Ersatz Coffee	German coffee made from acorns or other organic plants
ES	Equipment Support
Everest Carriers	Army radio set carrying equipment
Fairmile	Large Harbour Defence Motor Launch
Famagusta	Town in S/E Cyprus
Folboat	Folding Kayak
Force 133	SOE (Special Operations Executive)

Glossary

FSP	Field Security Police
Garrison	Body of troops stationed at a particular place
Gefreiter	German Military Rank equivalent to a Lance Corporal
Gestapo	Nazi Secret Police
GHQ	General Head-Quarters
Glubb's Girls	Nickname for Gen. John Glubb's Arab legion due to long hair and robes
GSB	Greek Security Battalion
Gulf of Doris	Now known as Gulf of Symi
HDML	Harbour Defence Motor Launch
Herrenvolk	German nation under Nazi Germany
HQ	Head-Quarters
HQMEF	Head Quarters Mediterranean Expeditionary Force
Imshi	Lets's be going (Arabic)
Jimmy	Nickname for First Lieutenant Navy
Joe	Nicknamed after Joseph Stalin
Junker	German transport aircraft
Junkers 88	German Multi combat aircraft
Knäckerbrot	Flat/dry crisp type bread
Kalimera ti kanis	Good morning, how are you? (Greek)
Leftheri	Cretan code name for Hugh Fraser
Lewes Bomb	Blast incendiary designed by Lt Jock Lewes
Livre	Lebanese currency during the Second World War
Lousiness	State of being lousy/poor quality
LRDG	Long Range Desert Group
LSF	Levant Schooner Force/Flotilla (Allied naval force used in covert operations)
Lubbers	Person unfamiliar with sailing
Luger	German Pistol
Magnum Opus	Most important work (of a chef)
Marlin	American Submachine gun
Matelot	Sailor
Mavrodaphne	Sweet red dessert wine
MEFHQ	Middle East Forces Head Quarters

Mersa Matruh	Coastal City of Egypt
Mills Bomb '36'	British hand grenade
ML	Motor Launch
MM	Military Medal
MO	Medical Orderly
MP	Military Police
Morse Code	Method of representing letters, numerals and punctuation marks by an arrangement of dots and dashes
MTB	Motor boat
M&V	Meat and Vegetables
Naval Pig	Navy Officer
NAAFI	Recreational establishment used by armed forces
NCO	Non Commissioned Officer
Nissen Hut	Barracks made of prefabricated metal
NOIC	Naval Officer In Charge
OC	Officer in Command
Oerlikon	20mm (diameter) Artillery Piece
OR	Other Ranks
Order arms	Military command to raise weapon to shoulder on a parade
Padrone	The Proprietor
Partisans	Yugoslav resistance fighters
Pillbox	Concrete guard post
PoW	Prisoner of War
PPP	Palestine Police Post
Predictor	Ack Ack term for calculating altitude, speed, direction of enemy aircraft
QM Store	Quartermaster store
Queen Bee	A low cost radio controlled 'target aircraft' for Artillery training
RA	Royal Artillery
RAF	Royal Air Force
RAMC	Royal Army Medical Corps
RE	Royal Engineers

Glossary

Recce	Reconnaissance
RFHQ	Raiding Forces Head Quarters
RSM	Regimental Sergeant Major
RTU	Return To Unit
RV	Rendezvous
Sariki	Headscarf made of crocheted cotton
SAS	Special Air Service
SBS	Special Boat Squadron/Service
Schmeisser	German Submachine gun
Springboks	South Africans
Skipper	Navy Captain
SM	Sergeant Major
SOE	Special Operations Executive
SSM	Staff Sergeant Major
Stanchions	Sturdy upright fixture that provides support to another object
Stand To	Stand ready for an attack
Sten	British Submachine gun
Stick	Line of Paratroopers
Stokes	Marine Technician
Swain	Boatswain/Bosun responsible for the hull
TA	Territorial Army
Toc H	An international Christian movement
TCV	Troop Carrying Vehicle
Tewfik	180-ton schooner
Time Pencil	A No 10 delay switch detonator
Tommy Cooker	a small compact metal fold up stove
Tommy Gun	US Submachine gun
Trieste **ship**	Italian cruising ship
UXB	Bomb disposal unit
Wadi	Dry valley or Ravine
Walther Automatic	German Semi-automatic pistol
WO	Warrant Officer
Yalla	Let's go Hebrew/Arabic

NOTES

Chapter 1

1. On 28 September 1942 the 85th Field artillery Regiment sailed out of Liverpool on board the *Highland Monarch*. The ship put into Belfast due to a submarine scare but by the 8 October was joined by the *Empress of Russia* and other vessels in the mid-Atlantic. On 18 October they arrived in Freetown, Sierra Leone then 3 days later sailed on to Durban arriving on 5 November. On 9 November they continued to Aden, refuelled then travelled up the Red Sea to Port Tewfik at the southern end of the Suez Canal. From there they transferred onto a train that took them to El Tahag mobilisation centre south of Cairo arriving by the end of November.

    On 3 January 1943 they left El Tahag heading east across the Suez, past Gaza, Beersheba and on to Tulkarn. After a further two days of travelling east through the Transjordan Desert and a stop at Mafrag they continued across the Iraqi Desert arriving outside Bagdad. On 12 January they set up camp at Latifya, 28 miles south of Baghdad. Their next move was a week spent in Kermanshah, Persia before returning to the Middle East. On 4 August the Regiment reached Wadi Mahmoudi then moved on to Damascus followed by a final move to Tripoli, Syria.
    Source: Goldstein, Wilf, '*Farewell Screw gun. The Tale of 85th Field/Mountain Regiment*' (Book Guild)

Chapter 3

2. 'Muscles' is most likely SBS PTI, Sgt. Douglas Blackett Henderson of the Argyll and Sutherland Highlanders.

Notes

Chapter 8

3. Sir John Bagot Glubb's Arab legion were known as 'Glubbs Girls' due to the length of their hair and long flowing robes. They were a few thousand finely trained and disciplined Bedouin tribesmen.
   Source: L.A. Times Archives.

Chapter 9

4. Des' Fairbairn-Sykes Fighting Knife. Manufactured by Wilkinson Sword Ltd and issued to British Commando's and SAS.

Chapter 11

5. The *Tewfik* set sail on 20 January 1944 with a cargo of 4700lbs of explosive.
   Source: Lodwick, John, *Raiders from the Sea*. (Greenhill Books) P.109

Chapter 14

6. Known as 'Operation Claymore' the raid on the Lofoten islands was carried out by No. 3 and No. 4 Commando, a Royal Engineers section, 52 men from the Norwegian Independent Company 1 and supported by the 6th Destroyer Flotilla and two troop transporters of the Royal Navy. They achieved their objective of destroying fish oil factories and 800,000 gallons of fish oil and glycerine used in the German war economy. 19,350 tons of shipping were destroyed and 225 Germans were taken prisoner.
   Source: *The London Gazette* 23 June 1948.

Chapter 15

7. The SBS patrol disembarked the HDML at Vassi Bay.
   Source: SBS Operational Report Stampalia

Chapter 17

8. Captain Anderson, Sgt Wilson, Stephenson and Kanakakis, stopped at a shepherd's house who then guided them all to the outskirts of Livadia village and the home of Athenae Patieyotis, cousin of Pepino Vasili, who they wished to make contact with.
   Source: SBS Operational Report Stampalia
9. This was most likely the same shepherd visited by Captain Anderson and the others the day before.
10. The full list of Patrolmen was,
    Captain Anderson, Sgt. Wilson, L/Sgt. Corner, Cpl. Asbery, L/Cpl Nixon, L/Cpl. Thompson, Pvt. Lock, Pvt. Rutter, Sgn. Webster, Sgn Marshall, Interpreters Sgn. Stephenson, Pte. Kanakakis.
    Source: SBS. Stampalia Operational report.
11. The Caiques were located in Marmari Bay.
    Source: SBS Operational Report.
12. Captain Anderson and L/Cpl Nixon were to attempt to enter Port Maltezana by folboat and destroy any fuel dumps there.
    Source: SBS Operational Report .

Chapter 18

13. The Doctor's name was Dr. Theophilos Kolletis. Along with him were Athenae Patieyotis, his son and Pepino Vasili. They retrieved medical supplies for the islanders that the SBS patrol had brought with them.
    Source: SBS Operational Report.
14. The Patrolman with malaria was L/Sgt. Bryson Corner 1437189 RA from Glasgow. Born 28 July 1916-1974.

Chapter 20

15. The sea plane was a Junkers Ju 52.
    Source: SBS Operational Report.
16. The charges on the seaplane were laid by Sgt. Wilson and Sgn. Les Stephenson.
    Source: SBS Operational Report.
17. With Jock Asbery were, Pvt. Rutter and L/Cpl. Thompson.
    Source: SBS Operational Report.

Notes

18. Kanakakis and Lock stayed on the beach as guards.
    Source: SBS Operational Report.
19. The friendly islander was Pepino Vasile.
    Source: SBS Operational Report

Chapter 21

20. Raymond Andrew Nixon 1438801. RA/SAS/SBS was later taken prisoner on an operation in Crete. July 1944. He and Captain John Lodwick escaped while being transported through Serbia after 134 days in captivity.
    Source: Lodwick, John, *Raiders From The Sea*. (Greenhill Books) p.171

Chapter 29

21. Inspector Robert Stacey Wilsher had in fact survived the war. Wounded in the hip on a commando raid in the Aegean October 44, he had to be left behind. Surviving out in the open for 3 nights he eventually managed to crawl to enemy lines. Unreported as a prisoner of war he was presumed dead. 4 months later his parents in Ramsgate, Kent received a letter from his hospital bed in Vienna. He and 3 others had been exchanged by the Germans for food and German/Italian POW's. He later received the British Empire Medal BEM and married Audrey Melville in January 1946.
    Source: 6/3/1946 *East Kent Times and Mail*.

Chapter 30

22. Captain Terence Bruce Mitford SOE/SBS. While in SOE he was given the task of maintaining a force of Kurds in Syria. 'A tough, cheerful lot, enormously strong with huge moustaches and lambskin Kalpaks' they were trained to sabotage the Turkish railway route into Iraq should Turkey enter the war on the Axis side. Not needed for this role, Bruce-Mitford redeployed his Kalpaks into the SAS/SBS.
    Source: The British Academy. Franz Georg Maier. Copyright 1982
23. Sgt John Richard Waterman 913296 Royal Corps of Signallers.
    Source: Nominal Roll of Special Raiding Forces Signal Squadron

Chapter 32

24. General Spears KBE CB MC (born Spiers) MP for Carlisle 1931-1945 and Minister to the Syrian and Lebanon Republic 1942-1944
Source: iwm.org.uk

Chapter 33

25. Pioneer Corps were made up of skilled labourers/worker fighters, that were used to build airfields, bridges, camps, fortifications, roads and clear rubble, roadblocks etc. Many were enlisted from the Commonwealth as well as enemy aliens from Germany, Italy and Austria and also Jews who had escaped from Nazi occupied Europe.
Source: royalpioneercorps.co.uk

Chapter 35

26. LEHI aka 'The Stern Gang' (Fighters for the Freedom of Israel) was a Zionist paramilitary organisation led by Avraham Stern. Its aim was to remove British authorities, 'the occupiers,' from Palestine by use of violence.
Source: Shapira, Anita, *Land and Power: The Zionist Resort to Force*, 1881-1948. *(Stanford University Press)* p.241
27. A twist on the John Milton (1608-1674) Poem; '*When I Consider How My Light is Spent*' aka 'On His blindness'

Chapter 37

28. Des' patrol were to target Armeni dump at the centre of the island.
Source: Lodwick, John, *Raiders From The Sea*. (Greenhill Books) p.166

Chapter 38

29. The patrol landed near Cape Kastellos on June 25th 1944. Most likely on Peristeres Beach. They brought with them an arms supply of 30 rifles and two Bren guns for the local resistance fighters (Andartes). Source (Hugh Fraser General Report. Archive File SOE Greece 859)

Notes

30. Hugh Fraser had landed on the island 3 June along with a 3 man party led by Colonel MacGlassen of the 'Organisation of Strategic Services'. the US equivalent of SOE.
    Source: Beevor, Antony, *Crete: The Battle and the Resistance*. (John Murray) p.320
31. The guide was George Psychoundakis.
    Source: Beevor, Antony, *Crete: The Battle and the Resistance*. (John Murray) p.321
32. This was most likely an area known as Kambia.
    Source: (Chris White. abductingageneral.info)

Chapter 39

33. The wireless operator's name was Cpl. Rooke.
    Source: (Hugh Fraser General Report. SOE Greece 859)

Chapter 40

34. The Cave was known as 'Skoteini' (The Dark One).
    Source: Psychoundakis, George, *The Cretan Runner: His Story of German Occupation* (Penguin) p.278
35. The bridge near Koufi is described in, Psychoundakis, George, *The Cretan Runner: His story of German Occupation* (Penguin) p.278

Chapter 43

36. Hugh Fraser feared the considerable risks of reprisals to the local population. He later discovered a reward of 10 Sovs and 2 sheep was placed on their own heads.
    Source: (Hugh Fraser General Report SOE Greece 859)
    On August 22nd the German forces began a reprisal drive through the Amari valley against the civilian population, destroying 9 villages and carrying out 164 executions.

Chapter 46

37. Lieutenant-General Scobie KBE, CB, MC was a senior British Army officer who fought in both the First and Second World Wars. From 11 December 1943 he

was given command of III Corps which was later sent to Greece to drive out the Germans but became embroiled in a power vacuum and in-fighting between the communist EAM-ELAS and nationalist EDES.
Source: Britanica.com

Chapter 47

38. Sir Archibold Hector McIndoe was a Plastic Surgeon from New Zealand who is credited with pioneering modern plastic surgery procedures during WW2 at the Queen Victoria Hospital, East Grinstead. Many of his patients were RAF pilots with severe skin burns.
Source: bbc.co.uk

BIBLIOGRAPHY

Books

Beevor, Antony, Crete: The Battle and the Resistance (*John Murray 1991*)
Lodwick, John, *The Filibusters: The Story of the Special Boat Service* (*Methuen & Co. Ltd.1947*)
Pitt, Barrie, *Special Boat Squadron: The Story of the SBS in the Mediterranean.* (Century Publishing Co. Ltd. 1983)
Mortimer, Gavin, *The SBS in World War II: An Illustrated History* (*Osprey Publishing 2013*)
Moss, W. Stanley, *Ill Met By Moonlight* (*George g. Harrap & Co Ltd. 1950*)
Psychoundakis, George, The Cretan Runner: His story of the German Occupation (*John Murray 1955*)
Warner, Philip, *The SBS: Special Boat Squadron* (*Sphere Books 1983*)
Goldstein, Wilf, *Farewell Screwgun: The Tale of 85th Field/Mountain Regiment* (*Book Guild*)
Shapira, Anita, *Land and Power: The Zionist Resort to Force, 1881-1948.* (*Stanford University Press*)

National Achives

WO 373/46/143
WO 373/46/164
WO 373/46/165
WO 373/46/166

Websites

www.specialforcesroh.com
https://uk.forceswarrecords.com
https://ww2talk.com/
www.thegazette.co.uk/London
https://discovery.nationalarchives.gov.uk
http;//littlegaddesdenchurch.org.uk

INDEX

Illustrations are in **Bold**

808 Plastic 146

Abbassia 19, 25, 27
Acre 144-45
Aden 238
Aegean 63, 68, 72, 84, 97, 104, 114-15, 209, 240
Albania 220
Aldis Lamp 47-8, 79
Allenby, General 24
Amadolakkos Taverna, Koufi 229
Amari Valley 243
Andartes 51, 161-64, 168-69, 171-72, 175-76, 180-83, 185, 191-92, 194-97, 201-207, 231
Anderson, Capt. Morris Elliott, MC **36**-8, 54, 57-8, 62, 64, 70, 74-7, 79-80, 239
Anogia 231
Araxos 210
Archontiki **170**
Argentina, The 49, 123
Argyropouli **170**
Arki Trieste 111, 115, 119, 122, 124-25
Armeni/Armenoi **173**, 242
Artists Rifles 225
Asbery, Cpl. William (Jock) MM **71**-2, 75, 80, 239-40
Asi Gonia 231
As-Luj 24
Astrakahn 183
Athens 211-14, 217-19, 223, 225

Athlit 24, 34, 56, 71, 128-29, 138, 142, 153
Avenue de Francais 44
Azzib 12, 14, 16-7, 26, 28-9, 31, 34-5, 38, 143-45

Bagot, Sir John 238
Balsillie, Keith 211
Bandy, Captured German Motorboat 82, 96, 107-108
Bari 209, 219-20
Barnett, Norman 'Barnie' **121**
Beaumont, 'Scruffy' 128
Bedouin 33-4, 238
Beersheba 24, 238
Beirut 11-2, 31, 34, 41-4, 46, 92, **102**, 109, 111, 117, 125, 128, 148, 151, **153**, 224
Belfast 238
Benzedrine 198-99
Berlin 115, 182, 231
Bimrose, Charles 211
Black, Battery Sgt. Major 1
Bob, Cpl 15
Bodrum 89
Bofors Gun 151
Bren Gun 151
Brenner Pass 221
British Army:
    4th Parachute Battalion 211-12
    III Corps 212, 242
    Intelligence Corps 225-26
    No. 3 Commando 239

No. 4 Commando 239
Parachute Brigade 128
Royal Artillery 6, 16, 32, 130, 240
   85th Field/Mountain Regiment **3**, **7**, **10**, **11**, 223, 238
Royal Corps. of Signals 24, 94, 241
Royal Corps. of Transport 226
Royal Engineers 226, 239
Raiding Support Regiment 14
Bucket-Force 210
'Bunny' Sgt 15-7, 19-22
Bustard's Plain, Salisbury 1

Caiques 52, 61-3, 70-4, **81**, 82, 84-7, 91-3, 100, 105, 110-11, 211
Cairo 19, 24, 25-9, 32, 35, 49, 51-2, 60, 68-9, 77-8, 86, 91, 94-5, 150, 164, 171-**3**, 202-03, 206, 238
Campion Dr 124
Canea/Chania **173**
Cape Krio 85
Carbine 19, 20, 99, 156, 185, 189-90, 217
Carmel Range 37, 130, 136, 141
Caspian Sea 182
Castelorizzo 52, 108-109, 118-19
Cetniks 220
Chatham 36
Churchill, Winston 209
Ciphers 154, 157, 164, 173, **208**
Clark, L. Cpl. Marine 'Nobby' 99, 156, 158, 161-62, 178, 185, 187, 191, 195, 198-99, 203
Colt.45 42, 157, 175, 216
Cordtex 185
Corinth 211
Corner, L/Sgt. Bryson 64-5, 68-9, 76, 239-40
Cos ((Kos) 98, 102, 109, 115
Coulter, Lt. Frank Norris 81
Cretan Runner Museum, The 231, 242
Crete 51, 144, 155-57, 159-63, 168, **173**, **176**-77, 179, 181, 184-86, 192, 203, 205-206, **208**-209, 227, 229, 231, 240, 242
Croatia 219
Croydon 218

Croydon, Dougie 122, 123, 126-28
Cyprus 49, 119, **121**, 125, 148, 151, 224

Dakota C47 plane 210, 219
Damascus 238
Davis Escape Apparatus 129
Dodecanese 14, 18, 53, 58, **93**, 148, 158, 167, 174
Dornier Do 17 4, 5
Duke of York Barracks 229, 231
Durban 238
Dusseldorf 116, 232

EAM 242
E. Boats 56, 159
EDES 242
Egypt 9, 19, 24, 47, 93, 153, 209
El Alamein 153
ELAS 210-11, 213-14, 217, 219
El Dabaa 153
El Qantara 25
El Tahag 25, 238
Empress of Russia 238
EPIP Tent 13, 129, 145
Episkopi **176**
Etna, Caique 84, 86, 88, 90, 92, 94, 97, 109, 111

Fairbairn – Sykes fighting Knife **ii**, 239
Fairmile, ML 345 158
Fallschirmjager 231
Famagusta 49, 52, **121**, 123-25
Field Security Police, FSP 122-24
Filibusters, The/ Raiders from the Sea, John Lodwick 97, 209
Florina 213
France 183-84, 209
Fraser, Capt. Hugh 'Leftheri' 161-64, 166, 168-69, 171-72, 174-75, 177-82, 185, 187-88, 190-91, 193-97, 201, **208**, 242
Freetown, Sierra Leone 238
Folboat, *see also* Jellicoe's Intruders 44, 52, 57, 74-5, 79-80, 83, 129, 139-40, 148-9, 239
Force 133, *see also* SOE 161, 206

Index

Gaza 238
Gefreiter 114-15, 191
German Forces:
   Army 182, 220-21
      Afrika Korps 188-89
   Luftwaffe 223
   Navy 220
Gestapo 196
Giorgio (Cretan Orchard Owner) 167, 169, 194
Glubb's Girls, (Arab Legion) 40, 238
Glubb, Sir John Bagot 238
Gorbals, The 44
Greece 47, 52, 184, 209-10, 212-15, 217-18, 220, 227, 242
Greek Sacred Squadron, GSS 109, 111
Greek Security Battalion 210-11
Gulf Of Doris 82, 85
Guncotton 146-7

Hadfield, Daphne 152
Hadfield, F.O. Lt. Harold 152
Haep, Hans 114-16, 126, 232
Haifa 11-3, 24, 29, 31-2, 34-5, 122-23, 125-26, 128, 130, 132, 136, 140, 142-43, 145, 153
Harbour Defence Motor Launch, HDML 46, 48, 50, 52-7, 75, 77-82, 92-3, 99-100, 105, 119, 148-49, 151, 156, 158-59, 161, 163, 209, 239
   ML1283 52, 80, 82
Harden, Lt. Dick 98-9, 156, **157**, 161-62, 166, 171-72, 174, 178, 184-93, 195, 197-200, 202-203, 205-207, **208**-209
Henderson, Sgt. Douglas Blackett 'Muscles' 15-6
Hickford Sub-Lt 99-100
Highland Monarch 238
Hills, Paddy **222**
Hitler, Adolf, Fuhrer 1, 116, 184, 231
Hitler Youth 114
Hotel Grand Bretagne, Athens 212
House, Angela 218
House, John 212, 217-18, 232
Howard, Peter **215**
Howitzer 10

Humphreys, Tom **155**
Hylands House, Chelmsford 223

Ill Met By Moonlight W. Stanley Moss 231
Iraq 9, 25, 238, 241
Iskandil Cape 115
Ismailia 25
Istria 219-**21**
Italian Forces 174, 189, 193
Italy 209-10, 218-**19**, 220

Jarvis, Jack 1
Jellicoe, Col. Lord George 'Duke' 32, 44, 94-8, 125, 156, 209-12, 217
Jellicoe, nee O'kane, Lady Patricia 125
Jellicoe's Intruders, *see also* Folboat 44
Jenin 39
Joe (Russian POW) 182-84, 195
Junkers Airplane:
   Bomber JU88 118
   Sea-Plane JU52 62, 70-4, 92, 240
   Transport JU52 187

Kalpaks 109, 241
Kambia 243
Kanakakis, Manoli 51, 61-2, **63**, 70, 75, 78, 174, **176**-79, 186, **228**-31, 239-40
Katakolon 210
Kayak 13
Kermanshah, Persia 11, 238
Kiervasilli Bay 82, 88, 105
King George V Battleship 152
Kingsbury, MO Sgt 99
Kleine, Waldemar 115
Kleine, Willi 115
Kolletis, Dr. Theophilos 64, 240
Koufi **173**, **176**, **186**, 229, 242
Kozani 212-13
Kreipe, Maj. General Heinrich 231
Kyrenia 150-51

Lamia 212
Latifya 238
Levant Coast 9
Levant Schooner Force, LSF 43, 46-7, **81**, 95

Lewes Bomb 146, 191
Leytonstone 224
Livadia 239
Liverpool 51
Lock, Pvt 239-40
Lockheed Hudson 132-33, 136-37
Lodwick, Capt. John 97, 209, 239-40, 242
Lofoten, Norway 54, 239
Lofty, Cook on ML1283 81
Lofty, Officer 142-47, 156
Long, Cpl 99
Long Range Desert Group, LRDG 25-6, 32, 209, 220-**221**
Luftwaffe 223
Luke, Curly **71**
Luxembourg 115
Lydda 24

MacGlassen, Col 242
Mackenzie, Wallie **228**
Maclean, Maj. Fitzroy 220
Mafrag, Jordan 238
Mandracchio, Nisero 98
Maric, Sgt. LRDG 26
Marko (andarte) 171, 201, 203, 206
Marlin M42 Machine-gun 185, 190
Marmari Bay, Stampalia 239
Marshall, Desmond Passim
Marshall Despo 223
Marshall, Iain **230**
Marshall, Jerry **228, 230**
Marshall, Joan (nee.Tingay) **4, 8, 18,** 223-24, 227, 229, 232
Marshall, Nicholas (Nick) **230**
Marshall, Robert **230**
Marshall, Stan **152**
Marshall, William 'Bill' 1, 6-7, **11-2, 71, 102**-103, 109-10, **112**, 117-18, **121**, 124, 130, 137-38, 148, 150, 152, 210, 213-**15**, 216, **218**, 220-23, 225, **227-28**, 232
McGonigal, Capt. Ambrose MC 220
McIndoe, Sir Archibald Hector 218, 243
Mediterranean 9, **47**, 117, 129, 162, 197, 209, 224, 231
Megara, Greece 211
Mena wireless station 27

Mersa Matruh 153-55, 158-59
Messerschmitt ME 210 4-6
Middle East Forces Headquarters, MEFHQ 27, 96, 128
Mills Bombs/ 36 Grenades 90-1
Mitford, Lt. Terence Bruce 241
Monopoli, Italy 219
Monte St Angelo, Italy 209
Monument To The Fallen, Anogia 231
Moran, MO Norman 217
Morphine 191-92
Morphou Bay, Cyprus 148-9
Motor Dory 52, 144
Motor Torpedo Boats, MTB 120
Mount Carmel 32, 37
Mount Hermon 37
Mount Ida 160
Munich Crisis 1
Murphy, Des **4**
Murphy, John 1
Mussolinni, Benito 'Duce' 143, 154, 159

NAAFI 154-55, 159
Nahariya, Egypt 14, 16
Narvik, Norway 54
Nazi 22, 114-15, 198, 221, 241
Newbury Park, Essex 223-24, **227**
Newlands, Sgt. Major 221
Nicosia Transit Camp, Cyprus 150
Nisero 36, **51**, 97-98
Nixon, L/Cpl. Raymond 74, 209, 239-40
Norwegian Independent Company 1 239
Norwich, Norfolk 21

Operational Wings document **112**
Operation Claymore 239
Operation Manna 209

Paiforce **10**; **11**
Palestine 11, 13, 24, 27-30, 32, 39, **71, 129,** **129, 138,** 144, 151, 153, 167, 224, 232, 241
Palestine Police 39, 140-43
Palo, Nisero 98
Parachute Brigade 128
Parachute Training 14-5, 130-38,
Patieyotis, Athenae 239-40

Index

Partisans, Tito's 220, **221**
Patmos **36**
Patras 210-11, 215
Patterson, Maj Ian Norman, MC 35-**6**, 48, **51**, 97-9, 101, 109, 210-11, 219-20
Peloponnese 210
Penzik Bay, Turkey 105
Peristeres Beach 242
Perth, WA 218
Pinckney, Capt. Philip 221
Pioneer Corps 126, 241
Piraeus 111
Piscopi **36**, **71**, 97
Pompforce 212-13
Port Deremen 109
Port Maltezana, Stampalia 239
Portsmouth 143
Port Tewfik, Egypt 238
Pserimos 36
Psychoundakis, George 231, 242
Psychoundakis, Nikos 231

Queen Elizabeth II 229
Queen Bee 3

Raiding Forces Headquarters 14, 19, 31-2, 35
Ramat David, British Parachute School 130, **138**
RAMC 124
Ras-en-Nakurah 13
Ramsaur, Lt. Commander 98-9
Red Devils, Grenades 139
Retimo/Rethymno **173**, 185, 194,
Rhodakino 181, 206-207
Rhodes 53, 98, 118
Rooke, Cpl. 'Yorkie' 164, 168-69, 171-72, 195, 206, 243
Royal Air force 3, 6, 130, 209, 212, 220, 223, 243
  2908 Sqn 210
Royal Air Force Bases UK:
  Beccles 6-7
  Bungay 6
  Duxford Aerodrome, RAF 4, 6
  Gorleston 6

Great Yarmouth 6
Holly Grove 7
Honington Aerodrome 3
King's Lynn 3
Marham Aerodrome RAF 3
Mildenhall, Aerodrome RAF 3
Oulton Broad, Suffolk 7
Ty Croes, Anglesey 6
Watchet 3
Watton Aerodrome 2
Royal Air Force Regiment 210-12
Royal Marines 35-6, 151-52, 156, 198, 210
  No. 40 Marine Commando 210
Royal Navy 52, 88, 105, 108, 123, **152**, 161, 206, 239
  6th Destroyer Flotilla 239
Rutter, Micky Pvt **71**, 239, 240

Salamina Bay, Greece 211
Samakh 36, 40, 128
Sans Rival 44
Sardinia 128
Schmeisser 19, 23, 99, 124, 127, 156, 185, 189, 216-17
Schneider, Rudolf 115-16
Schooners 43, 46-8, 82, 92-3, 95, 105-108, 110-11, 113, 118-20
  LS5 48
  LS9 95, 108-11
  Arki Trieste 111, 119, 124-25
  Tewfik 46, **48**, **52**, 82-3, 87, 94, 99, 101-102, 105-106, 109-11, 238-39
Scobie, Lt. General KBE CB MC 212, 214, 242
Sea Of Galilea, Lake Tiberius 36
Seligman, Lt-Cdr Adrian 95-6, 107-108, 151
Sennybridge, Training Area, SENTA 7
Serbia 209, 240
Seven Kings, Essex 223
Sherman tank 214, 217
Silk Maps 47, **160**, 162, **219**
Simi, Greece 115, 117
Skoteini Cave, Andarte HQ **170**, 171, 181, 243
Slovenia 219

Sofia, Bulgaria 209
Spears, General 125, 241
Special Air Service, SAS 11, 14, 19, **100**, 209, 217, 219-21, 223-**24**, 225, 227-**28**, 229, 231, 240-41
    1st SAS 225, 223
    21st SAS 224
    Association 227, **229**
    Australian Association 218
    Reunions **228, 229**, 231
Special Boat Section 11-2, 14
Special Boat Squadron Passim
    Squadrons, L 35, 148, 209-10, 214, 219-21
        S 109
        M 220
Special Operations Executive SOE,
    see also Force 133 231, 241-42
Spitfire 6, 210, 212
SS EOLA 125
Stampalia, (Now Astypalaia) **36, 51**, 54, 56, 62, 68, **71**, 72, 156, 239
Stephenson, Leslie Norman DCM 46, **51**-2, 61-**3**, 98-101, 156, 158, 161-62, 166, 171-72, 174-78, 180-81, 185, 188, 190, 193, 195, 197-99, 202-204, 206-207, 213, **218**, 239-40
Stern Gang, LEHI 142
Stewart, Jock 215
St. Botolph's Church, London 224
St. Peter & St. Paul's Church, Ilford 224
Stratford 1
Suda Bay, Crete 187
Sudetenland, Czech Rep 115-**16**
Sutherland, Col. David 'Dinky' 220
Syria 13-4, 24, 98, 109, 111, 115, 238, 241

Tabor, refugee camp 39
Tel Aviv, Palestine 29
Tewfik 46, **48, 52**, 82-3, 87, 94, 99, 101-102, 105-106, 109-11, 238-39
Thebes, Greece 211

Thompson L/Cpl 239-40
'Tito', Josip Broz 220
Tobruk, Libya 158-60
Tommy Cooker 65, 145, 167
Tommy Gun 50, 64, 100, 127, 185
Tripoli, Lebanon 11, 238
Trunks Telephone Exchange 8
Tulkarn, Palestine 238
Turkey **48**, 52, 77, 80, 82-**3**, 86, 92, 109, 115, 241

US Navy 98

Vasili, Pepino 23,
Vassi Bay, Stampalia 239
Vathi Bay, Turkey 52
Victoria Cross, VC 14
Volga River 183

Wadi Mahmoudi 238
Wakefield, Arthur **10**
Walther Automatic Pistol 191
Wanstead Flats 1, 224
Waterman, Sgt. Jack/John 109, 11, 115, 122-23, 126, 28, 241
Webster, Jim 84, 88, 95-6, **155**, 239
Wehrmacht 231
Wilsher, 'Shorty' Robert Stacey 105, 240
Wilson, Sgt. 'Tug' 75-6, 84, 87-8, 90, 239-40
Windom Aerial 154
Wireless 3, 14-6, 20, **25**, 26-8, 32, 37-9, 52-3, 57, 59-60, 63, 75, 77, 80, 83-4, 86, 94, 107, 109, 154, 157-58, 161, 164, 168, 171-72, **173**, 195, 201, 206, 220
Wren 152
Wynne, Sqn. Ldr 210

Yugoslavia 184, 213, **219**, 220-21

Zaghoria. Lebanon 9